ALSO BY JACK CASHILL

POPES AND BANKERS

WHAT'S THE MATTER WITH CALIFORNIA?

SUCKER PUNCH

HOODWINKED

RON BROWN'S BODY

FIRST STRIKE

2006: THE CHAUTAUQUA RISING (*NOVEL*)

DECONSTRUCTING
OBAMA

THE LIFE, LOVES, AND LETTERS
OF THE FIRST POSTMODERN PRESIDENT

JACK CASHILL

THRESHOLD EDITIONS

NEW YORK LONDON TORONTO SYDNEY

Threshold Editions
A Division of Simon & Schuster, Inc.
1230 Avenue of the Americas
New York, NY 10020

First Threshold Editions hardcover edition February 2011

THRESHOLD EDITIONS and colophon are trademarks of Simon & Schuster, Inc.

For information about special discounts for bulk purchases,
please contact Simon & Schuster Special Sales at 1-866-506-1949
or business@simonandschuster.com.

The Simon & Schuster Speakers Bureau can bring authors to your live event. For
more information or to book an event contact the Simon & Schuster Speakers Bureau
at 1-866-248-3049 or visit our website at www.simonspeakers.com.

Designed by Ruth Lee-Mui

Manufactured in the United States of America

10   9   8   7   6   5   4   3   2   1

Library of Congress Cataloging-in-Publication Data

Cashill, Jack.
    Deconstructing Obama : the life, loves, and letters of America's first postmodern
president / Jack Cashill. — 1st Threshold Editions hardcover ed.
      p.   cm.
    Includes index.
    1. Obama, Barack—Literary art.   2. Obama, Barack—Authorship.
3. Obama, Barack—Friends and associates.   I. Title.
    E908.3.C37   2011
    973.932092—dc22   2010038341

ISBN 978-1-4516-1111-3
ISBN 978-1-4516-1113-7 (ebook)

To Margaret and Flannery

CONTENTS

CONTENTS

II. THE WILDERNESS CAMPAIGN, 2009–2010

INTRODUCTION

Christmas 2009

S eptember 23, 2009, was Christmas Day for me, and I woke to find an official Red Ryder carbine-action two-hundred-shot Range Model air rifle under my tree. Not a real tree, mind you, nor a real air rifle, but a gift in my inbox even better than an air rifle, specifically a cluster of emails, all of them pronouncing some joyous variation on the theme "Did you see *Hannity* last night!!!!"

I had not, but in the age of the Internet, it was simple enough to find the clip in question. The guest on Sean Hannity's Fox News show was celebrity biographer Christopher Andersen. An establishment journalist with credentials of the first order—*Time, People, Vanity Fair*—Andersen had written some thirteen *New York Times* bestselling biographies in the past twenty years.

He appeared on the *Hannity* show to promote the fourteenth, *Barack and Michelle: Portrait of an American Marriage*. If Andersen did not fire his publicist after the show, he should have. The natural audience for his book skews female and left. *USA Today* had accurately described it as "A glowing 'Portrait' of the Obamas' rock-solid marriage," and yet here was Hannity pounding on one of the book's few unfriendly revelations, namely Barack Obama's friendship with terrorist emeritus Bill Ayers. For those who have been comatose the last several years or stuck on NPR, Ayers is the Weather Underground veteran who made *unrepentant* a household word. His relationship with Obama would bedevil the candidate throughout the 2008 campaign.

I had observed the campaign at a safe remove until, in September 2008, the literary detective work I had been doing led me to suspect a heretofore unimagined intimacy between erstwhile terrorist and candidate. Indeed, I had come to believe that Ayers had been deeply involved in the writing of Obama's acclaimed 1995 memoir, *Dreams from My Father.* I went public with my suspicions in September 2008 and for my troubles I endured a year of sustained abuse from all corners of society, polite and otherwise.

And then Chris Andersen showed up on *Hannity*. I watched the clip with the kind of awe I once felt for the first moon landing and the Miracle on Ice. On air, Hannity quoted Andersen's claim that "literary devices and themes [in *Dreams*] bear a jarring similarity to Ayers's own writings." Asked Hannity, "Bill Ayers helped him with his book?" Andersen answered in the affirmative and then anxiously changed topic. Hannity, sensing perhaps he had gotten all he could, let Andersen move on, but the proverbial cat had crept rather publicly out of the bag.

I immediately headed to my local Barnes & Noble and bought the book. By late afternoon, I had consumed it. The Ayers bombshell was no minor aside. Andersen spends some six pages on the story. He details the how, when, and why of Obama's collaboration with Ayers on *Dreams*.

Andersen wrote from within the gates. He had no agenda. His book is as softly liberal and sympathetic to the Obamas as his previous book had been to Christopher and Dana Reeve. He interviewed some two hundred people for the book, many of them close to the

Obama family, at least two of whom talked to him about Ayers's role in *Dreams*, possibly Bill Ayers himself. The Obamas had likely given their tacit blessing to the project. Andersen had no reason to invent facts that would alienate his base. Nor does he have a track record of doing so.

In the immediate aftermath of the Andersen revelations, friends advised me to start writing my Pulitzer speech, but by this time I knew better. Too much depended on Obama's authorship of *Dreams*. In their reading of the book, the world's literary gatekeepers, an influential subset of the Obama faithful, had convinced themselves that Obama was too smart, too sensitive, too skilled as a writer to need anyone's assistance. They believed this deeply enough to have built Obama's foundational myth around his presumed literary genius.

Obama encouraged them. "I've written two books," he told a crowd of teachers in Virginia in July of 2008. The crowd applauded. "I actually wrote them myself," he added with a wink and a nod, and now the teachers exploded in laughter. They got the joke: Republicans were too stupid to write their books.

Although no one much cared about Obama's second book, a first-person memoir / policy brief published in 2006 and titled *The Audacity of Hope*, *Dreams* had emerged as the sacred text in the cult of Obama. "There is no underestimating the importance of *Dreams from My Father* in the political rise of Barack Obama," David Remnick would later write in his exhaustive look at Obama's life and career, *The Bridge*.

Thanks in no small part to *Dreams*, Obama had been anointed perhaps the smartest would-be president of all time. The Obama campaign machine, Organizing for America, did not shy from saying so. It had shamelessly encouraged its minions to "get out the vote and keep talking to others about the genius of Barack Obama." This, I sensed from the beginning, was a myth that one challenged at his own peril.

As I half expected, the media ignored Andersen's bombshell. Scores of major media outlets reviewed *Barack and Michelle*, among them CBS News, *USA Today*, the *Chicago Sun-Times*, the *Seattle Times*, the *Atlanta*

Journal-Constitution, the *Chicago Tribune*, and the *Telegraph* of London. Yet incredibly, despite Andersen's insights, despite the research that my co-conspirators and I had done on this topic, I could not find a single outlet that so much as mentioned the *Dreams* controversy, the most newsworthy item in the book.

By September 2009 I knew well that this controversy involved more than authorship. It involved the very content of *Dreams* and the character of the man who put his name on it. Proving Ayers had helped write it would make a statement but would not be statement enough. To move this story onto the main stage, I had to dig deeper and "deconstruct" the life of our first postmodern president.

A serious student of literature, Ayers has written a good deal about the postmodern perspective, specifically in the writing of a memoir. Like pornography, postmodernism is one of those things that is hard to define, but you know it when you see it, and Ayers's version is not all that hard to spot. Like many on the left, he rejects the possibility of an objective, universal truth, either the "modern" scientific perspective of the Enlightenment or the God-centered perspective of the Judeo-Christian tradition. In its stead, he argues for a more personalized reality, one whose "narrative" we each "construct" as we journey along.

Ayers's own memoir, the 2001 *Fugitive Days*, is laced with repeated references to what he calls "our constructed reality." So too is *Dreams*. "But another part of me knew that what I was telling them was a lie," writes Obama, "something I'd constructed from the scraps of information I'd picked up from my mother." (For simplicity's sake, I will refer to "Obama" as the author of everything that appears under his name.) If the role of the postmodern writer is to construct a reality, the role of the postmodern critic is thus to "deconstruct" it.

To help sort out the lies and the half-truths from the truth, I return to the words that Obama has spoken or written or had written for him. Of these, *Dreams* is the most telling, but *Audacity* is not without its revelations. Significant too are Obama's half-dozen or so defining speeches. More quietly critical is an enigmatic poem published under the name of the nineteen-year-old Obama called "Pop." If *Dreams* serves as sacred text, "Pop" is the Rosetta stone, the key to decrypting Obama's shrouded past, his fragile psyche, and his uniquely cryptic political life.

In unlocking that past, I have discovered that the story that Obama has been telling all his life varies from the true story in ways big and small. I suspect that in other times and places a man as enigmatic and ambitious as Obama could emerge as president or caliph or czar, but only in contemporary America could a scrappy band of everyday Joes take him on and actually hope to prevail.

I

The Political Campaign of 2008

10,000 HOURS

This adventure began all so innocently. In June 2008 a friend sent me some excerpts from *Dreams from My Father* and asked if they were as radical as they sounded. I had not yet read the book, but I found myself bookless in the Detroit Metro Airport awaiting America's least glamorous flight—Detroit to Buffalo—and decided to buy a copy.

Besides, the bookstore provided escape from the billboard-size TV screens that dominate each successive chamber in Detroit's then Northwest, now Delta terminal. A few years earlier, just prior to the 2004 election, I experienced what, for me at least, was the very essence of Orwellian terror. While walking through the terminal, I looked up and saw the surreal, snarling, Rushmore-sized head of certifiable political madman James Carville.

I looked away, of course, but Carville's ragin' Cajun cackle trailed me from speaker to speaker as I walked ever faster through this seemingly endless chamber of horrors. Finally, I passed under the screen and breathed a sigh of relief only to be confronted in the next massive chamber by another talking billboard filled still with the same monstrous, gleaming Carvillian head. On my way to a nightmarishly distant gate, in fact, I passed through about ten more such chambers and under ten more colossal Carvilles until I finally reached the gate and ducked into the bookstore, the only refuge I could find without a urinal in it.

For the record, Carville was then co-host of the CNN show *Crossfire*. Until that moment, I had not really noticed that CNN had infiltrated every major airport in America. This service, launched in 1992, is called the CNN Airport Network. When last I checked, 1,775 airport gates in thirty-nine of America's leading airports showed CNN news and no other show but CNN news, all the time.

Upon inquiring, I discovered that major airports were contractually bound well into the future to force-feed a captive audience the politically loaded CNN twenty-four hours a day, arguably the most comprehensive monopoly in the history of the American media. One can imagine the outcry if the airports switched to a new station that people actually watched, like Fox News, for instance.

The airport bookstore drove me nearly as batty as the terminal. There were Obama books everywhere I looked: hardcover, softcover, coffee-table books, coloring books, you name it. Given my biases, I found myself as uneasy in buying *Dreams* as I had been when I bought my first copy of *Playboy* many moons ago. "What if someone sees me?"

The clerk, a young black woman, beamed at me for my purchase, and I felt squeamish no longer. Like so many of my fellow citizens, I had a momentary flash, however delusional, of the racial harmony that would settle upon the land if Obama were elected. The extent of the delusion became clear some months later when I told this story on the air and was promptly called a racist for either experiencing it or telling it. I wasn't sure which, maybe both.

I also bought a yellow highlighter, a complicated one that collapsed into itself like a low-grade Transformer toy. Once on the plane, I commenced to read the book—the cover kept discreetly down—find the passages in question, and highlight them. What I found disappointed my friend. "As far as I can tell," I emailed her back, "the excerpts all seem to be taken out of context. They are not as radical as they sound." Most, in fact, were quotes by other people that Obama had captured. They did not express his own thoughts.

The content of *Dreams* did not strike me then as terribly controversial. In paperback, the book runs 442 pages. The first section, called "Origins," begins with Obama as a twenty-one-year-old learning of his father's death and quickly backtracks to cover his family's history on either side. This 126-page section takes Obama through his childhood in Hawaii and Indonesia, his college years in Los Angeles and New York, and ends with the twenty-four-year-old Obama on the verge of moving to Chicago.

The 162-page second section, "Chicago," reads as though it were written to be part of some other book. It mercilessly details the three years Obama spent as a community organizer before climaxing with Obama's weepy embrace of something like Christianity at Reverend Jeremiah Wright's church. Yet, despite its length, the section does little to advance the primary thrust of the book—Obama's search for identity.

The third section, "Kenya," picks up the identity theme again. Its 131 pages dwell on Obama's first trip to Kenya in what would appear to be 1988, the summer before he begins Harvard Law School. A short epilogue wraps up the rest of Obama's brief life, including his Harvard experience and his marriage to Michelle in 1992.

Early on in the first read, the quality of the writing caught my attention. Although the book lacks discipline and occasionally grinds on in useless detail, long stretches of *Dreams* are very well written. In my twenty-five-year career in advertising and publishing, I have reviewed the portfolios of at least a thousand professional writers. Not a half dozen among them wrote as well as the author of the book's best passages, and these were professionals, not presumed amateurs like Obama.

To be sure, political celebrities routinely use ghostwriters. This kind of low-level subterfuge is as common in Washington as hair dye. But that an aspiring state senator of modest means and minimal reputation could afford such a quality professional touch-up impressed me as an angle worth examining.

Many critics of my research have failed to recognize that some people have a keener eye for style than others. I learned this the hard way. A few years ago, a visiting artist friend zeroed in on a portrait of Teddy Roosevelt hung on my living room wall. I had painted it as a high school student in New York at a salon overseen by Helen Farr Sloan, the widow of famed American painter John Sloan, and herself a painter of no small talent.

"Who did that?" my friend asked upon seeing the painting.

"I did," I answered proudly.

"I can believe you did the face," said my friend, a funny, blunt guy. "That sucks. But who did the eyes?"

"I did," I answered. He stared at me hard. "I had help," I added sheepishly.

"You had more than help."

He was right. Helen Sloan had touched up the eyes after I proved unable to bring them to life. Who knows how many hundreds of people had looked at my TR painting without spotting the difference in quality between her eyes and my face. My artist friend saw it in a second. The painting now hangs in my basement.

Not long ago my wife asked me if I wanted to go to an Eric Clapton concert. "Why do I want to pay seventy bucks a ticket to see Eric Clapton?" I asked. "He's the best guitarist in the world," she answered. "We'd waste the investment," I countered. "I couldn't tell the world's best guitarist from the fourteenth-best guitarist in Kansas City."

If I cannot tell the great from the good in art or music, I can do just that when it comes to writing. I read a hundred or so nonfiction books a year. I have taught writing of all sorts at all levels. I have a Ph.D. in American studies with a literature emphasis. I write for a living. I have "doctored" books by people you have heard of. And I have recently written a book on literary and intellectual fraud, *Hoodwinked* by name. I can spot the "eyes" of a book and recognize a literary Eric Clapton, often at a glance. I am hardly unique. Others can do the same, but they have to be willing to look. Precious few have looked.

Not too long ago I volunteered to teach a writing class at a local high school. I met with the same small group of kids once a week for three years. They tried hard, and after three years all wrote better than they had at the beginning. But none wrote appreciably better, and the skill differential among them had not shifted a whit. As all teachers will attest, to make an ordinary writer an extraordinary one is nearly impossible.

Even a gifted student writer must work hard to reach the next level. In his bestseller *Outliers*, Malcolm Gladwell painstakingly lays out what he calls the "ten-thousand-hour rule." He quotes neurologist Daniel Levitin to the effect that "ten thousand hours of practice [in any subject] is required to achieve the level of mastery associated with being a world-class expert" and cites example after example to make his case.

In his recent memoir, *Hitch-22*, British-born journalist Christopher Hitchens details what that ten-thousand-hour rule might look like in the life of a writer. Hitchens spends page after page documenting his early awakening to the craft, his first efforts, his influences, his successes, his failures, his strengths, his failings. Obama's Hawaii mentor, Frank Marshall Davis, does the same in his useful memoir, *Livin' the Blues*, published posthumously in 1992. Davis incorporates several of his poems into the text. He talks at length about his influences, his honors, his early infection with "journalitis," his publications, his ambitions.

In *Dreams*, there is none of this. Gladwell's ten thousand hours gets whittled down to about one hundred implied hours of journal entries and "very bad poetry." And then, without further ado, Obama produces what the estimable Joe Klein of *Time* magazine calls "the best-written memoir ever produced by an American politician." To put this in another context, imagine that your double-bogey golfing buddy shows up one day at your country club wearing a green jacket and claiming to have won it at the Masters. Would you not be a little suspicious? Surely, the editors of *Golf Digest* would be. From the looks of his literary scorecard pre-*Dreams*, Obama was a double-bogey writer. If anything, given his skill base, it would have been easier for him to make the cut at the Masters than to write a minor political masterpiece.

After reading *Dreams*, I thought there would be chat rooms filled with people who shared my suspicion. Not so. The literati had already embraced Obama as one of their own. On the strength of *Dreams*, noted British author Jonathan Raban called Obama "the best writer to occupy the White House since Lincoln." Added Raban, "Every sentence has its own graceful cadence! He could as easily be a novelist as a politician!"

Raban was in good company. "Whatever else people expect from a politician," wrote Oona King in her London *Times* review, "it's not usually a beautifully written personal memoir steeped in honesty." The American literary crowd was just as enamored. "I was astonished by his ability to write, to think, to reflect, to learn and turn a good phrase," said Nobel Prize–winning novelist Toni Morrison of *Dreams*. "I was very impressed. This was not a normal political biography." Implicit in every review I read was that Obama penned the memoir himself. One amateur reviewer nicely captured the left's shared faith in Obama's talent: "Wow. The man can *write*."

I had a full plate in the summer of 2008, so I did just a little dabbling in literary detection. I began by picking out a series of distinctive poetic phrases from *Dreams*—"ragged laughter," "unadorned insistence," "the landscape of my heart," and the like—and began Googling to see if I could find any matches online. I found no pattern. The best I could find I summarized in an email headed "Long Shot" to an online buddy, a boxing promoter and all-around good spirit who has the same last name as my two suspects. To protect identities, I will change their shared name to "Tarleton."

> Donald, I am doing some literary detective work on Obama's Dreams From My Father, which I am sure he did not write. My best guess is that it was written by a couple: Bill and Slyvia [sic] Tarleton. Actually, I am not sure that they are a couple but one distinctive Omaba [sic] phrase shows up in Bill's work and another in Sylvia's. Do you know either of these people?

Donald did not know them at all. My next trick, a fairly lame one, was to send an email to Bill Tarleton. As I incorporate my name in my email address, the email could not come from me. So I asked my web-master to send it, a useful ruse given that her hosting site at the time was "sfsu.edu." The exchange went as follows:

> Hi Bill,
>
> Long time! Just got to the Obama book. Great job. Regards to Sylvia.
>
> Debra

> Debra,
>
> Please, what Obama book? Who is Sylvia?
>
> Nice to get praise, but I have no idea who you're talking about. San Francisco State University, sfsu?
>
> Bill

Bill,

Oops. Sorry. I was looking for another Bill Tarleton.

Debra

Debra

How can there be another Bill Tarleton?

Oh, yeah, my son Bill is another Bill Tarleton.

Just to let you know, we are Obama people.

Bill

In looking over Bill Tarleton's writings, I had presumed he was an Obama person, which is why I used a cutout to approach him. He could have Googled me as easily as I Googled him and discovered that I was probably not an Obama person. In any case, he had fully convinced me of his innocence.

Unable to identify a collaborator, I plunged deeper into *Dreams* and into the language Obama used in spontaneous interviews. I first publicly voiced my suspicions on July 31, 2008, in a *WorldNetDaily* (*WND*) column titled "Who Wrote *Dreams from My Father*?" Quoting my painter friend, I argued that Obama "had more than help," much more. The real question, I asked, was where did that help come from and why. At the time, I did not suspect Bill Ayers at all.

THE STORY

The story that Barack Obama tells in *Dreams* is a story that he had been telling with some variation all his life and always to good effect. When Obama hooked up with campaign guru David Axelrod in his 2004 race for the U.S. Senate, his story crystallized into a marketing strategy. Packaging was Axelrod's strong suit.

Guided by Axelrod, Obama held off in his breakthrough keynote speech at the 2004 Democratic convention for all of forty-six words—including "Thank you. Thank you so much. Thank you so much"—before sharing his story with the world. At the 2008 Democratic National Convention in Denver, Obama leaped into the story in the very first sentence. "Four years ago," he began, "I stood before you and told you my story—of the brief union between a young man from Kenya and a young woman from Kansas who weren't well-off or well-known, but shared a belief that in America, their son could achieve whatever he put his mind to."

In between the two convention speeches, the story of Obama's birth was told more often than that of anyone since Jesus. No one, of course, told it as convincingly as Obama himself, especially in his game-saving Philadelphia speech, immodestly titled "A More Perfect Union." In this speech, delivered to negate the baleful impact of the Jeremiah Wright videos, Obama attributed his faith in the American people to his "own American story." He reminded those few registered voters who might somehow have forgotten, "I am the son of a black man from Kenya and a white woman from Kansas."

Obama and his operatives would invest enormous political capital in what David Remnick calls his "signature appeal: the use of the details of his own life as a reflection of a kind of multicultural ideal." From the beginning, Obama's handlers worked hard to protect their investment. This "carefully constructed narrative," confirmed Toby Harnden of the U.K. *Telegraph*, was "guarded assiduously by his campaign staff." As Harnden and others discovered, Obama staffers would do what they had to do to keep the storytellers in line.

As Obama told the story at the 2004 convention, his father had grown up in Kenya "herding goats." His mother's roots he traced to Kansas, as he always did. "My parents shared not only an improbable love," Obama continued, "they shared an abiding faith in the possibilities of this nation." Obama refined his story for a critical speech in Selma, Alabama, in March 2007, a speech that would define his presidential campaign. "My very existence might not have been possible had it not been for some of the folks here today," Obama told the civil rights veterans gathered to mark the events of "Bloody Sunday" forty-two years prior.

"Something happened back here in Selma, Alabama," Obama said. This something "sent a shout across the ocean," which inspired Barack Sr., still "herding goats" back in Kenya, to "set his sights a little higher." This same something also "worried folks in the White House" to the point that the "the Kennedys decided we're going to do an airlift."

As the saga continued, Barack Sr. got a ticket on the airlift and met Obama's mother, a descendant of slave owners. "There was something stirring across the country because of what happened in Selma, Alabama, because some folks are willing to march across a bridge," preached Obama. "So they got together and Barack Obama Jr. was born. So don't tell me I don't have a claim on Selma, Alabama. Don't tell me I'm not coming home to Selma, Alabama."

Something about Selma apparently inspired Obama to embellish more than usual. For starters, herding goats in his father's town was like delivering newspapers in an American one. Everyone did it as a kid. Obama's grandfather was the most prosperous guy in the village. Indeed, the photo of Barack Sr. as a toddler on the cover of *Dreams* shows him in Western clothes. He grew up speaking English and attending Christian schools. He was working as a clerk in Nairobi, not a goatherder in the Kenyan bush, when he applied for the first airlift in 1959. The Republican Eisenhower, not the Democrat Kennedy, was the president when he came to the United States.

Although born in Kansas, Stanley Ann Dunham, Obama's mother, was not exactly Dorothy. She spent her formative years in the state of Washington under the tutelage of some hipster teachers. If there ever was a romance between her and Barack Sr.—and much more on this later—the record of the same is elusive. In any case, Selma had nothing to do with Obama's birth. He was conceived four years before anyone outside Alabama ever heard of the town. By the time of the march, Barack Sr. had long since abandoned Ann and baby Barry for Harvard, where he hooked up with another American woman.

No matter. Well before Obama launched his presidential campaign, Axelrod had come to understand that a popular Democrat, especially if black, could craft his own mythology and get away with it. He had learned from the master, Bill Clinton, whose 1996 campaign he had helped shape.

Almost exactly ten years before Obama's election to the presidency, author Toni Morrison had famously anointed Clinton "our first black president." Wrote Morrison in her much-discussed *New Yorker* article, "Clinton displays almost every trope of blackness: single-parent household, born poor, working class, saxophone-playing, McDonald's-and-junk-food-loving boy from Arkansas."

In August 1998, the same month as Clinton's ill-tempered and ill-received public apology for *l'affaire Lewinsky*, Clinton's approval rating among African Americans registered an astonishing 93 percent, higher even than Jesse Jackson's. Indeed, black support for Clinton had been critical at every step of his presidency. This kind of support was possible for one reason: the media had allowed Clinton to craft a fictional account of his own life.

Although his actual story mirrors Obama's in some interesting ways—the missing father, the wandering mother, the nurturing grandparents, the unreliable stepfather, the elite education—Clinton spun his tale nearly as far from the truth as Obama did. Clinton did not exactly grow up, as the public was told, in an archetypal poor, single-family household with a brutal stepfather. The old man may have been a drunk, but he was a largely benign one. Clinton's strategic exploitation of his drinking problems on the campaign trail maddened the extended Clinton family.

"Nobody ever loved Bill Clinton more than Roger did," wrote Clinton's mom, Virginia, about Roger Clinton, her new, well-heeled husband. In fact, both Clinton parents doted on Bill. They turned the living room of their comfortable home into a veritable "shrine" to the lad's many accomplishments, writes the *Washington Post*'s David Maraniss. "The refrigerator was stocked to his taste." His bedroom, and he never had to share one, was the largest in the house. He had his own bathroom, perhaps the only teen in the state so blessed.

Meanwhile in the Clinton carport sat the black-finned Buick that young Bill drove to segregated Hot Springs High School. For special occasions, like a trip to the whites-only country club, he could always finagle the family's cream yellow Henry J coupe. By nineteen, Clinton was driving a white Buick convertible with red interior. If these were really the "tropes of blackness," Jesse Jackson would have had to find a new hustle a half century ago.

In Clinton's defense, he may have shaded a fact or two, but he never denied his inner redneck. What you saw was what you got. When Clinton quoted Bible verses or sang country songs, it came from the heart. Not so for Obama. When he cited Moses and Joshua at Selma or sang the wonders of America, he sounded as though he were speaking a second language, one whose accent he had nearly mastered—but not quite.

BURYING PERCY

The blogosphere abhors a vacuum. So when the mainstream media (for simplicity's sake, going forward, "the media") leave holes in a given narrative—in this case, the biography of a presidential candidate—bloggers individually, incrementally, and indefatigably strive to fill them in.

Although I am not a blogger per se, I do occasionally orbit the blogosphere through a weekly column for the long-running *WorldNet-Daily* and through occasional think pieces for the aptly named online journal *American Thinker*. Like most in this sphere, I do not get paid. I justify the time invested by imagining that the exposure will help me sell my books and videos, but I really contribute for the same reason most others do, namely the itch to shake things up and shape the debate.

I trace that itch to my days as a paperboy who consumed his own product, the Newark *Star-Ledger*. Like every other kid in America with a Mick or two in the family tree, my first preteen political passion was JFK. Unlike the others, I can still name his first cabinet. When Kennedy was killed in 1963, I transferred my affection to his brother Bob. As the decade wore on, however, and the city crumbled around us, even an adolescent could see the consequences of liberal misrule.

I was nineteen in the summer of '67 and working at an institution for troubled city kids. The place was co-ed, multiracial, and "progressive" in any number of interesting ways. For a self-identified Democrat eager to sample the perks of "the revolution" and not at all above its pretenses, it seemed a likely place to be.

When the Newark riot broke out, I watched the news on a kitchen TV with my co-workers, most of them either garden-variety potheads or revolutionary wannabes. Although my cop father had died the same year as JFK, my cop uncle was in the thick of it. As events unfolded, I understood quickly and clearly that my co-workers and I saw the world through different eyes. Where I saw relatives and friends, they saw "pigs." They weren't shy about saying so. It was the first time I had heard that slur within striking distance, and it almost came to that. By the time the smoke had cleared, so had my illusions. I did not know what I was politically, but I knew what I was not.

More to the point of this story, I saw for the first time up close how and why the media choose sides. Like Procrustes, the mythological innkeeper who stretched his victims or severed their limbs to make them fit his iron bed, the media were making a fluid set of facts fit their iron perspective. At the time, this shocked me. I had trusted newspeople the way I trusted Bishop Sheen or Davy Crockett. I had no reason to suspect mischief.

Over time, the media would grow more Procrustean still. Refitting the bed were people like Tom Hayden, who, in the progressive tradition, was not about "to let a serious crisis go to waste." Hayden had drafted the Port Huron statement, the defining document of Students for a Democratic Society (SDS), the outfit that would nurture the young Billy Ayers. Within months of the riot, Hayden and

Vintage Books had elevated the mayhem in my hometown into *Rebellion in Newark*.

As George Orwell acknowledged in his timeless 1946 essay, "Politics and the English Language," intellectuals have long manipulated words to make an alien ideology palatable. "Political language," he argued, was "designed to make lies sound truthful and murder respectable, and to give an appearance of solidity to pure wind."

The budding intellectuals of the New Left might disagree on intent but not on the manipulation. "We invented words," Bill Ayers would later write; "we constructed culture." Calling a riot a "rebellion," however, did not make it "an organized attempt to overthrow a government or other authority by use of violence." It was nothing of the sort. Hayden knew that. No, Newark was a riot, exactly as the dictionary defines *riot*, namely "a public disturbance during which a group of angry people becomes noisy and out of control, often damaging property and acting violently."

By 2008, the Tom Haydens of the world and those they influenced, if not intimidated—the potheads and revolutionary wannabes now all grown up—largely controlled the media flow. Although they rarely fabricated news, they decided what information was allowed through the sluices and what was not. And in the case of the Obama campaign, there was a whole lot of raw data that was not allowed to become "news."

Having made little headway in my search for Obama's muse in the summer of 2008, I was tipped to a story that the media were scrupulously ignoring. It involved the venerable African American entrepreneur and politico Percy Sutton. A Manhattan borough president for twelve years and a credible candidate for mayor of New York City in 1977, Sutton had appeared in late March 2008 on a local New York City show called *Inside City Hall*.

When asked about Obama by the show's host, Dominic Carter, the octogenarian Sutton calmly and lucidly explained that he had been "introduced to [Obama] by a friend." The friend's name was Dr. Khalid al-Mansour, and the introduction had taken place about twenty years earlier. Sutton described al-Mansour as "the principal adviser to one of the world's richest men." The billionaire in question was Saudi prince Al-Waleed bin Talal.

For the record, bin Talal was the very same Saudi who had offered New York $10 million to help the city rebuild after 9/11, but who had his gift refused by Mayor Rudy Giuliani. In September 2001, Giuliani was in no mood to hear even a billionaire blame America for inciting the attacks with its pro-Israel stance, no matter how deep his pockets.

According to Sutton, al-Mansour had asked him to "please write a letter in support of [Obama] . . . a young man that has applied to Harvard." Sutton had friends at Harvard and gladly did so. Although Sutton did not specify a date, this would likely have been in 1988, when the twenty-six-year-old Obama was applying to Harvard Law School.

Khalid al-Mansour was a piece of work. Although impressively well connected, the Texan-born attorney and black separatist had yet to meet a paranoid racial fantasy unworthy of his energy. His books included myopic classics like *The Destruction of Western Civilization as Seen Through Islam* and *Will the West Rule Forever?*

Several of his speeches can still be seen on YouTube. In one named "A Little on the History of Jews," he shares his distinctive insights into the creation of Israel. "God gave you nothing," al-Mansour lectures the world's Ashkenazi Jews. "The children from Poland and Russia were promised nothing. But they are stealing the land the same as the Christians stole the lands from the Indians in America."

No matter how many books he had written, al-Mansour himself lacked the wherewithal to have written or even helped with *Dreams from My Father*. What interested me at the time, however, was that he seemed to be one of many people in Obama's network with enough money and/or influence to get the book of an unknown author written and published.

I had hoped that the blogosphere would force the Sutton story into the larger media. Three months before the election it should have mattered that a respected black political figure had publicly announced that a wild-eyed conspiracy theorist, backed by an ambitious Saudi billionaire, had been guiding Obama's career perhaps for the last twenty years. It apparently did not matter to the gatekeepers. The story died a quick and unnatural death.

Moving in swiftly for the kill were *Politico*, an insider D.C. journal run by *Washington Post* alums, and Media Matters, an alleged watchdog group founded by the recovering Troopergate author, David Brock. Since the reporters from neither entity could deny what Sutton had said, they claimed instead that he had insufficient marbles to be taken seriously.

Ben Smith of *Politico* took the lead. Shortly after the story broke, Smith ran the disclaimer that "Barack Obama's campaign is flatly denying a story told by former Manhattan Borough President Percy Sutton." The Obama camp, in fact, denied that Obama even knew al-Mansour. Smith then talked to al-Mansour. At first, al-Mansour avoided contradicting Sutton's story out of respect for Sutton, "a dear friend." When pressed, however, al-Mansour disowned Sutton's story. "The scenario as it related to me did not happen," he reportedly told Smith.

A self-appointed "spokesman for Sutton's family" by the name of Kevin Wardally put the penultimate nails in this story's coffin with an email to Smith that read in part:

> The information Mr. Percy Sutton imparted on March 25 in a NY1 News interview regarding his connection to Barack Obama is inaccurate. As best as our family and the Chairman's closest friends can tell, Mr. Sutton, now 86 years of age, misspoke in describing certain details and events in that television interview.

For Smith, even though Wardally had gotten Sutton's age wrong by two years, this email was proof enough that Sutton's highly specific claim was manufactured. Wrote Smith, Wardally's email "seems to put the story to rest for good." Media Matters meanwhile scolded those conservative bloggers who did not accept the various denials at face value.

Like the man about to be carted away in *Monty Python's Holy Grail*, the Percy Sutton story was not quite dead yet. *Newsmax*, a conservative satellite in the blogosphere, contacted Wardally. Unconvincingly, he claimed that a nephew of the elder Sutton had retained his services. Sutton's son and daughter, however, told *Newsmax* that no one in their family even knew who Kevin Wardally was, let alone authorized him to speak on behalf of the family. When *Newsmax* contacted al-Mansour, he repeatedly declined to comment on what Sutton had said and, contrary to the line from the Obama camp, claimed to know Obama personally.

"I'm getting better," pled Monty Python's nearly dead man. No he wasn't. Nor was this story. With Hillary out of the race, no newsroom in America felt compelled to dig up dirt that could sully Obama. At the time this story was gelling, in early September 2008, the media were doing all their digging in Alaskan Dumpsters.

At the time, I thought that the premature burial of this story merely *seemed* coordinated. In March 2009, however, Michael Calderone of *Politico* revealed the existence of a four-hundred-member-strong online meeting space called "JournoList." Calderone described the participants as "left-leaning bloggers, political reporters, magazine writers, policy wonks, and academics." Given that three *Politico* writers, Ben Smith among them, contributed to the "JList," as well as David Brock, Calderone wrote approvingly of an enterprise unabashedly designed to elect Barack Obama president. It was not until the content of several group discussions was published in July 2010 that the outside world could see how effectively JList participants had steered the national discourse in Obama's favor.

The books that might have shed some light on the Percy Sutton incident have not done so. John Heilemann and Mark Halperin's comprehensive look at the 2008 campaign, *Game Change*, does not so much as mention Percy Sutton. Nor does David Remnick. The Pulitzer Prize winner and *New Yorker* editor has proved particularly disappointing. *The Bridge* stands as the authoritative book on Obama's "life and rise," but he only inadvertently addresses the question of how Obama got into Harvard Law.

The eighty-nine-year-old Sutton would pass away in December 2009, but the story had died long before he did. With his death, there was no chance the tale would come back to haunt the president. The media gatekeepers in the age of Obama had done their job.

AMIABLE DUNCES

A short time back, an eye-popping documentary about the Moinjang tribe of the White Nile stopped me dead in my channel-surfing tracks. For about a half hour, I watched in awe as several hugely tubby guys wandered around town stark naked, covered in dust, eating everything in sight.

As I learned, the men were participating in an ancient tribal custom, roughly translated as "the fattest man in the land competition." Apparently the competitors eat all they can for about a year, and at the end of the year the biggest lard butt wins. This was billed as "a high-stakes contest" and with good reason: at least one unlucky contestant fell over dead when his stomach exploded. Still, the narrator described the whole phenomenon in the kind of hushed tones one reserves for incomprehensible third-world rituals and/or major golf tournaments.

Oh, that such a respectful documentary crew would have come to Kansas! Instead, in the wake of Thomas Frank's soft-core Marxist bestseller, *What's the Matter with Kansas?*, we got smarmy know-it-alls from either coast. They came not to learn about our humble customs, but rather to tell us what's wrong with the customs we have.

I say "we" reservedly. Although Frank deemed me the embodiment of what was the matter with the Sunflower State, the person in whom "all the contradictions come together," I have spent fewer nights in Kansas (three) than I occupy pages in Frank's book (ten). Details! Details! I live and work in Missouri and was born and raised in New Jersey. Had I been cited as "what's the matter" with either of those two states I would have been honored, but to have been cited as "what's the matter" with Kansas left me feeling mostly just confused.

To help me work through the confusion, the Kansas delegation invited me to attend the 2008 Republican National Convention as their guest, an honorary Kansan. Not having attended a convention before, I happily accepted. A few days beforehand, however, I almost changed my mind. The rumor started seeping out that John McCain was about to pick Joe Lieberman as his running mate, a decent fellow as far as Democrats go, but a Democrat. Unless I misremembered, he had been Al Gore's VP choice in 2000.

Always a contrarian, McCain shocked the media by choosing Sarah Palin. The choice left me feeling very smart. In early June, at lunch with some of my political buddies, I was asked whom I thought McCain would pick as a running mate. "Sarah Palin," I said. They said, "Sarah who?" Now they were all emailing me, "How did you know?" I didn't. I just guessed, but why tell them?

While driving north through Iowa—America's prettiest state in August and September—on that uneasy Labor Day of 2008, I station-surfed to keep abreast of the news. It was all Palin all the time and just about all negative. Like the TV crews that came to Kansas, the radio talking heads were busy telling Republicans how they ought to think and what they ought to do, namely dump Sarah Palin. What with that Marge Gunderson accent and University of Idaho diploma, not to mention the slutty daughter, Sarah Palin was just another lowbrow off the Republican assembly line, no more ready to serve as vice president than Daisy Mae Yokum.

None of this surprised me. The left, through its control of the media, including the entertainment media, has been rigging political IQ tests for the last half century, if not longer. Those Republicans who were not evil geniuses—Nixon, Cheney, Rove—the media have painted as blithering idiots. Dwight Eisenhower was doddering and incoherent. Gerald Ford, perhaps the best athlete to occupy the White House, was a bumbling fool. "I wanted [Jimmy] Carter in and I wanted [Ford] out," comedian Chevy Chase would later admit of his mocking Ford impersonation on *Saturday Night Live*, "and I figured look, we're reaching millions of people every weekend, why not do it."

Ronald Reagan, in the memorable words of Clark Clifford, was an "amiable dunce." The senior George Bush was so out of touch he was ambushed by a grocery scanner. Dan Quayle could not spell *potato*. George W. Bush inspired the popular bumper sticker "A village in Texas is missing its idiot," as well as charming websites like "president moron.com." And now Sarah Palin—the hillbilly who could allegedly "see Russia from my house"—was being anointed Bush's idiot successor.

In a 2010 tour of the White House, my former favorite Beatle, Liverpool High grad Paul McCartney, would capture the pop zeitgeist perfectly both in terms of content and dopy condescension. Said McCartney, in a graceless dig at George Bush, an avid reader and Harvard MBA, "After the last eight years, it's great to have a President who knows what a library is."

Democratic politicians, by contrast, have been "scary smart," too bright for an undeserving American citizenry. Adlai Stevenson was an "egghead." JFK was a Pulitzer Prize–winning author. Eugene McCarthy was professorial. George McGovern was cerebral. Bill Bradley was a Rhodes scholar. So was Bill Clinton. Hillary Clinton was the smartest woman on the planet. Gary Hart, Michael

Dukakis, and Al Gore were all big-brained wonks. John Kerry was so finely educated that when smearing American troops, he remembered to pronounce the name Genghis "jenghis." And Obama, of course, as historian Michael Beschloss put it, was "probably the smartest guy ever to become president."

Most Americans never got to hear that Ted Sorensen wrote Kennedy's *Profiles in Courage* or that Bill Bradley scored a lowly 485 on his SAT verbals or that John Kerry's grades at Yale were "virtually identical" to George W. Bush's. Given the protection the media afforded Democratic candidates, exposing the shaky foundation of Obama's genius would not be easy, regardless of the evidence. With Palin's nomination, the job had just gotten harder. To undermine his bona fides would be to elevate hers, and for many in the media, including some influential conservatives, that would sting doubly.

Although I cannot vouch for Palin's IQ, she is surely smart enough. This I got to confirm firsthand. Despite the merry time we Kansans were having in St. Paul—luncheons, receptions, cruises down the Mississippi flanked by gunboats—we all worried about the pressure on Palin. If she screwed up her big Wednesday night speech, the race was over.

I stayed off the convention floor that evening and sat up in the mezzanine, hard by the bar. Before Palin emerged, I watched a whole parade of women speakers make their pitches—Meg Whitman of eBay, Carly Fiorina of Hewlett-Packard, Governor Linda Lingle of Hawaii. All were a bit dull and stiff but competent. They read from their teleprompters without incident. I remember hoping that Palin could just do as well as they did.

As history will record, she did hugely better. She was sharp, sexy, funny, and utterly charming. Under enormous pressure, she had served up a convention speech as dazzling and unexpected as any in modern political history—including Obama's 2004 keynote—and she did so before a malfunctioning teleprompter. "I knew the speech well enough that I didn't need it," she would say. At night's end every guy I talked to wanted to marry her and have her babies.

Had Obama's teleprompter malfunctioned at the 2004 convention, he would not be president. He has always depended on the eloquence of others. So thoroughly hooked on the teleprompter is Obama that the irrepressible Joe Biden jokes about it. "What am I going to tell the president?" Biden asked the crowd at the Air Force Academy after a teleprompter blew over. "Tell him his teleprompter is broken? What will he do then?"

BEAUTIFUL OLD HOUSE

In early September 2008, while still scouting about for hints as to who might have served as Obama's literary muse, I came across a photo floating through the blogosphere taken during an Arab American community dinner in Chicago in 1998 on the fiftieth anniversary of the Palestinian *nakba*, or disaster, also known as the birth of Israel.

The photo shows Obama sitting next to Edward Said (pronounced "sigh-EED"), seemingly engaged in an animated conversation at dinner. The intimacy surprised me. At the time of the photo, Obama was an obscure state senator while Said, according to the *Nation*, was "probably the best-known intellectual in the world" and star of that evening's show. He would speak on this occasion, as the *Los Angeles Times* would later report, "against settlements, against Israeli apartheid."

I presumed it possible that the pair had met when Obama was a student and Said a professor at Columbia University, but the information known at the time about Obama's New York years was, for a presidential candidate, uniquely sketchy. In late October 2007, the *New York Times* had run a telling article on that period headlined "Obama's Account of New York Years Often Differs From What Others Say." Given that he was an announced candidate for president, the *Times* expected Obama to welcome the chance to reconcile his account in *Dreams* with the accounts of those who knew him. "Yet he declined repeated requests to talk about his New York years, release his Columbia transcript or identify even a single fellow student, co-worker, roommate or friend from those years."

A campaign spokesman, Ben LaBolt, offered a conspicuously lame explanation for Obama's reticence. "He doesn't remember the names of a lot of people in his life." Lame or not, it worked. Obama's indifference to the facts on the ground may have shocked the *Times*, but it did not exactly shock the *Times* or any other media outlet into action.

Nearly three years later—and eighteen months after the election— David Remnick would offer the first serious inquiry into those years and would confirm that Obama had indeed taken a course in modern fiction from Said at Columbia. Although Remnick reports that Obama was not keen on the course, Obama may have absorbed more from Said about modern fiction than Remnick suspects.

Said, you see, lived an almost entirely fictional life. In 1978, he had published his masterwork, *Orientalism*, a book so influential that it changed the very direction of Middle Eastern studies. "*Orientalism* is written out of an extremely concrete history of personal loss and national disintegration," Said observes in the Afterword of the book's 1994 edition. It is this sense of loss that gives the book its spirit of righteous certainty.

Not unlike Obama, Said used his childhood as the central metaphor for his significant life work. "Mr. Said was born in Jerusalem and spent the first twelve years of his life there," confirmed the *New York Times* in a flattering 1998 article. His family left the house and "fled" Palestine for Cairo in late 1947, "five months before war broke out between Palestinian Arabs and Jews over plans to partition Palestine."

Throughout his career, Said returned again and again to the source of his own moral power—the forced exile from "my beautiful old house." For Palestinians and postmodernists, the house at 10 Brenner Street in Jerusalem was at least as iconic as a certain stable in nearby Bethlehem. The Palestinian Heritage Foundation honored Said with a portrait of the house. *Harper's Magazine* commemorated Said's celebratory visit to the house. The BBC featured the house in a documentary, which showed, among other indignities, Said fussing to get it back from the Israeli authorities.

Although the house would stand, the fable Said had constructed was about to be deconstructed. By 1998, the year of the documentary and the year he and Obama schmoozed in Chicago, an Israeli scholar named Justus Reid Weiner had already done two years of hard-nosed research on the excellent adventures of Edward Said. "Virtually everything I learned," Weiner would write, "contradicts the story of Said's early life as Said has told it."

Weiner released his findings a year later in the September 1999 issue of the influential Jewish magazine *Commentary*. As Weiner revealed, Said's early life was even more charmed and elitist than Obama's own and his origins story just as shaky. Yes, Said was born in Jerusalem in 1935 but only because maternity care—Jewish doctors?—was better there than in Egypt. After his birth, the family hightailed it back to Cairo, where his father, a naturalized American citizen, had been living for the last decade and continued to grow his prosperous office supply business.

A Christian and an American citizen from birth, Said attended the best British schools in Cairo before leaving for the Mount Hermon School in Massachusetts, Princeton University, and ultimately Harvard. The famed house, Weiner learned, belonged to Said's Jerusalem relatives. It was sufficiently small that the affluent Cairo cousins may never have even stayed there.

Said was busted big-time. Weiner had proved beyond doubt that America's most celebrated Palestinian refugee was not really a Palestinian or a refugee, let alone a Muslim. The whole moral basis for his postcolonial posturing as victim seemed shot. To its credit, the *New York Times* gave Weiner's exposé decent coverage and confirmed his findings.

Not surprisingly, however, when Said died four years later, the media buried the fraud along with his body. In a glowing obituary, the *New York Times* revived Said's imaginary past, claiming in the obit's opening that he had "spent his childhood" in Jerusalem and fled with his family "to Cairo in 1947 after the United Nations divided Jerusalem into Jewish and Arab halves." The *Times* mentioned the Weiner research dismissively two thousand words into an otherwise laudatory 2,600-word obituary.

The lack of diversity at the cultural gates makes cases like Said's much more common than they ought to be. The gatekeepers tend to think scarily alike on social and political issues. Not unnaturally, they promote individuals who think as they do and they protect those from people who think otherwise. In their eyes, a favored artiste could do almost anything shy of telling a racial joke and not lose standing. And in the fall of 2008, no one was more favored—or less likely to tell a racial joke—than Barack Obama. Taking him on would not be easy.

FUGITIVE DAYS

lthough I continued to dabble in literary detective work that
September, I spent most of my spare moments on the Khalid
al-Mansour angle. I strongly suspected that Obama had help
with *Dreams*, but I saw no easy way of proving it or identifying his
muse. I was more interested in how he had gotten into Harvard.

One diary entry that I found caught my attention. Radical-turned-
actor Peter Coyote entered it at the time of the 1996 Democratic Na-
tional Convention. "After that," Coyote wrote, "I inform Martha that
I'm dragging her to the apartment of old friends, ex-Weathermen,
Bernadine [*sic*] Dohrn and Bill Ayers, hosting a party for Senator
Leahy. Perhaps Edward Said will be there." I still don't know who
Martha is, but the entry got me to wondering whether an Ayers-
Obama-Said-al-Mansour cabal had formed in the early 1980s back in
New York City. If so, such a combine might have generated enough
momentum to push Obama's career along.

To see if Obama and Ayers had crossed paths before Chicago, I ordered a copy of Bill Ayers's 2001 memoir, *Fugitive Days*. The book had a memorable marketing history. In August 2001, *Chicago* magazine helped launch it with a color photo of Ayers, hands in pockets, face alight with his superior wisdom, feet firmly planted on an American flag. The article is aptly titled "No Regrets," and the sympathetic author suggests no reason why Ayers should harbor any.

The *New York Times* followed soon thereafter with a lengthy article of its own. Dinitia Smith begins her review of the book and its author with a now-famous quote from Ayers. "I don't regret setting bombs," Ayers tells her. "I feel we didn't do enough." Smith interviewed Ayers in his unproletarian "big turn-of-the-19th-century stone house" in Chicago's Hyde Park.

In the book, Ayers traces his career arc from his upbringing in a prosperous Chicago suburb to his emergence as a campus radical to his ten-year stint in the Weather Underground as a part-time bomber and full-time fugitive. As Smith notes, Ayers plays with the truth. Of the events related in the book he writes, "Is this, then, the truth? Not exactly. Although it feels entirely honest to me." When questioned by Smith as to why someone should read a less than honest memoir, Ayers answers, "Obviously, the point is it's a reflection on memory. It's true as I remember it."

Given Ayers's career as a bomber, the review is sober, lengthy, and exquisitely nonjudgmental. Despite the occasional quibble about Ayers's career choices, Smith allows him the last word. "I was a child of privilege," he tells her, "and I woke up to a world on fire. And hope and history rhymed." If Ayers told Smith he lifted the "hope and history" line from Seamus Heaney's *The Cure at Troy*, she neglected to mention it.

Under normal circumstances, a lengthy *Times* article titled "No Regrets for a Love of Explosives" would have propelled *Fugitive Days* onto the bestseller lists. But there was nothing normal about the day of this article's publication. Within hours of the paper's release, the world, or at least the Lower Manhattan part of it, was literally on fire.

On this memorable September 11, more competent terrorists than Ayers had suddenly thrown his "love" into disrepute. If not literally, certainly emotionally, Ayers was forced underground again.

The specter of Bill Ayers resurfaced dramatically during an April 2008 presidential debate broadcast live on ABC. Moderator and former Clinton aide George Stephanopoulos threw Obama a curve that he likely expected at some point, but not on his home turf, a primary debate on network TV. His checked swing would mark his character as surely as Bill Clinton's memorable whiff on the subject of "that woman, Ms. Lewinsky."

While addressing the "general theme of patriotism," Stephanopoulos asked Obama about Ayers. "He was part of the Weather Underground in the 1970s," Stephanopoulos reminded the audience. "They bombed the Pentagon, the Capitol, and other buildings. He's never apologized for that." He then asked Obama, "Can you explain that relationship for the voters and explain to Democrats why it won't be a problem?"

If Obama was caught asleep at the plate, there was a good reason why. David Axelrod thought he had retired the Ayers issue two months earlier. In February, Ben Smith of *Politico* had reported as gospel Axelrod's claim that Obama scarcely knew Ayers. Their children "attend the same school," said Axelrod, but the relationship went no deeper. When a reader alerted Smith that Ayers's youngest child was twenty-three when Obama's oldest child started kindergarten, Smith added a comically circuitous "update," but the media shied from chasing the story or even chiding Axelrod. It was clear they wanted no part of Ayers.

The Stephanopoulos question put Obama on the spot. "I know not the man," he replied—no, excuse me, that was Peter on the subject of Jesus. On the subject of Ayers, Obama proved only slightly more straightforward. "This is a guy who lives in my neighborhood," said Obama for the ages. "He's not somebody who I exchange ideas from [*sic*] on a regular basis." Obama then went on to scold Stephanopoulos for daring to ask a question about a man who "engaged in detestable acts forty years ago, when I was eight years old." To suggest that this relationship somehow reflected on him and his values, huffed Obama, "doesn't make much sense."

Following the debate, just about every chatterbox in the chattering class fueled what the *Los Angeles Times* called a "storm of criticism." Their rage was directed not at Obama for his evasiveness, but at Stephanopoulos for his effrontery. How dare he confront Obama with "such tired tripe," said the *Washington Post*'s Tom Shales. How dare he ask Obama about an "obscure sixties radical," said Michael Grunwald of *Time*.

A *Huffington Post* blogger likened Stephanopoulos to the inevitable Joe McCarthy. He was one of many to do so. In the unkindest of cuts, several pundits accused him of conspiring with Sean Hannity. "The real story of this debate," snarled MSNBC's ever-suspicious Keith Olbermann, may be "where one of the moderators found his questions."

Not surprisingly, the ABC debate proved to be one of the topics about which the participants in the notorious JournoList had conspired. Before the conspiracy unraveled, Michael Calderone of *Politico* would classify Stephanopoulos's grilling of Obama on Ayers and Jeremiah Wright as sixth among the "top ten media blunders of 2008."

If Ayers was marginally in play before the debate, he was clearly out of bounds afterward, at least in the mainstream arena. Obama had established his distance from this guy in the neighborhood, and God help the reporter or vice presidential candidate who imagined them more closely together.

That kind of imagining was left to folks like myself in the blogosphere. Reading *Fugitive Days* recalled for me that eerily unstable age. I had just started graduate school at Purdue when Mark Rudd stopped by on the way to Chicago to recruit young Boilermakers for the now-infamous "Days of Rage." Although I went to hear him, I was not tempted to join his children's crusade. I knew only one Weather guy personally, but I knew the type well: soft, suburban, spoiled, self-righteous, petulant, pissed off at the old man. Circa 1969, universities abounded in revolutionary fodder.

At the time, Ayers had a lower public profile than Rudd, who had held center stage at the Columbia University protests, and a much lower one than his future wife, Bernardine Dohrn, the miniskirted guerrilla hottie with her killer bod and folk-singer hair. In 1969, Dohrn attained a new level of notoriety at a Michigan "War Council." Here she challenged her comrades to take aim on "Amerikkka" and wreak havoc within the "belly of the beast." Dohrn then raised three fingers in a "fork salute" to Charlie Manson, recently arrested for the murder of pregnant actress Sharon Tate and seven others. "Dig it," shrieked Dohrn. "First they killed those pigs, then they ate dinner in the same room with them, they even shoved a fork into a victim's stomach! Wild!" Years later, Dohrn would say she was just kidding.

At the time, however, the young woman who held Ayers's heart was the more demure—who wasn't?—Diana Oughton. In *Fugitive Days*, he speaks of her as reverentially as Al once did of Tipper. "Diana was fair with glowing cheekbones, prominent forehead, powerful arms and legs," Ayers writes. "She was somehow both elegant and simple, her golden hair and classic good looks balanced by a gaze that beamed out with unexpected intensity."

The prelude of *Fugitive Days* opens with Dohrn informing Ayers that Oughton had been killed in the explosion of a Greenwich Village bomb factory. Oughton and her comrades had been simply and elegantly plotting to plant an antipersonnel bomb at a dance for noncoms and their dates in nearby Fort Dix, New Jersey. This is a fact that Ayers readily concedes. Had they succeeded, we would remember Ayers today the way we remember Timothy McVeigh, and any kind of relationship with the man would have cost Obama a gig as alderman, let alone president.

"The woman on the other end of the phone would save me soon," writes Ayers of Dohrn, "and soon after that we would plunge together into a subterranean river, the strong, swift brown god of life pulling us forward for decades to come." The guy that readers of *Fugitive Days* meet in this subterranean swamp is not someone they would probably want their president palling around with.

Ayers may have outgrown his affection for violence, but his attraction to radical politics smoldered on. Like so many on the hard left, he supported those politics with whatever historical invention he could get away with. "If there is no God," said Jean-Paul Sartre in his famous paraphrase of Dostoyevsky's Ivan Karamazov, "everything is permitted."

Ayers admits as much. "The old gods failed and the old truths left the world." He continues: "Clear conclusions were mainly delusional, a luxury of religious fanatics and fools." Having declared truth obsolete, Ayers goes on to say pretty much whatever serves his political purpose. "He was not interested in finding the truth but in proclaiming it," British historian Paul Johnson said of Karl Marx, but he might as well have been talking about Ayers. To justify his bombing of the Pentagon, for instance, Ayers tells the reader that a century earlier abolitionist John Brown had "shot all the members of the grand jury." Brown, of course, did no such thing.

Nowhere is an ill word said about the demonstrably murderous thugs Ayers holds up as heroes: Castro, Che, Ho Chi Minh, or even Mao, arguably the greatest monster of the 20th century. As to Oughton and her two comrades who blew themselves up, Ayers wonders out loud how long it will take before America "imagines their actions as heroic."

The question that those of us not on the JournoList were asking in the fall of 2008 was how Obama responded to after-dinner stories chez Ayers that ended with the punch line "Kaboom." Did he too imagine the Weather pals' actions as "heroic"?

One cultural artifact that sheds light on Obama's milieu is *Weather Underground*, a watchable 2002 documentary on the soi-disant Weathermen and their times. Although superficially objective, the film allows the final comment of Rudd to stand as something of a thesis statement.

"It was this knowledge that we couldn't handle," says Rudd, explaining the group's turn to violence. "It was too big. We didn't know what to do. In a way I still don't know what to do with the knowledge."

The Russian equivalent for Rudd's "big" knowledge is *pravda*, as in "larger truth" or "truth and justice." In the Soviet era, Communists hammered the facts Procrustes-style until they fit the "truth." Small *c* communists like Rudd and Ayers still do. By contorting every fact that did not naturally fit their template, the Weathermen and their allies concluded, in Ayers's words, that America's "intentions were evil and her justifications dissembling, her explanations dishonest, her every move false." This was the "knowledge" uniquely intuited by the hard left that Rudd and his colleagues found "too big" to handle.

In *Weather Underground* not one of the seven or eight Weathermen interviewed in 2002 questions this assumption about America and the Vietnam War. Neither do their liberal critics in the film, nor do the filmmakers for that matter. All that anyone questions are the futile ends to which the Weathermen applied their superior insights.

The film offers no hint that Cambodia sunk into horrific genocide and Vietnam into a repressive Stalinist state after the Weathermen's Communist heroes took over. No hint that the antiwar left ignored, or cheered, the horrific consequences of America's withdrawal. In sum, no hint that the Weathermen's larger truth was largely false.

More troubling, in neither of their memoirs does either author give any sense that his "big" knowledge is any less true or relevant today than it was forty years ago. America was and remains, in Rudd's words, "racist" and "imperialist." It must be thus, as Ayers declaimed in a 2006 speech in Venezuela, because "capitalism promotes racism and militarism—turning people into consumers, not citizens." In a 2006 essay, he describes America as "still the biggest threat to a world at peace and in balance."

If there is any one chapter in *Dreams* that shows how seamlessly Obama could have embraced this worldview, it is the one that documents his life in Indonesia, ages six to ten. Much has been made of his education as a Muslim during those years but not enough of his grooming as a secular humanist with a deeply ingrained contempt for his fellow Americans.

The chapter reads like an extended parable on the subject of American imperialism. No doubt, terrible things happened in Indonesia shortly before Obama's arrival in 1967. As intimated in *Dreams*, the United States, "obsessed with the march of communism through Indochina," instigated a coup that resulted in the installation of a corrupt military dictatorship and the subsequent slaughter of perhaps a half million otherwise innocent communists.

In reality, however, the Indonesian military led a counterrevolution to suppress a bloody coup by the huge and restless PKI, the communist party of Indonesia. Islamic political organizations took advantage of the upheaval and began slaughtering communists wherever they could find them. In those places like Bali, where Hindu groups ruled, the Hindus led the anti-PKI pogroms. One gets the sense that in Indonesia no one much liked the communists.

Obama's mom, the wide-eyed Ann Dunham Obama Soetoro, stumbled into the country just as the dust was settling on this mayhem. As attracted as she was to the multicultural ideal, she didn't much like Indonesian health care or, come to think of it, Indonesian education. These Western weaknesses, however, did not prevent her from feeling purer than her fellow Americans. When her then husband Lolo Soetoro asked her to meet some of "her own people" at the American oil company where he worked, she shouted at him, "They are not my people." In the midst of all these "ugly Americans," Ann remained, in Obama's words, "a lonely witness for secular humanism, a soldier for New Deal, Peace Corps, position-paper liberalism."

As a boy, Obama learned that perhaps the only thing exceptional about America was Barack Hussein Obama. Back in Hawaii, his communist mentor, Frank Marshall Davis, reinforced his mom's ugly-American riff, and Obama soaked it in. In *Dreams*, he describes the Americanization of Hawaii as an "ugly conquest." Missionaries brought "crippling diseases." American companies carved up "the rich volcanic soil" and worked their indentured laborers of color "from sunup to sunset." And during the war, of course, the government interned Hawaii's "Japanese-Americans."

In Obama's account, as in the standard progressive retelling of American history, facts are bent to serve a larger purpose. In the litany above, Obama bends one fact beyond the breaking point. In reality, more than 99 percent of Hawaii's Japanese and Japanese Americans were *not* interned. After the horrors of Pearl Harbor, the American response suggested not racism or oppression, as Obama implies, but enlightened restraint.

After hitting the mainland Obama surrounded himself with leftists well versed in the knowledge too big to handle. "I chose my friends carefully," he writes in *Dreams*. "The more politically active black students. The foreign students. The Chicanos. The Marxist professors and structural feminists and punk-rock performance poets." With his new friends, Obama discussed "neocolonialism, Franz [*sic*] Fanon, Eurocentrism, and patriarchy" and flaunted his alienation.

The literary influences Obama cites include radical anti-imperialists like Fanon and Malcolm X, communists like Langston Hughes and Richard Wright, and tyrant-loving fellow travelers like W. E. B. Du Bois. "Joseph Stalin was a great man," Du Bois wrote upon Stalin's death in 1953. "Few other men of the 20th century approach his stature."

In *Dreams*, Obama gives no suggestion that this reading was in any way problematic or a mere phase in his development. He moves on to no new school, embraces no new worldview. At least five of the authors he cites—Wright, Fanon, Hughes, Malcolm X, and James Baldwin—Bill Ayers cites in his writings as well. (As an aside, both Obama and Ayers misspell Fanon's name in the same way, as "Franz.")

Obama unwittingly gives the game away in *Audacity*. When scolding his fellow liberals for not facing up to current international threats, he writes, "It's useful to remind ourselves that Osama bin Laden is not

Ho Chi Minh." No, of course not. In Hyde Park, Ho is the kind of murderous thug kids still look up to, sort of like Che, just not cute enough to put on a T-shirt. In 2008, some Obama campaign workers in Texas proudly tacked Che posters to the wall, blissfully unaware that communist executioners lack red-state crossover appeal.

Not surprisingly, given his inputs, Barack Obama has embraced a vaguely Marxist, postcolonial view of the capitalist enterprise. In the 2004 preface to *Dreams*, written after his keynote speech at the Democratic convention, he describes an ongoing "struggle—between worlds of plenty and worlds of want." America, he implies, prospers only at the expense of the rest of the world, a zero-sum fallacy common among those who refuse to understand the way free enterprise works.

"I have seen, the desperation and disorder of the powerless: how it twists the lives of children on the streets of Jakarta or Nairobi in much the same way as it does the lives of children on Chicago's South Side," Obama continues. When the powerless strike back, the powerful respond with "a steady, unthinking application of force, of longer prison sentences and more sophisticated military hardware."

By equating Chicago with the third world, Obama endorses the link between racism and imperialism, the presumed motive for America's involvement in Vietnam. Later in *Dreams*, he makes this point more explicitly when he talks about righteous insurrections in "Soweto or Detroit or the Mekong Delta." For the left, racism at home parallels imperialism abroad, one or both of which must inevitably underwrite the capitalist adventure.

To be fair, the "Detroit" and "Mekong Delta" references—the whole preface, for that matter—are more likely to have come from Bill Ayers's pen than Obama's, but if so, Obama surely felt comfortable with Ayers's conclusions. And from all evidence, even after two years as president, he still accepts the left's relentless anticapitalist, anti-American agitprop as "knowledge."

THE WORD-SLINGER

As much as I disagreed with Ayers on the issues, I had to admit that *Fugitive Days* was well written, so well written, in fact, that I thought he too must have had a ghostwriter. For whatever reason, one sentence caught my attention. It reads, "I picture the street coming alive, awakening from the fury of winter, stirred from the chilly spring night by cold glimmers of sunlight angling through the city."

The sentence reminded me of one I had read in *Dreams*. I pulled out my dog-eared copy and thumbed through the highlighted passages until I found this one: "Night now fell in midafternoon, especially when the snowstorms rolled in, boundless prairie storms that set the sky close to the ground, the city lights reflected against the clouds."

These two sentences struck me as similar in their poetic flow, their length, and their gracefully layered structure. When I ran them through a simple test available on Microsoft Word, the Flesch Reading Ease Score (FRES), something of a standard in the field, they tabulated nearly identical scores. The *Fugitive Days* excerpt registered a 54 on reading ease and a twelfth-grade reading level, the *Dreams* excerpt a 54.8 on reading ease and a twelfth-grade reading level as well. Scores can range from 0 to 121. Hitting a nearly exact score mattered at least enough to keep my attention.

Another little thing that struck me was the word *midafternoon*. I had never used that particular locution. Although more expansive dictionaries include the word as written in *Dreams*, it was distinctive enough that my Microsoft Word program underlined it in red, meaning misspelled or not a word. None of this would have mattered much save that Ayers used *midafternoon*, too, as in "I had the thing mostly memorized by midafternoon."

At this point, I had my first eureka moment, albeit a dumb one—Gosh, I thought, they both live in Chicago. They must have shared the same ghostwriter! As I continued reading Ayers's memoir, however, I began to sense a real stylistic difference between the two books: *Fugitive Days* is infused with the authorial voice in every sentence. It is fierce, succinct, and tightly coiled throughout. "What makes *Fugitive Days* unique," wrote Edward Said in a blurb, "is its unsparing detail and its marvelous human coherence and integrity." If "integrity" means sticking to one's guns regardless of facts or fashion, there is no denying what Said says. Say what one will about Ayers, he did live an eventful life at a dramatic moment.

At that time, September 2008, I had no idea that Ayers was an accomplished writer and editor, but he is. By this point in his career, he had written three mainstream books on his own and, importantly, edited or co-authored at least twice as many more. His style and tone remain consistent throughout his books and articles, and there can be little doubt that he wrote them himself.

Ayers's affection for language dates back at least to his days in the Weather Underground. "We were ill-equipped gunslingers," he writes in the introduction to the 2006 book *Sing a Battle Song*, "and we became word-slingers instead." He clarifies: "The Weatherpeople were all talkers—we already loved words and we read widely." In this same passage, Ayers observes that words "tumbled from us in a crazy flash flood." In *Dreams*, as it happens, "words tumbled out of [Obama's] mouth" as well, and memories come in a "flood."

Although the media were at pains to minimize the connection between Ayers and Obama—Remnick dismisses as "preposterous" the notion that the two "were ever close friends or shared political ideas"—there was enough known about their relationship by September 2008 to suggest a motive for Ayers's involvement in *Dreams*. Stanley Kurtz had been doing yeoman research on this subject for the *National Review*.

As Kurtz reported, the then little-known Obama assumed the chairmanship of the Chicago Annenberg Challenge (CAC) only months before he launched his first state senate campaign in 1995. The Annenberg Foundation had breathed the CAC to life that same year with a $50 million grant to be matched by $100 million from other sources. The money was to fund educational reform projects.

Ayers was the co-founder and guiding force behind this massive slush fund. Not surprisingly, as often happens, the money Republicans like Annenberg earned, progressives like Ayers and Obama spent. Ayers's own radical projects received enough funding to raise eyebrows even within the CAC. As a chairman more than a little indebted to Ayers, Obama seemed indifferent to possible conflicts of interest as he happily signed off on Ayers's adventures.

When Ayers helped launch the Obama campaign in September 1995 with a fund-raiser chez Bill and Bernardine, it was surely more than the neighborly gesture that both Ayers and Remnick suggest. Kurtz more accurately pegs the fund-raiser as "further evidence of a close and ongoing political partnership."

In the spirit of fairness, Kurtz asked the Obama campaign to respond to his findings, and the campaign did so in some detail. The spokesperson minimized the relationship between Ayers and Obama, cited the Annenberg fund's Republican genesis, and claimed, rather boldly, "Ayers had nothing to do with Obama's recruitment to the Board." As even the Obama-friendly Remnick concedes, however, "Ayers helped bring Obama onto the Annenberg board."

Kurtz would slice and dice the Obama rebuttal into a thousand little pieces and prove, through the board's own documentation, that the CAC "was largely Ayers's show." What caught my attention about this budding relationship was the timing. Ayers maneuvered Obama onto the board in February 1995. He hosted a campaign kickoff for Obama in September 1995, and *Dreams* was published in June 1995. Michael Milken was sent to the slammer for collusion on less evidence.

Those inclined to believe that Ayers was prepping Obama for the presidency, however, inflate the vision of both Ayers and Obama. Although seriously calculated, *Dreams* is too revealing in too many troubling ways—drugs, Jeremiah Wright, Frank Marshall Davis—to boost an aspiring presidential candidate. More likely, Ayers thought he was grooming a future mayor of Chicago.

"I met [Obama] sometime in the mid-1990s," Ayers would later tell *Salon*. "And everyone who knew him thought that he was politically ambitious. For the first two years, I thought, his ambition is so huge that he wants to be mayor of Chicago." Obama friend Cassandra Butts traced that ambition back at least to Harvard. "He wanted to be mayor of Chicago and that was all he ever talked about as far as holding office," she would tell Chicago reporter David Mendell, author of the valuable 2007 biography *Obama: From Promise to Power*.

The young Obama was modeling his career on that of his political hero, the late Chicago mayor Harold Washington. Washington had moved from the Illinois state senate to Congress to the mayoralty. *Dreams* roots Obama in the Chicago experience and in the progressive tradition thereof. As such, it seems finely calibrated to attract the black/lakefront liberal coalition needed for a Democrat not named Daley to achieve high office in Illinois. As Chicago mayor, Obama could have been very helpful to the parochial power broker Ayers. As the president of our "marauding monster" of a country, Obama causes him only a mess of philosophical and emotional problems.

Eight weeks shy of a hugely consequential election, no one was even raising as a possibility what to me now seemed probability—Ayers helped Obama write *Dreams*. Kurtz, for instance, would write that Ayers had emerged as "a sort of father-figure" in the radical community, one who routinely helped edit the collections of "like-minded authors," but neither he nor anyone else at *National Review* was hinting Obama might be one of those authors. I seemed to have uniquely chanced upon a genuine October surprise. The only problem—rather a major one—was that no one else could see it.

POETIC TRUTHS

I t just so happened that Barack Obama was not the only black icon in his neighborhood to write a bestselling memoir. Boxing great Muhammad Ali produced one long before Obama, and he too with more than a little assistance. In Ali's case, that assistance has been well documented by black scholar Gerald Early.

According to Early, the Nation of Islam oversaw the entire production of *The Greatest: My Own Story*. The NOI newspaper's Marxist editor, Richard Durham, taped any number of conversations with the nearly illiterate Ali or between Ali and others and then gave them to an "editor" for writing. That editor was a young Toni Morrison. Ali's is surely the only boxing autobiography ghosted by a future Nobel Prize winner. NOI honcho Elijah Muhammad's son Herbert reviewed every page. As one might expect, Ali's Muslim helpmates rendered his story poorer, tougher, and blacker than the truth would bear.

The editing collective had no use for Ali's white ancestors, his middle-class home, his loving parents, his Olympic gold, the glorious reception in hometown Louisville, the generous white sponsors, and the inevitable pink Cadillac. The true story did not make anyone angry enough to dial 1-800-FARRAKHAN. So for *The Greatest*, Ali and his handlers had to imagine a grievance ugly enough to undo Ali's obvious blessings. For symbolic reasons, they zeroed in on the Olympic gold.

In the approved NOI version, Ali, wearing his gold medal, stops at a Kentucky diner to duck an impending rainstorm. The manager, true to stereotype, has no use for the man the whole town just honored, gold medal or no gold medal. "We don't serve no niggers," he drawls ominously.

"Suddenly I knew what I wanted to do with this cheap piece of metal and raggedy ribbon," says Ali. He heads toward a bridge over the Ohio River. To reach the bridge, though, he and a buddy have to fight their way past the local racist motorcycle gang. The gang dispatched, Ali throws the medal into the river. True to form, the *New York Times* described *The Greatest* as "honest" and "very convincing." Ali's sidekick Bundini Brown knew better. "Honkies sure bought into that one," he would tell *Sports Illustrated*. In reality, the instinctively patriotic Ali wore the medal until the gold rubbed off.

As I was coming to believe, whoever guided Obama steered him toward a grievance narrative like Ali's, if not quite as obvious or extravagant. Unlike Ali, however, Obama occasionally acknowledges the slightness of his racial traumas. Still, he revels in describing them. The most dramatic of these has the nine-year-old Obama visiting the American embassy in Indonesia. While waiting for his mother, he chances upon "a collection of *Life* magazines neatly displayed in clear plastic binders." In one magazine, he reads a story about a black man with an "uneven, ghostly hue," who has been rendered grotesque by a chemical treatment.

"There were thousands of people like him," Obama learned, "black men and women back in America who'd undergone the same treatment in response to advertisements that promised happiness as a white person." Obama's attention to detail is a ruse. *Life* never ran such an article. When challenged, Obama claimed it was *Ebony*. *Ebony* ran no such article, either. Among the thousands of black people I saw in Newark, New Jersey, where I lived at the time, I never saw anyone so disfigured. Besides, in 1970, black was beautiful.

Most of the racial slights Obama recounts in *Dreams*—and there are several—seem equally counterfeit and even more trivial. On one occasion a tennis coach touches Obama's skin to see if the color rubs off—and this in a state where whites are in the minority, mind you. On another mystifying occasion, Obama barely refrains from punching out a white school chum because the kid makes a sympathetic allusion to Obama's outsider status. On a few occasions, Obama scolds his mother for romanticizing the black experience, and then, of course, he chastises his grandmother Madelyn Dunham, aka Toot, first in the book, and later before the world, for daring to let a black panhandler intimidate her.

Remnick concedes that many of these grievances are "novelistic contrivances," but if Obama "darkens the canvas" or "heightens whatever opportunity arises" to score a racial point, he does so, according to Remnick, "obviously" because he is going "after an emotional truth."

Shelby Steele, who is biracial himself, has seen these kind of "truths" played out around him from the time he was a boy in a still-segregated world. In his underappreciated 2008 book, *The Bound Man: Why We Are Excited About Obama and Why He Can't Win*, Steele dissected Obama's soul with more precision than anyone has before or since, and he did so before Obama had won a primary. The book's subtitle, by the way, only seems to suggest a miscalculation on Steele's part. The "win" does not refer to the election.

Obama's dilemma, as Steele sees it, is that in his quest to seem an "authentic" black man, Obama feels compelled to exaggerate the state of black victimization. Rather than fixing problems, many of which are spawned within the black community, the newly authentic Obama fixes blame. When Obama has attempted to tackle moral issues, some more seemingly authentic black leader can be counted on to whittle Obama down to size.

"I wanna cut his nuts off," said Jesse Jackson, almost on cue, when in July 2008 Obama gingerly addressed the issue of parental responsibility. Despite his accidentally televised threat, Jackson somehow stayed on the Obama campaign, and Obama got back to blaming the government. Obama's deterministic approach to racial issues, says Steele, "commits him to a manipulation of the very society he seeks to lead."

Unfortunately, Obama did not look to Shelby Steele as a potential mentor, and although he did look to Frank Marshall Davis, Davis died before he could instruct the lad in the art of memoir writing. The contrast between *Dreams* and Davis's own memoir, *Livin' the Blues*, is stark. Growing up in small-town southern Kansas in the early years of the 20th century, Davis endured more racist crap in a given day than Obama endured in his entire life.

As a high school basketball player, Obama was known to pout when benched, thinking his race the reason why. Davis suffered no such confusion. When white schoolmates threw a rope around his neck and played at lynching, he knew the reason why. Yet Davis exaggerates his gripes not at all and exonerates the whites around him when exoneration is due. Unlike the doggedly humorless Obama, Davis writes about his life with a comic flair and a healthy sense of the absurd.

Davis died in 1987, two years after Obama arrived in Chicago. For guidance in the Windy City, Obama looked to people like Jeremiah Wright, who relentlessly instructed his congregants, says Steele, "to think and act as if the exaggerated poetic truth of white racism is the literal truth." Writing well before anyone had seen those telltale videos, Steele asks a fundamental question: how could Obama "sit every week in a church preaching blackness and not object"?

Even on a first reading of *Dreams*, I could see that Obama's muse proved particularly eloquent on the subject of the angry black male.

Phrases like "full of inarticulate resentments," "knotted, howling assertion of self," "unruly maleness," "unadorned insistence on respect," and "withdrawal into a smaller and smaller coil of rage" lace the book. Yet in the several spontaneous interviews Obama had given on the subject of race, I had not seen a glimpse of this eloquence and insight. The good reverend, as I could see, had the requisite anger in surplus but lacked the editorial chops to bring this project to life. At the time I had no idea who had both.

The evidence, however, was leading me toward an odd conclusion: the man who lent Obama his voice on the subject of blackness gave all appearances of being white. The more I researched Bill Ayers's background, the less unlikely this seemed. Skin color aside, Ayers and Obama had much in common. Both grew up in comfortable white households, attended idyllic, largely white prep schools, and have struggled to find an identity as righteous black men ever since.

"I also thought I was black," writes Ayers only half jokingly. He read all the authors Obama did—James Baldwin, LeRoi Jones, Richard Wright, Malcolm X. As proof of his righteousness, Ayers named his first son "Malik" after the newly Islamic Malcolm X and the second son "Zayd" after Zayd Shakur, a Black Panther killed in a shootout that claimed the life of a New Jersey state trooper. Just as Obama resisted "the pure and heady breeze of privilege" to which he was exposed as a child, Ayers too resisted "white skin privilege," or at least tried to.

Tellingly, Ayers, like Obama, began his career as a self-described "community organizer," Ayers in inner-city Cleveland, Obama in inner-city Chicago. In Chicago, Ayers also found a strategic ally in Jeremiah Wright, a man he called a "distinguished theologian and major intellectual," meaning that Wright too spelled "Amerikkka" with three *k*'s. In short, Ayers was fully capable of crawling inside Obama's head and relating in superior prose what Obama calls, only half ironically, a "rage at the white world [that] needed no object."

In *Fugitive Days*, "rage" rules. Ayers tells of how his "rage got started" and how it evolved into an "uncontrollable rage—fierce frenzy of fire and lava." In fact, both Ayers and Obama speak of "rage" the way that Eskimos do of snow—in so many varieties, so often, that they feel the need to qualify it, as Obama does when he speaks of "impressive rage," "suppressed rage," or "coil of rage." The real roots of Obama's rage trace back not to his father in Kenya, but to his pal in Hyde Park.

This rage leads Ayers to a sentiment with which Obama was altogether familiar. Ayers writes, "I felt the warrior rising up inside of me—audacity and courage, righteousness, of course, and more audacity." Ayers had likely pulled the concept of "audacity" from the same source Jeremiah Wright did, Martin Luther King. Something apparently got lost in translation.

Although Ayers rages at "structural racism" in all of his books, that rage approaches primal scream in *Race Course: Against White Supremacy*, a book he co-wrote with wife Bernardine *after* Obama's election. One would think that victory would have eased the pain, but it has done no such thing for Ayers and any number of other radicals, black and white.

Among the eternally irritated is Tim Wise, author of *Between Barack and a Hard Place: Racism and White Denial in the Age of Obama*. Self-described as an "Angry White Male" in the title of one of his earlier works, Wise penned his jeremiad post-election precisely to deny whites even a moment of self-congratulation.

In his book, Wise quickly reassures his audience that the "deep-seated cultural malady" of racism has been "neither eradicated nor even substantially diminished by Obama's victory." To support his arguments, he marshals the most outlandish set of statistics I have seen in a book that was not self-published.

Scarier still, the copy of the book I bought online had been previously owned by a student assigned to read it, likely by Wise himself, a former "distinguished visiting scholar for Diversity Issues" at Washburn University in my native Kansas. Even scarier, she seems to have bought into his malarkey. The student writes, among other silly notes, "great simile" in the margin where Wise compares the oppression of witches in 17th century Salem with that of blacks in contemporary America. I wish I were kidding. Wise, like Ayers, like Wright, like all believers in institutional racism, sees remediation only through "productive anti-racism and social justice work."

In a similar spirit, Ayers rejects any easy "end-of-white-supremacy narrative." He fears that Obama's victory may actually set back the cause of social justice by taking black concerns off the table to preserve the illusion of racial harmony. For Ayers, social justice means nothing less than communism, albeit with a small *c*. In 1993, a year before *Dreams* was finally written, Ayers would concede in an interview for the book *Sixties Radicals, Then and Now*, "Maybe I'm the last communist who is willing to admit it." Outside of Cuba, North Korea, and the occasional American campus, he still may be.

Listening to these radical voices, Steele believes, has kept Obama a "bound man." He is not allowed to extrapolate from his own experience and preach the value of education, marriage, family, ambition, and success. At exactly the wrong moment, Ayers crawled into Obama's head, much as Elijah Muhammad had crawled into Ali's, and shielded his charge from his better angels.

Ayers had the chance to help Obama establish himself as his own man, but instead, like Wright and so many others, he insisted that, to be authentic, a black man must rage at the machine. If Obama argued for redemption through self-help, his core supporters, black and white, would deny him his authenticity. For someone who has struggled so long and hard to establish an identity, that denial is scarier than defeat. This is why, implies Steele, "He Can't Win."

CRYSTAL CHAOS

On October 2, 2002, at an impromptu rally staged by Chicagoans Against the War in Iraq, Barack Obama gave a speech second in career importance only to the 2004 DNC keynote. This was the speech that enabled his handlers to position him on the credibly sane left flank of naïfs like Hillary Clinton and John Edwards "who took the president at his word" and voted for the war in Iraq.

Although effective, this speech was factually adrift in any number of key details and sneakily anti-Semitic. In Obama's defense, he may not have sensed the anti-Semitic riff, either because he was parroting what he had heard others say or because someone else had inserted the telltale phrase for him. I suspect the latter.

The rally was the handiwork of Chicago's vestigial radical community. Two of the key organizers were proud veterans of the militant Students for a Democratic Society, Carl Anderson and Marilyn Katz, the latter a friend of Bill Ayers since her teen years. As Katz tells it, she was one of a group of five individuals who put the rally together, and they did so on just ten days' notice.

David Mendell, who was close to the action, does the best job of tracking Obama's recruitment. According to Mendell, heiress and activist Bettylu Saltzman, who had long been "enraptured" by Obama, called and asked whether he wanted to participate. At the time, Obama was keen on taking a shot at the U.S. Senate in 2004. He envisioned as his base of support blacks and lakefront liberals like Saltzman, the former for their votes, the latter for their money. When he asked adviser Dan Shomon whether he should accept the invite, Shomon told him it was a "no-brainer." Obama could not risk alienating Saltzman, especially given her close relationship with media guru Axelrod, whom Obama was then courting. That much said, Shomon advised Obama to be cautious given the "political ramifications to whatever you say."

Obama got the message. There was no point risking his future to please a bunch of crazies in Chicago. So he spoke, but cautiously. Indeed, in the very first sentence of the speech, Obama offered the unlikely caveat that he was "not opposed to war in all circumstances," a point that he was at pains to reinforce. Obama promptly cited the American Civil War as a war he could support. That the war led to a bloody, twelve-year occupation and Iraq-style insurgency, which ended only when the U.S. military yielded to the insurgents, was likely something Obama and helpmates had not thought through even by 2008.

Obama also gave his belated approval to World War II and sang the praises of his grandfather, who fought in Patton's army and "heard the stories of fellow troops who first entered Auschwitz and Treblinka." By Memorial Day 2008, however, Obama was claiming that it was his "uncle" who was "part of the first American troops to go into Auschwitz." When reminded that his mother was an only child and his father a Kenyan, Obama designated his "great uncle" as the liberator of Auschwitz. This proved problematic as well because Auschwitz, as the Republican National Committee gleefully pointed out, was actually liberated by the Soviets.

The media dependably liberated Obama from the Republican siege. "What's worse," opined the *Los Angeles Times:* "Obama's apparent gaffe or the RNC pouncing on a Holocaust-related historical mistake for political advantage?" What was worse actually was that Obama used his "uncle" to make the point that America ignored its traumatized war vets. "The story in our family," Obama told the 2008 Memorial Day crowd in New Mexico, was that when his "uncle" came home from the war, he promptly went up to the attic and did not come down for six months. One would think Obama might have remembered this striking detail in 2002 when he attributed the liberation of Auschwitz not to his notoriously deranged uncle, but to his grandfather's "fellow troops."

In June 2008, speaking before a veterans' group, Obama would make the opposite claim. "My father served in World War II," he told the veterans theretofore unaware that Kenyan third graders fought in the big one. "And when he came home," Obama continued, "he got the services that he needed. And that includes, by the way, posttraumatic stress disorder." He was likely referring to his traumatized, Auschwitz-liberating great-uncle, whose malleable history had just been reshaped to bash the Bush administration. As was their wont, the media let this gaffe, if that's what it was, pass unremarked.

As to why Obama opposed the war in Iraq six months before it began, there is some confusion. Six years later, he would tell Rick Warren's Saddleback forum that he "was firmly convinced at the time that we did not have strong evidence of weapons of mass destruction." This point would have delighted the crowd at Chicago's Federal Plaza had he made it, but he did not. In October 2002, Obama made a more politic claim entirely, namely that although Saddam "butchers his own people" and has "developed chemical and biological weapons and coveted nuclear capacity," the war was "dumb" nonetheless.

If later confused about his motives, Obama could never forget the speech's emotional toll. He would tell Warren, in fact, that protesting the war was his most "gut wrenching decision," largely because of its "political consequences." Obama's official 2008 website attested to the anguish. "As a candidate for the United States Senate in 2002," the website claimed, "Obama put his political career on the line to oppose going to war in Iraq." Obama would likewise tell Mendell that this was his "most courageous" speech, unaware that Mendell himself saw the speech as "a political calculation." Indeed, given the political drift of Obama's intended base, *supporting* the war in 2002 would have been the courageous thing to do.

In Chicago, whatever his motives, Obama traced his early opposition to intelligence that had apparently escaped the attention of Clinton and Edwards. Nearly six months before the war began, Obama had sniffed out "a cynical attempt by Richard Perle and Paul Wolfowitz," the only two officials in the defense hierarchy cited, "to shove their own ideological agendas down our throats."

Aiding and abetting the neocons, of course, was Bush adviser and all-purpose progressive punching bag Karl Rove. As Obama told it, Rove was banging the war drum to distract America from, among other things, "a stock market that has just gone through the worst month since the Great Depression." In reality, the Dow Jones had been fairly flat since July 2002 and would gain more than 10 percent in that very October of Obama's discontent.

Although Bill Ayers attended the rally, neither Mendell nor Remnick connect him in any way to Obama's speech. After agreeing to participate, writes Mendell, Obama "wrote the speech long hand in a single evening." Obama told Mendell that he found the speechwriting "liberating" because "I said exactly what I truly believed." Parsing Obama's thoughts, Mendell later questions whether saying what he believed was an exception for Obama rather than the rule.

Yet despite Obama's claims to unique authorship, one senses a radical contribution to the speech. On his own, he would not likely have made the quietly anti-Semitic reference to Perle and Wolfowitz, two names in common parlance only on the hard left. A less sophisticated protestor might have blamed the anticipated war on Cheney,

Rumsfeld, Bush, Rice, or Tenet, not two obscure Jews from within the bureaucracy.

Soon after publishing my thoughts on this, I heard from one of my better correspondents, a Conrad scholar who prefers to be called "Ishmael." His reason for choosing anonymity was not hard to understand. "Like just about everyone else," he wrote, "I dread the scrutiny received by Joe the Plumber."

For those of short memories, on October 12, 2008, Joe Wurzelbacher had a chance encounter with Barack Obama, who had descended on Joe's small Ohio town to campaign. When Joe asked whether Obama's tax policy would impede his intended purchase of a small business, Obama responded in part, "I think when you spread the wealth around, it's good for everybody." By standing up to the seemingly indomitable Obama and sparking his socialist instincts, this ordinary Joe turned overnight into a cable-TV David.

Wurzelbacher paid for his boldness. The media immediately commenced to comb through his and his employer's financial records as though Joe were the guy running for president. Meanwhile, employees of Ohio's Department of Job and Family Services dug into the state databases for some useful dirt. On October 16, ABC broke the news, such as it was, that a judgment lien had been filed against an Ohio plumber for nonpayment of $1,182 in state income taxes, a lien that Wurzelbacher himself had not yet been made aware of.

The *New York Times* and other news outlets spent more resources investigating Joe's plumbing license than they had Obama's birth certificate. "An official at Local 50 of the plumber's union, based in Toledo," intoned the *Times* solemnly, "said Mr. Wurzelbacher does not hold a license. He also has never served an apprenticeship and does not belong to the union." As proof of its solemnity, the *Times* added the qualifier that Local 50 was supporting Obama. You can't make this stuff up.

Although the state employees would later be fired, the damage had been done, not so much to the resilient Wurzelbacher, but to the vox populi. Any number of my correspondents cited Joe when they declined my offer of credit. University correspondents did not need Joe's example to keep their mouths shut. Their reticence would become an issue in a growing campaign to out the muse who inspired *Dreams*.

A fan of the late political philosopher Leo Strauss, Ishmael would provide some useful insights along the way. "You are the only person to note that in Obama's anti-war speech he gave in 2002, he singled out two Straussians, Richard Perle and Paul Wolfowitz," he wrote. "You're right that there is absolutely no way Obama would have chosen those names himself." He added that only someone like Ayers, Said, or some other fellow traveler would have zeroed in on a pair of Jews. "A political climber like Obama," he noted, "would not have risked the charge of anti-Semitism."

In an extended quote from the Mendell book, Obama hints that he may indeed have had help. "That's the speech I'm most proud of. It was a hard speech to give," he tells Mendell. He adds, "And it was just, well, a well-constructed speech. I like it." Obama had to "give" the speech himself, and of this he is proud, but he describes the "well-constructed" text as though it had been handed to him, which it may have been.

Whatever his contribution to the speech, if any, Ayers knew whom to blame for Iraq. "Let's look forward to the day Wolfowitz will be tried as a war criminal," Ayers would insist some years later. He also had an historic fondness for Middle Eastern Jew haters. In 1974, he and his pals dedicated the Weather manifesto, *Prairie Fire*, to, among others, Sirhan Sirhan, the raging anti-Semite who assassinated Robert Kennedy. More than thirty-five years later, he and Dohrn would help organize the Free Gaza Movement, whose six-ship flotilla tried to bust the Israeli blockade.

Still, Ayers was no garden-variety anti-Semite. His lakefront liberal allies were predominantly Jewish. Then too, there were any number of ethnic Jews in the Weather Underground. Curiously, however, just about all of them—Terry Robbins, Ted Gold, Mark Rudd, Kathy

Boudin, Laura Whitehorn, and Bernardine Dohrn—came into the world with Anglicized names and moved through it even more deracinated than their parents.

They would have to have been totally severed from their roots, however, not to be disturbed by one passage in *Fugitive Days*. "The streets became sparkling and treacherous with the jagged remains of our rampage," writes Ayers of his window-breaking spree through the streets of Chicago in the famed "Days of Rage." Then Ayers lovingly describes the scene, in a trope that has to chill the blood of any Jew, as "crystal chaos." Just thirty years prior, the Nazis had called their sparkling rampage through the streets of Germany "Kristallnacht," or "Crystal Night" in English.

Ayers knew what he was saying. Whether Obama did is another question.

CONSPIRACY COMMERCE

In 1997, the Clinton White House so feared what Hillary Clinton would label the "vast right-wing conspiracy" (VRWC) that it put out a 332-page report specifying how the conspiracy worked. In its unblinking paranoia, the *Communication Stream of Conspiracy Commerce* recalled nothing so much as the final days of the Nixon White House.

According to the document, well-funded right-wing think tanks and individuals underwrote conservative fringe publications, whose stories were passed along on the still-mysterious Internet, where they were picked up by the right-wing British press, then passed back across the ocean to semi-respectable conservative publications stateside and from there into Congress, "finally to be covered by the remainder of the American mainstream press as a 'real' story."

In late 2009, on *Meet The Press*, NBC's David Gregory raised the specter of conspiracy with former president Clinton. "As you look at this opposition on the right to President Obama, is [the VRWC] still there?" Gregory asked with a straight face. "Oh, you bet," said Clinton. "Sure it is."

A few weeks earlier, Gregory and his guests—Tom Friedman of the *New York Times* and NBC's anchorman emeritus Tom Brokaw—were fretting openly about the VRWC's communication stream. In lamenting the fate of former "green jobs" czar Van Jones, whom the conspirators had exposed as a believer in the 9/11 "inside job" theory and other mumbo jumbo, Gregory worried, "You can be a target real fast."

"A lot of people will repeat back to me and take it as face value something that they read on the Internet," cautioned Brokaw. "And my line to them is you have to vet information." Not to be out-preached, Friedman countered, "The Internet is an open sewer of untreated, unfiltered information, left, right, center, up, down, and requires that kind of filtering by anyone." And my wife wonders why I refuse to watch Sunday morning TV?

To be fair, the mechanics the White House's *Communication Stream* described in 1997 were not entirely fanciful. The Clinton White House failed to address, however, what Gregory and pals failed to address twelve years later: namely, were these stories true and, if so, why was so circuitous a stream necessary?

While doing research for my books, I have stumbled across any number of eye-popping media oversights. As I learned from reading a roll of the Waco dead, for instance, more than half of those killed during the misbegotten tank attack in 1993 were racial or ethnic minorities, 39 out of 74 to be precise, six of them Hispanic, six of Asian descent, and a full 27 of them black, ages six to sixty-one. The Clinton White House, aided and abetted by the media, shielded black America from the bad news.

The Waco dead did not commit suicide à la Jonestown in 1978. Neither did about a third of the Jonestown dead commit suicide à la Jonestown. Three-year-olds typically don't know how. Authorities dumped the bodies of more than 250 of these children, almost all of them black, into a mass grave in Oakland's Evergreen Cemetery. There they lie to this day, unsung and unmourned because their death serves no useful political purpose. Their killer, Jim Jones, a self-professed "communist," commanded a two-thousand-strong bloc of ballot-stuffing automatons. Every relevant Democrat from Harvey Milk to Walter Mondale had courted him. This is not a story that bears retelling.

When it has been newsworthy, I have tried to share my info with the major media—occasionally at high levels and sometimes in person—but their reporters tend to resist stories that imperil the fortunes of the Democratic Party, especially those stories that threaten the party's hold on black America.

For instance, in reading the twenty-two-volume U.S. Air Force report on the 1996 plane crash that killed black secretary of commerce Ron Brown and thirty-four others, I learned something that had never been reported: Clinton had dispatched Brown to Croatia to broker a sweetheart deal between the country's neofascist president and the Enron Corporation. Even when Enron topped the news, this fresh angle attracted the major media not a whit. To the best of my knowledge, no media outlet had even bothered to request the USAF report, including the *New York Times*, one of whose reporters died in the crash.

In their coverage of the Obama campaign, the media undid whatever was left of their reputation. Their refusal to probe their man's shrouded past was becoming obvious even to themselves. Given my own research, I was less curious about the much-discussed birth certificate than I was about Obama's SAT scores, his college theses, his LSAT scores, his college grades, his Illinois bar scores, anything that spoke to his abilities as writer or scholar.

An impressively incurious media, alas, were not asking to see any of this. Although I had a helpful contact at the *New York Times*, I had no reason to believe that she could—or anyone else in the media would—pursue a story with what Remnick calls so much "diabolical potency," namely the possibility that Ayers helped Obama write *Dreams*.

Fortunately, I had a platform, specifically a weekly column in *WorldNetDaily*. *WND*'s publisher, Joseph Farah, was among those cited in the 1997 conspiracy commerce report and was still bristling for a good fight. A New Jersey native of Arab descent, Farah came up through mainstream ranks, first as executive news editor at the *Los Angeles Herald Examiner* and then as editor of the *Sacramento Union* before launching the Western Center for Journalism in 1991. The Clinton years proved fruitful for those keen on doing actual reporting, and in 1997 Farah spun out *WorldNetDaily* from the Western Center's side. Thirteen years later—an eternity on the Internet—*WND* remains profitable and widely read. If there is an independent online journal of longer standing, I do not know what it is.

I had been writing a regular column for *WND* since 2005 and semiregularly for five years before that. As I had seen firsthand, the Internet represents a radically new—and potentially superior—journalistic model. The writer no longer depends on the support of a newsroom, but rather on the support of a potentially vast community of participants, many of them with direct knowledge and/or useful expertise. Once I went public with my suspicions about *Dreams*, I knew others would join in the hunt. First, though, I wanted to see what I could learn about the book's genesis. To that end, a 2006 article by publisher Peter Osnos proved very helpful. More recent sources have helped flesh out this account.

As Osnos relates, a 1990 *New York Times* profile on the *Harvard Law Review*'s first black president caught the eye of hustling young literary agent Jane Dystel. Dystel persuaded Obama to put a book proposal together, and she submitted it. Poseidon Press, a small, now-defunct imprint of Simon & Schuster, signed on and authorized a roughly $125,000 advance in November 1990 for Obama's proposed memoir.

With advance in hand, Obama repaired to Chicago, where the University of Chicago offered him a stipend, benefits, and an office to help him write what Obama told the administrators would be a book on race and voting rights. When he switched topics to pure memoir, Remnick reports, the university law school brass were "unfazed." They were mostly just glad to have Obama in their midst. Some of his new colleagues at Davis, Miner, Barnhill & Galland, the town's leading civil rights firm, were less than thrilled to see their young associate, feet up on his desk, doodling on his memoir on company time. The named partners, however, indulged him.

Writes Remnick, "His intelligence, charm, and serene ambition were plain to see." If I may digress, Remnick makes more references to the intelligence of his subject, Obama, than Walter Isaacson does to the subject of his recent bestseller, Albert Einstein. Count them.

In the spring of 1992, on top of his existing obligations, Obama was offered the opportunity to head up Project Vote, a nonpartisan voter-registration effort designed to herd thousands of fresh Democrats to the polls come November. If Obama accepted the offer, he would have still another excuse for not being able to meet his June 15 manuscript deadline despite the generous eighteen months he had been allotted. He took the job and missed the deadline. Simon & Schuster extended it.

In October 1992, he and Michelle married. After their honeymoon, in order to finish without interruption, Obama decamped to Bali for a month. Nothing happened. Those in Obama's circle have been at pains to excuse his inability to honor his contract. Intimate friend Valerie Jarrett would tell Remnick, "He had to come to terms with some events in his life that some people pay years of therapy to get comfortable revealing." She adds, "The writing went slowly because everything was so raw."

There is a simpler explanation. The writing went slowly because Obama was not a writer. During the 2008 presidential campaign, the *Times* ran an article on what psychologists call the "impostor phenomenon." To measure it, they ask test subjects to respond to statements like "At times, I feel my success has been due to some kind of luck" or "I can give the impression that I'm more competent than I really am."

Although the article had nothing to do with Obama, he would surely have scored off the charts had he responded honestly. He was a reasonably bright guy but not nearly as "brilliant" as white liberals thought him to be. His "luck" derived from the fact that he grew up almost exactly as those liberals had but in the body of a black man. Hearing him they heard themselves. Seeing him say what he said surprised them, validated them, delighted them with its freshness. Although they would be the last to admit it, they suffered conspicuously from what George W. Bush has called "the soft bigotry of low expectations."

In speaking of Obama in early 2007, Joe Biden framed those expectations with dunderheaded clarity. "I mean, you got the first mainstream African-American presidential candidate who is articulate and bright and clean and a nice-looking guy." Not to be outgaffed, Senate majority leader Harry Reid found comfort in Obama's having "no Negro dialect." The always-observant Shelby Steele, writing before anyone doubted Obama's credentials, summed up the phenomenon: "Blacks like Obama, who show merit where mediocrity is expected, enjoy a kind of reverse stigma, a slightly inflated reputation for 'freshness' and excellence because they defy expectations."

That reverse stigma has encouraged the faithful to think their man a much better writer than he ever was or would be. "Obama had missed deadlines and handed in bloated, yet incomplete drafts," Remnick tells us. Bali or not, advance or no, he could not produce. He was surely in way over his head.

Simon & Schuster lost interest. After it closed its Poseidon imprint in the summer of 1993, the publishing house ditched those books that showed little promise, Obama's prominent among them. According to Christopher Andersen, the publisher allowed Obama to keep the advance on his unfulfilled contract when he pled poverty due to "massive student loan debt." At the time, the combined salary for the still-childless Obamas ranged well into six figures.

As Osnos tells it, Dystel did not give up. She solicited Times Books, the division of Random House at which Osnos was publisher. He met with Obama, took his word that he could finish the book, and authorized a new advance of forty thousand dollars.

During this same period, Obama was working as a full-time associate at Davis Miner, teaching classes at the University of Chicago Law School, and spinning through a social whirl that would have left Scarlett O'Hara dizzy.

Writes Remnick, "He and Michelle accepted countless invitations to lunches, dinners, cocktail parties, barbecues, and receptions for right minded charities." Obama had also joined the East Bank Club, a combined gym and urban country club, and served on at least a few charitable boards.

If these distractions were not burden enough, Obama's Luddite approach to writing slowed him down all the more. "I would work off an outline—certain themes or stories that I wanted to tell—and get them down in longhand on a yellow pad," he would later relate to Daphne Durham of Amazon. "Then I'd edit while typing in what I'd written."

In late 1994, Obama finally submitted his manuscript for publication. Remnick expects the public to take an awful lot on faith: specifically, that a slow writer and sluggish student who had nothing in print save for a couple of "muddled" essays, who blew a huge contract after nearly three futile years, who turned in bloated drafts when he did start writing, who had gotten married, and who had taken on an absurdly busy schedule somehow suddenly found his mojo and turned in a minor masterpiece. Obama fans believe this to a person. No one else could.

Remnick quotes Henry Ferris, the Times Books editor, to bolster Obama's claim to authorship. Ferris "worked directly with Obama," Remnick tells us, but Ferris edited in New York while Obama wrote in

Chicago. Ferris would have had no way of knowing just how much of the editing or writing Obama was doing himself. Osnos, too, offhandedly notes that the writing of *Dreams* was "all Obama's," which means only that, if the book had been doctored, the doctoring was done before it reached the publisher.

Andersen based his account of *Dreams'* creation on two unnamed sources within Hyde Park. By any standard, it rings truer than Remnick's. According to Andersen, Obama found himself deeply in debt and "hopelessly blocked." At "Michelle's urging," Obama "sought advice from his friend and Hyde Park neighbor Bill Ayers." What attracted the Obamas were "Ayers's proven abilities as a writer" as evident in his 1993 book, *To Teach*.

On September 6, 2008, I sent an email to Dystel under the heading "Serious Inquiry." In the body of it, I wrote the following:

> Having written a book on intellectual fraud, "Hoodwinked," and being something of a literary detective, I have some real issues with Dreams From My Father. I would perfectly understand if you told me to take a hike, but I promise total discretion if you care to talk.

I referred Dystel to the earlier article I had written on the subject and offered my cell number if she chose to call. I had some reason to hope Dystel would respond. As Osnos relates, Obama dumped her after *Dreams* took off in 2004 and signed a seven-figure deal with Crown, using only a by-the-hour attorney. In order to avoid congressional disclosure and reporting requirements, Obama inked the deal after his election but before being sworn in as senator. An honest liberal, Osnos publicly scolded Obama for his "ruthlessness" and his "questionable judgment about using public service as a personal payday."

And a major payday it proved to be. In 2008, Obama pocketed $1,512,933 for *Audacity of Hope* and another $949,910 from *Dreams*. In 2007, his book royalties had been $3.9 million; in 2006, $570,000;

in 2005, $1.4 million. In sum, Dystel's 15 percent would have netted her at least another $500,000 in royalties had Obama not forsaken her. Dystel did not return my email or my subsequent phone call. Nor has she spoken publicly on this subject with anyone else. Hell, I am told, hath no fury like an agent scorned, but Dystel, to Obama's good fortune, has held her tongue.

BALLAST

Starting on September 18, 2008, *WorldNetDaily* ran a three-part series of mine with the speculative title "Did Bill Ayers Write Obama's 'Dreams'?" In the series, I highlighted the parallels in the lives of the two neighbors, their shared affection for postmodern concepts of truth and memory, the Osnos revelations, the lack of an Obama paper trail, and some comparable stylistic turns. Although my motivation was openly partisan, I had no interest in being wrong. To spread my research beyond the right half of the blogosphere, I would have to be accurate, and to prove my accuracy I would need lots of help.

The world did not stop spinning with this series. I did not expect it to. Although the preponderance of evidence favored my thesis, enough perhaps to win a lawsuit, I had not proved it beyond a reasonable doubt. From the emails I could tell that readers, though favorably disposed, had their doubts as well. They are much more discerning and demanding than schoolmarms Brokaw and Friedman choose to believe.

A few readers were intrigued enough to start digging on their own. Among them was Boston-area writer and composer Jay Spencer, who sent me a matched pair of sentences that struck me then and now as almost enough to convict. The first comes from *Fugitive Days*, when Ayers finds himself engulfed in an antiwar protest.

> The confrontation in the Fishbowl flowed like a swollen river into the teach-in, carrying me along the cascading waters from room to room, hall to hall, bouncing off boulders.

The second comes from *Dreams*. While talking to his African relatives about his family history, Obama experiences a remarkably similar information overload:

> I heard all our voices begin to run together, the sound of three generations tumbling over each other like the currents of a slow-moving stream, my questions like rocks roiling the water, the breaks in memory separating the currents. . . .

It is hard to ignore the parallels between these two sentences. Not only is the imagery the same—the flowing water broken by rocks or boulders—but so also is the structure. Each sentence begins with a standard verb phrase, embellished by a series of participles: *tumbling, roiling, separating* in the one; *carrying, bouncing* in the other.

These sentences reinforced a thread that I had already discerned. A particular sentence in *Dreams* had alerted me to it, and I led with the sentence in my regular *WND* column a week later: "A steady attack on the white race . . . served as the ballast that could prevent the ideas of personal and communal responsibility from tipping into an ocean of despair."

I had highlighted this sentence on my first pass of *Dreams* because it was among those sentences that seem radical when taken out of context. After reading *Fugitive Days*, however, it took on a new significance. It seems that shortly before getting into the revolution business, Bill Ayers had taken a job as a merchant seaman. "I'd thought that when I signed on that I might write an American novel about a young man at sea," says Ayers in *Fugitive Days*, "but I didn't have it in me."

The open sea can intimidate. Years later, Ayers would recall a nightmare he had while crossing the Atlantic, "a vision of falling overboard in the middle of the ocean and swimming as fast as I could as the ship steamed off and disappeared over the horizon." Although Ayers has put his anxious oceangoing days behind him, the language of the sea has not let him go. Indeed, it infuses much of what he writes. This is only natural and often distinctive, as in an appealing Ayers metaphor like "the easy inlet of her eyes."

"I realized that no one else could ever know this singular experience," Ayers writes of these adventures. Yet it struck me as entirely curious that much of this "singular" language flows through Obama's earthbound memoir. Despite growing up in Hawaii, Obama gives little indication that he has had any real experience with the sea or ships beyond bodysurfing at Waikiki. Ayers, however, knows a great deal about both.

"Memory sails out upon a murky sea," Ayers writes at one point in *Fugitive Days*. Indeed, both he and Obama are obsessed with memory and its instability. The latter writes of its breaks, its blurs, its edges, its lapses. Obama, like Ayers, has a fondness for the word *murky* and its aquatic usages. "The unlucky ones drift into the murky tide of hustles and odd jobs," he writes, one of four times *murky* appears in *Dreams*.

Ayers and Obama also speak often of waves and wind, Obama at least a dozen times on wind alone. "The wind wipes away my drowsiness, and I feel suddenly exposed," he writes in a passage that sounds as though he had just been called from sleep to man a late watch. In these two wind-conscious memoirs, the word *flutter* appears often and imaginatively.

Not surprisingly, Ayers uses *ship* as a metaphor with some frequency. Early in the book he tells us that his mother is "the captain of her own ship." For Obama, it is his father who acts like a "sea captain." Ayers imagines the family ship as "a ragged thing with fatal leaks" launched into a "sea of carelessness." In another stressful instance, he feels as if he were "going over the side of a sinking ship."

Obama too finds himself "feeling like the first mate on a sinking ship." He writes of a "silent sea" and a "tranquil sea." More telling still is Obama's use of the word *ragged*, as in the poetic "ragged air" or "ragged laughter." In *A Kind and Just Parent* Ayers also uses "ragged" metaphorically, as in the phrase "a ragged mess."

Ayers and Obama each use *storms* and *horizons* as both substance and as symbol. Ayers writes of an "unbounded horizon," and Obama weighs in with "boundless prairie storms" as well as "eastern horizon," "western horizon," and "violet horizon." Both use the words *current* and *calm* as nouns, the latter word more distinctively, as in Ayers's "pockets of calm" and Obama's "menacing calm." Their imaginative use of the word *tangled* suggests a nautical genesis, as in Ayers's "tangled love affairs" and "tangled story" and Obama's "tangled arguments."

In *Dreams*, we read of the "whole panorama of life out there" and in *Fugitive Days*, "the whole weird panorama of my life." Ayers writes of still another panorama, this one "an immense panorama of waste and cruelty." Obama employs the word *cruel* and its derivatives no fewer than fourteen times in *Dreams*. On at least twelve occasions, Obama speaks of "despair," as in an "ocean of despair." Ayers counters with a "deepening despair," a constant theme for him as well. Both distinctively pair "violence and despair." Obama's "knotted, howling assertion of self" sounds like it had been ripped from the pages of Jack London's *The Sea Wolf*, or, more proximately, from *Fugitive Days*, where Ayers too uses *howling* metaphorically, as in "the unleashing of a howling political storm." The word *knot* or its derivatives, an Ayers favorite, is used eleven times in *Dreams*.

In *Fugitive Days* Ayers uses the word *moorings* on two occasions, both times figuratively but precisely, as with, "in time words lost their moorings and floated away." Obama uses the word literally and too knowingly. "The boats were out of their moorings," he writes, "their distant sails like the wings of doves across Lake Michigan." In his book *A Kind and Just Parent*, which I had secured and read by this point, Ayers speaks lovingly of his bike rides along Lake Michigan, "a shining sea of blues and greens." He knew the lake well. In this book, too, Ayers fuses his anger with his seamanship to create the memorable "whirlpools of rage."

At the end of the day, I found in both *Dreams* and in Ayers's several works the following shared words: *fog, mist, ships, sinking ships, seas, sails, boats, oceans, calms, captains, charts, first mates, floods, shores, storms, streams, wind, waves, waters, anchors, barges, horizons, harbor, bays, ports, panoramas, moorings, tides, currents, voyages, narrower courses, uncertain courses*, and things *howling, wobbling, wind-whipped, fluttering, sinking, leaking, cascading, swimming, knotted, ragged, tangled, launched, boundless, uncharted, turbulent*, and *murky*.

Not unlike Ayers, I had had my own intimidating encounter with the sea. Each summer of my childhood, my parents would unearth their squirreled-away poker earnings to rent a bungalow in Ortley Beach, New Jersey, for as long as the money held out. (Ortley, by the way, borders the now-infamous Seaside Heights, the setting for the rococo MTV reality show *Jersey Shore*.)

The summer I was seven, two hurricanes hit the shore back to back. When the skies cleared, thousands of us, the governor included, drove up to Point Pleasant to watch the dramatic return of a fishing boat all had thought lost. The boat rolled violently as it approached the inlet, the crow's nest very nearly touching the sea, first on one side, then on the other. The scene affected me. Not a month goes by that I do not dream about being at the shore as a storm brews and the waves mount.

After noticing the nautical thread in both *Dreams* and *Fugitive Days*, I checked to see if my own semi-memoir, *Sucker Punch*, was similarly threaded. It is not. The book makes reference to precious few of these words precious few times in any context, and yet I have spent a good chunk of every summer of my life at the ocean and many a day on a boat. As an additional point of comparison with *Dreams* and *Fugitive Days*, in *Sucker Punch* there are no contrived memories, no composite characters, no phony names, no jacking with the timeline, no postmodern quibbles about truth. In this regard, mine is like most memoirs, Frank Marshall Davis's included.

Even if there were no other evidence, the frequent and sophisticated use of nautical terms in *Dreams* makes a powerful case for Ayers's involvement. One passage in particular caught my attention. It is the one with which I introduced this theme, namely the notion that for black nationalists, a steady attack on the white race "served as the ballast that could prevent the ideas of personal and communal responsibility from tipping into an ocean of despair." As a writer, especially in the pre-Google era of *Dreams*, I would never have used a metaphor as specific as *ballast* unless I knew exactly what I was talking about. Seaman Ayers most surely could.

SECRET SHARER

After publishing an article on the nautical theme, I heard from several correspondents almost simultaneously on a likely inspiration for the Ayers-Obama project, the Anglo-Polish author Joseph Conrad. In the way of background, Conrad retired from the British merchant marine in 1894 after sixteen years in the service. It was only then, in his late thirties, that he began his formal literary career, one that would result in any number of classic novels and short stories, *Heart of Darkness* foremost among them.

My Conrad scholar correspondent "Ishmael" saw the Conrad touch all throughout *Dreams*. "It's apparent that Joseph Conrad was a considerable influence on whoever wrote *Dreams*," Ishmael wrote. I had already been thinking along those lines. Obama refers to Conrad on three occasions in *Dreams*, none of them convincingly. "While we packed, my grandfather pulled out an atlas and ticked off the names in Indonesia's island chain: Java, Borneo, Sumatra, Bali," Obama writes. "He remembered some of the names, he said, from reading Joseph

Conrad as a boy." Obama was six years old at the time. He was as un-likely to have remembered a specific allusion to Conrad as his grandfa-ther was to have made one.

The second and third reference derived from Obama's own reading of Conrad's *Heart of Darkness*, reportedly as an assigned text at Occi-dental College in Los Angeles. It is possible that he did read the book, but it is more likely that he would have read it at Columbia in the modern fiction class taught by Edward Said, who had himself written a book titled *Joseph Conrad and the Fiction of Autobiography*. "To post-modernists," observed Ishmael wryly, "it's understood that all autobi-ography is fiction. Regular Joes, however, who have purchased *Dreams of my Father* [*sic*] probably think otherwise."

A serious student of literature, Ayers had a relationship with Ed-ward Said dating back to his New York days, and he had a particular interest, like Said, in the art of the memoir. As Ishmael noted, there is a highly favorable blurb on the back of *Fugitive Days* by Said. Although Ayers does not acknowledge Said as having read the manuscript, Ish-mael has to wonder whether Said contributed any editorial advice prior to its publication. Regardless, Ishmael was convinced that Con-rad influenced Ayers. "Ayers became a merchant seaman like Conrad," he wrote. "Ayers also became involved in an underground terrorist or-ganization not unlike the one found in Conrad's *The Secret Agent*."

In terms of style, Ishmael pointed out, Conrad is perhaps best known for his use of triple parallels unbroken by a conjunction. Not surpris-ingly, the signature rhetorical flourish for both Ayers and the Obama of *Dreams* is the triple parallel unbroken by a conjunction. Ishmael pro-vided scores of samples from all three books, a few of which follow:

From *Heart of Darkness*:

. . . a treacherous appeal to the lurking death, to the hidden evil, to the profound darkness of its heart.

The man filled his life, occupied his thoughts, swayed his emotions.

It was an affirmation, a moral victory paid for by innumerable defeats, by abominable terrors, by abominable satisfactions.

From *Fugitive Days:*

He inhabited an anarchic solitude—disconnected, smart, obsessive.

He continued, outlining a bottle, roughing in the bottom two thirds with diagonal lines, blocking out the remaining third with horizontals.

We swarmed over and around that car, smashing windows, slashing tires, trashing lights and fenders—it seemed the only conceivable thing to do.

... trees are shattered, doors ripped from their hinges, shorelines rearranged.

From *Dreams:*

... the mixed blood, the divided soul, the ghostly image of the tragic mulatto trapped between two worlds.

Her face powdered, her hips girdled, her thinning hair bolstered, she would board the six-thirty bus to arrive at her downtown office before anyone else.

... his eyes were closed, his head leaning against the back of his chair, his big wrinkled face like a carving stone.

Bruce Dunstan of Sydney, Australia, also intuited the Conrad influence on *Dreams* before I had written about the same. "I'm reading *Dreams* right now and amazed at the nautical metaphors right in the intro, stunning writing," he wrote. "But it reminds me of Conrad's *Heart of Darkness*." Dunstan saw an ironic parallel between the book's brilliant and charismatic character, "Mr. Kurtz," and our own Mr. Obama. Says the book's protagonist, Charles Marlow, of Kurtz:

The point was in his being a gifted creature, and that of all his gifts the one that stood out preeminently, that carried with it a sense of real presence, was his ability to talk, his words—the gift of expression, the bewildering, the illuminating, the most exalted and the most contemptible, the pulsating stream of light, or the deceitful flow from the heart of an impenetrable darkness.

Blogger Bob Calco found still another fascinating Conrad parallel, and this with his short story "The Secret Sharer." In this case, as Calco argues, Ayers made no conscious effort to evoke Conrad. Rather, his relationship with Obama had come to mirror the relationship between the murderer "Leggatt" and the unnamed narrator of "The Secret Sharer," an inexperienced and insecure young sea captain.

As the story unfolds, the new captain surprises his skeptical veteran crew by taking a night watch alone. During the watch, he discovers a naked young man clinging to the bottom rung of the ship's ladder. He helps him on board, dresses him in his own clothes, and hears out his tale. What Leggatt tells him is that as first mate of a ship, now anchored nearby, he got into a fight with an insolent sailor during the frenzy of a storm, strangled him, and was promptly locked up by his own captain.

Leggatt makes no attempt to deceive. He expects to be tried and executed. He has escaped his own ship and swum to this one expecting little more than a moment of freedom, but the young captain senses "a mysterious communication" between him and the fugitive and decides to shelter him. "He appealed to me as if our experiences had been as identical as our clothes," observes the captain. He decides to hide Leggatt, not only from his own crew but also, and more perilously, from the visiting captain of the ship that Leggatt had escaped.

Upon rereading Conrad's story, I imagined Ayers as Obama's Leggatt, his "second self," one who put Obama at risk much as Leggatt did the captain. "An accidental discovery was to be dreaded now more than ever," fretted the captain, and I suspect Obama felt much the same after Ayers's September 2001 comments had made him something of a pariah.

Like Leggatt, however, Ayers had been at least partially misunderstood. In numerous letters to various editors after September 11, he protested that he had never meant to endorse "terrorism," which he defined as the commission of "random acts of terror against people." He was being at least halfway sincere. After the Greenwich Village bomb factory disaster in 1970, the Weather Underground chose to avoid human targets.

In *Fugitive Days*, published before September 11, Ayers had made this same case: "We simply didn't have it in us to harm others, especially innocents, no matter how tough we talked." In the 2004 preface to *Dreams* while discussing September 11, Obama echoes Ayers's concern in language that sounds very much like Ayers's own: "My powers of *empathy*, my ability to reach into another's heart, cannot penetrate the blank stares of those who would murder innocents with abstract, serene satisfaction."

Killing "innocents" is wrong. Both *Fugitive Days* and *Dreams* make this clear, but there is another, more salient observation that both make: "real" terrorists, those who kill innocents, hide behind a blank, impenetrable veil. If in *Dreams* Obama cannot "penetrate the blank stares" of the September 11 terrorists, in *Fugitive Days* Ayers cannot "penetrate" what the American terrorists in Vietnam "have posited as impenetrable," namely their "smug veil of immutability." For Ayers, Americans will always remain the real terrorists. Even in his exculpatory letters, he cannot resist equating the terrorism of September 11 with the "terrorism . . . practiced in the countryside of Vietnam by the United States."

For all his protestations, Ayers had already been convicted of terror, at least in the court of public opinion. After September 11, Obama had little choice but to keep their relationship quiet. So well did he distance himself that Mendell, who covered Obama closely beginning in 2003, does not so much as mention Ayers in his 2007 book. Unlike the young sea captain, however, Obama could never be sure that his hidden partner would keep their shared moment forever secret.

THE POSTMODERN
PRESIDENT

As much for fashion's sake as for ideology, leftist literati like Edward Said and Bill Ayers have grabbed the banner of post-modernism and waved it proudly. Whether Ayers recruited Obama to his larger worldview is arguable. That he schooled him in its language—at least in *Dreams*—is all but beyond debate.

Before *Dreams*, Obama showed no hint of a postmodern flair. In fact, only one real prose sample of Obama's writing would surface prior to the 2008 election. In 1988, a journal called *Illinois Issues* had published his essay "Why Organize?" In 1990, the University of Illinois at Springfield included it in a collection titled *After Alinsky: Community Organizing in Illinois*. Although the essay covers many of the issues raised in *Dreams* and uses some of the memoir's techniques, it does so without a trace of style, sophistication, or promise. Earnest to a fault, the essay would pass unnoticed in a freshman comp class.

In this essay, Obama re-creates dialogue, a technique used to somewhat better effect in *Dreams*. Here his ungainly conjuring of black speech in a conversation between himself and a neighborhood woman would have gotten an organizer with *two* white parents fired:

> "I just cannot understand why a bright young man like you would go to college, get that degree and become a community organizer."
>
> "Why's that?"
>
> "Cause the pay is low, the hours is long, and don't nobody appreciate you."

Dreams was published just five years down the road from *After Alinsky*. America was asked to believe that Obama metamorphosed in these few short years from an awkward amateur into what the *New York Times* has called "that rare politician who can actually write . . . and write movingly and genuinely about himself."

A much more likely explanation is that Ayers transformed the stumbling literalist of "Why Organize?" into the sophisticated post-modernist of *Dreams*. What is undeniable is that their two memoirs follow oddly similar rules. The evidence is in the text. Ayers describes his as "a memory book," one that deliberately blurs facts and changes identities and makes no claims at history. Obama says much the same. In *Dreams*, some characters are composites. Names have been changed. Events occur out of precise chronology.

Remnick concedes that *Dreams* is not to be taken at face value. He calls it a "mixture of verifiable fact, recollection, recreation, invention, and artful shaping." The same could be said for James Frey's best-selling memoir, *A Million Little Pieces*. For no clear reason, however, Frey's many inventions, when revealed in 2006, incensed the literary gatekeepers.

None reacted more fiercely than chief Obama cheerleader Oprah Winfrey. When she finished drawing and quartering Frey before her national TV audience, the janitor with the sawdust was needed to mop up the pieces. Ace *New York Times* columnist and Obama fan Maureen Dowd cheered the dismembering on:

> It was a huge relief, after our long national slide into untruth and no consequences, into Swift boating and swift bucks, into W.'s delusion and denial, to see the Empress of Empathy icily hold someone accountable for lying.

And Frey, at least, had written his own books!

Dowd herself would soon enough contribute to the long national slide. In May 2009, she was accused of lifting a paragraph from the blog of *Talking Points Memo* editor Josh Marshall. "I was talking to a friend of mine Friday about what I was writing," Dowd said in her own defense. Apparently, this friend "suggested I make this point, expressing it in a cogent—and I assumed spontaneous—way and I wanted to weave the idea into my column." If you are expecting some rough approximation of Marshall's blog, brace yourself. Here is what Dowd wrote:

> More and more the timeline is raising the question of why, if the torture was to prevent terrorist attacks, it seemed to happen mainly during the period when the Bush crowd was looking for what was essentially political information to justify the invasion of Iraq.

Here is what Marshall had written earlier. See if you can spot the difference.

> More and more the timeline is raising the question of why, if the torture was to prevent terrorist attacks, it seemed to happen mainly during the period when we were looking for what was essentially political information to justify the invasion of Iraq.

Dowd had matched every single word, even every single comma, but changed "we" to "the Bush crowd." Then she just flat-out lied about what she had done. The gratuitous Bush-bashing likely saved her career. A less prominent or politically useful columnist would have been dispatched to the 4 A.M. shift on the delivery trucks, if not drummed out of the building.

Remnick cuts Obama a whole lot more slack than Dowd or anyone else cut James Frey. What makes *Dreams* "exceptional," he observes, is "not that Obama allows himself these freedoms, but, rather, that he cops to them right away." Not that exceptional. Ayers cops to these freedoms right away, too. He asks of his own memoir, "Is this then the truth?" He answers, "Not exactly. Although it feels entirely honest to me." The reader knows that Ayers—with some justification—has much to hide. He senses that Obama does, too, but he is never quite sure why.

In early October 2008, a correspondent alerted me to an essay by Ayers titled "Narrative Push/Narrative Pull." The lessons that Ayers offers on the art of the narrative seem to have found their way into *Dreams* unmolested. The Ayers quotes come from this essay unless otherwise specified. Obama quotes come from *Dreams:*

AYERS:

The hallmark of writing in the first person is intimacy. . . . But in narrative the universal is revealed through the specific, the general through the particular, the essence through the unique, and necessity is revealed through contingency.

OBAMA:

And so what was a more interior, intimate effort on my part, to understand this struggle and to find my place in it, has converged with a broader public debate, a debate in which I am professionally engaged. . . .

Our trials and triumphs became at once unique and universal, black and more than black.

AYERS:

Every narrative is, of course, necessarily incomplete, each a kind of distortion. Reality is always messier. . . .

OBAMA:

I understood that I had spent much of my life trying to rewrite these stories, plugging up holes in the narrative. . . .

I had felt my voice returning to me that afternoon with Regina. It remained shaky afterward, subject to distortion.

AYERS:

Narrative inquiry can be a useful corrective to all this.

OBAMA:

Truth is usually the best corrective.

AYERS:

The mind works in contradiction, and honesty requires the writer to reveal disputes with herself on the page.

As far as race in America was concerned, the problems and contradictions were all taken care of in the deep past. (*Teaching Toward Freedom*)

OBAMA:

But I suspect that we can't pretend that the contradictions of our situation don't exist. All we can do is choose.

AYERS:

The reader must actually see the struggle. It's a journey, not by a tourist, but by a pilgrim.

OBAMA:

But all in all it was an intellectual journey that I imagined for myself, complete with maps and restpoints and a strict itinerary.

AYERS:

Narrative writers strive for a personal signature, but must be aware that the struggle for honesty is constant.

OBAMA:

I was engaged in a fitful interior struggle. I was trying to raise myself to be a black man in America.

AYERS:

But that intimacy can trap a writer into a defensive crouch, into airing grievances or self-justification.

OBAMA:

At best, these things were a refuge; at worst, a trap.

AYERS:

Forgetting can be confused with remembering—the fictions we force ourselves to carry replace the facts we are hiding from the world, facts buried within fictions. (*Fugitive Days*)

OBAMA:

I know how strongly Gramps believed in his fictions, how badly he wanted them to be true, even if he didn't always know how to make them so.

AYERS:

When history is being rewritten in the interest of a smoother, less troublesome tale . . . (*Fugitive Days*)

OBAMA:

It corresponds to what I know about my grandfather, his tendency to rewrite his history to conform with the image he wished for himself.

Although I cite no more than two examples for each, *Dreams* offers many more. There are ten "trap" references alone and nearly as many for "narrative," "struggle," "fiction," and "journey." With less frequency, the two authors dabble in advanced postmodern slang as well—the "grooves" into which they have fallen, the "poses" they assume, and even the "stitched together" nature of the lives they or their relatives lead.

This postmodern posturing leads to the frequent manipulation of dates and numbers to score political points, a sleight of hand that Ayers justifies in *Fugitive Days:* "I've come to see, in any case, that fiction does a better job with the truth in almost every instance."

When citing numbers to make a point, Ayers is as reckless as an Enron accountant. In the "rotten and unjustifiable" Vietnam War, he tells us, America was responsible for the "indiscriminate murder of millions of Vietnamese." During the American bombing along the Cambodian-Vietnamese border, he insists, "perhaps three-quarters of a million peasants were murdered cleanly from the air." This figure represents many more people than lived in the area and more than 10 percent of the Cambodian population. In reality, fewer than 750,000 Cambodians died violently during that whole era from all causes.

Date changes allow for symmetry in the storytelling, but they can also enhance the propaganda value of the story. "I saw a dead body once, as I said, when I was ten, during the Korean War," writes Ayers in *Fugitive Days*. This correlation is important enough that Ayers mentions it twice. The only problem is that Ayers was eight when the Korean War ended.

Obama tells us that when he was ten, he and his family visited the mainland. The date of the visit is specific: "during the summer after my father's visit to Hawaii, before my eleventh birthday." This was 1972. Traveling around the country on Greyhound buses with his mother, grandmother, and baby sister, the ten-year-old Obama and his family "watched the Watergate hearings every night before going to bed."

Only the cruelest of ideologues would force her children to watch Senate hearings before bedtime, but Ann had no opportunity to play mommy dearest. She and her family took this trip a year before the Watergate hearings, which actually began in the late spring of 1973. This is not an isolated misrepresentation.

According to *Dreams*, the little family with one-year-old Maya in tow made an improbable long-distance detour from the obvious places they might visit—Seattle, Disneyland, the Grand Canyon, Yellowstone—to spend three days in Chicago. Obama mentions a Kansas City stop along the way, and Madelyn's youngest brother in suburban K.C. would later provide photographic evidence of the same. He confirms the year as 1972. Why they would have traveled an additional five hundred miles each way beyond Kansas to spend three dreary days in a motel in the South Loop is anyone's guess.

In Chicago, Obama's most vivid memory is of seeing the shrunken heads on display at the Field Museum. Yes, the museum did have those heads on display. Examining them, according to one source, was a "crucial rite of passage for generations of Chicago kids." Ayers was one such kid. He grew up in suburban Chicago.

In *Dreams*, Obama remembers the heads to be of "European extraction." The man looked like a "conquistador" and the woman had "flowing red hair." This reversal of Euro-fortune struck the precocious ten-year-old as "some sort of cosmic joke." This memory too is thoroughly contrived. That some conquistador would wander into the Ecuadorian jungle with a woman in tow, let alone Rita Hayworth, and end up as a shrunken head defies all probabilities. No source on the Field exhibit even hints that these were Europeans. In fact, one source suggests that the tribe in question vanished seven hundred years before the first European arrived.

Ayers, however, has something of a fascination with headhunting. In *Fugitive Days*, he recounts a 1965 antiwar protest on the University of Michigan campus that proved formative in his own radicalization. At the protest, Ayers saw a series of photos that moved him. One showed "four American boys kneeling in the sun, bare-chested, smiling broadly." Although these soldiers looked like the kind of guys Ayers had grown up with, they "cradled in their hands now, the severed heads of human beings, their dull, unseeing eyes eternally open, their ears cut off, strung into a decorative collar worn around one smiling kid's neck." That this photo never made its way beyond this particular protest testifies to the easy malevolence of Ayers's imagination.

Obama would claim to return to Chicago as an adult "fourteen years later." In fact, Obama arrived in Chicago thirteen years after his presumed 1972 visit or twelve years after the Watergate hearings. This error struck me as no more than careless data transmission between co-authors. Ayers seemed to be taking the raw data of Obama's life and improvising as he saw fit, often without checking facts.

While driving around town upon his arrival in Chicago in 1985, Obama found himself sharing magically in the black oversoul, as he recounts in *Dreams:*

> I remembered the whistle of the Illinois Central, bearing the weight of the thousands who had come up from the South so many years before; the black men and women and children, dirty from the soot of the railcars, clutching their makeshift luggage, all making their way to Canaan Land.

In 1988, Obama had tried to voice a similar cultural memory in "Why Organize?" This awkwardly structured excerpt likely does capture the real voice of Obama:

Through the songs of the church and the talk on the stoops, through the hundreds of individual stories of coming up from the South and finding any job that would pay, of raising families on threadbare budgets, of losing some children to drugs and watching others earn degrees and land jobs their parents could never aspire to . . .

"Threadbare budgets"? It is remarkable how much better a writer Obama would become in the next few years. The pages in *Dreams* reminiscing about the Chicago return end thus: "I imagined Frank in a baggy suit and wide lapels, standing in front of the old Regal Theater." The point is made: Obama was not merely moving to Chicago in 1985. He was returning home as spiritual heir to progressive black Chicago icon Frank Marshall Davis. We will hear more about "Frank" later.

WEIRD SCIENCE

As soon as I started writing on the authorship subject, correspondents began to advise me of computerized programs designed to sniff out literary mischief, like the one that tagged *Time* magazine's Joe Klein as the author of the Clinton-era novel *Primary Colors*.

I was wary of such science for any number of reasons. Most practically, I did not believe that Ayers wrote *Dreams* the way Klein wrote *Primary Colors*. Rather, my belief was that he served as Obama's muse, editing the book lightly in some parts, heavily in others, and taking over principal writing duties in others still. This pattern, I suspected, would defy existing forensic programs.

I knew too that controversy dogged the whole field of literary forensics. The case of Don Foster, the Shakespearean scholar and Vassar professor who helped uncover Joe Klein, is instructive. Using computer analysis, Foster was the first to attribute to Shakespeare an otherwise anonymous poem, "A Funerall Elegye in memory of the late

Vertuous Maister William Peeter." This being the first new Shake-speare find in more than a century, Foster received a good deal of international acclaim.

Not everyone agreed, however, that Foster deserved the honor. In 2002, one such critic, Gilles Monsarrat, made such a compelling case for John Ford as the poem's author that Foster yielded to Monsarrat's argument. In a rare moment of academic grace, Foster wrote, "No one who cannot rejoice in the discovery of his own mistakes deserves to be called a scholar."

I labored under no illusion that the media would greet my challenge to Obama with anywhere near that level of civility. Given their barrels of ink and reels of tape, I wanted to know what kind of science they might use to undercut me. So before proceeding further, I decided to seek out expert advice. Among those I contacted was Patrick Juola of Duquesne University, the author of two highly regarded books on the subject of authorship attribution. My query and his thorough response both took place on September 27, 2008:

Patrick

> *You come highly recommended as someone who might help me solve a linguistics challenge on which I have been hacking: the authorship of Barack Obama's memoir, "Dreams From My Father." I have no idea of your politics. If you reject this challenge out of hand I would understand. If, however, you have an interest in influencing history, this might be fun. What makes the project particularly intriguing is that I firmly believe that the primary author is Bill Ayers.*

> *I had written an earlier book on intellectual fraud called "Hoodwinked," but I am in over my proverbial pay grade on things like QSUM analysis. What follows are some introductory articles I have written. I can also provide pdfs of "Dreams" and "Audacity of Hope" and extensive notes on Fugitive Days.*

> *Thanks*
> *Jack*

Dear Mr. Cashill,

Thank you very much for the extremely interesting opportunity, but—politics aside—I don't think that the technology is currently available to do what you would like. Not to put too fine a point on it, the accuracy simply isn't there. The best-performing methods we know about can get 90%+ accuracy, but can also get 50% or less (and we don't yet understand the conditions that cause that to happen) which means that for high stakes issues (such as national politics), the repercussions of a technical error could be a disaster (in either direction). In fact, this is what much of my research is on—trying to improve the accuracy rate of these techniques so that they can be used reliably in important cases, or at least to understand when these techniques can be used with safety.

If you go to my home page, http://www.mathcs.dug.edu/~iuola, you will be able to download a copy of a recent book of mine, called "Authorship Attribution." (I encourage you to do so, and don't worry, it's free. Special deal with the publisher.) I talk a bit on page 11–13 about a couple of well-publicized failures (including a failure of the QSUM technique you mentioned on national TV, where the researcher Morton "could not distinguish between the writings of a convicted felon and the Chief Justice of England.") I hope you understand my reluctance to be pilloried as Morton was (or as Don Foster later was over the _Elegy_).

Having said that, . . . I will happily offer you a couple of cautionary notes and travellers' tales that might help your search for evidence. My first suggestion is simply to look at my book, particularly chapters four and five, which might help you understand better the type of stuff that people have been doing since the fall of QSUM. (And in particular, don't bother with QSUM; it simply doesn't work.) In general, single-valued measures such as average word length, average sentence length, or mean "reading level" tend not to work as well as multivariate measures, where you measure lots of different properties of the text, such as the frequencies of fifty or a hundred different words. There's even some software out there that might be able to help you in the analysis; I have the JGAAP program available for download and I believe David Hoover has a "Delta Spreadsheet" that also does authorship analysis. But a better approach is simply to do what you're already doing (as far as I can tell from the columns you were so kind as to send)—good old-fashioned literary detective work. If you can get Dystel or Osnos into the metaphorical back room and ask them some hard questions, that's the sort of thing that would be much more convincing than an abstract numerical argument based on something like "entropy" that no one really understands anyway. . . .

Warmest regards,
Patrick (Juola)

Shortly before I talked to Juola, an experienced systems designer named Ed Gold had volunteered to run a QSUM scan on multiple excerpts from both memoirs. He reported in after my conversation with Juola. Although I shared Gold's conclusion with my readers, I cautioned them about the reliability of such studies.

"I have completed the analysis," Gold had written me, "and I think you will be pleased with the findings." In assessing the signature of sample passages from *Dreams*, Gold found "a very strong match to all of the Ayers samples that I processed." Like Juola, Gold recognized the limitations of the process and of his own resources.

Going forward, I took Juola's advice and plowed on the old-fashioned way. Helping me now, though, were literary Hardy Boys and Nancy Drews from throughout the world. In time, I would receive useful tips from correspondents in Australia, Switzerland, Israel, South Africa, Hawaii, and all over the mainland, some from within the academy, many from without. Most preferred anonymity. Almost to a person, they cited the same reason—the media hell that had rained down on "Joe the Plumber."

ACKNOWLEDGMENTS

In early October 2008, a correspondent sent me an unusual clue from an unexpected source, Rashid Khalidi. Khalidi now serves as the Edward Said Professor of Modern Arab Studies at Columbia University, an appropriate posting as his background is nearly as contrived as Said's. Once considered a spokesman for the Palestine Liberation Organization and typically designated as a "Palestinian-American," Khalidi was born in New York to a Saudi diplomat and a Lebanese American Christian. That the Saudi father was born in Jerusalem apparently gives the American son Palestinian griping rights. In reality, I have better claim to speak for the IRA than he does for the PLO.

Khalidi achieved some small notoriety during the 2008 campaign. In April of that year, Peter Wallsten of the *Los Angeles Times* wrote a lengthy article titled "Allies of Palestinians see a friend in Obama." The article pulled some of its information from a video shot at a 2003 farewell dinner for Khalidi. Khalidi, who had spent several years at the University of Chicago, was leaving for New York.

At the dinner, reportedly attended by Ayers and Dohrn as well, Obama thanked Khalidi and his wife for the many meals they had shared chez Khalidi and for reminding him of "my own blind spots and my own biases." Obama hoped that "we continue that conversation— a conversation that is necessary not just around Mona and Rashid's dinner table . . . [but around] this entire world."

Wallsten acknowledged that during this "celebration of Palestinian culture" some of the guests made hostile comments about Israel. One recited a poem accusing the Israeli government of terrorism, with the implicit threat that Israel "will never see a day of peace." Another compared "Zionist settlers on the West Bank" to Osama bin Laden. If worse had been said, or if Obama had applauded these comments, the world beyond the *Los Angeles Times* newsroom would not be allowed to know.

The *Times*, which endorsed Obama for president, steadfastly refused to share the videotape despite the demand by the McCain camp and others to release it. "A major news organization is intentionally suppressing information that could provide a clearer link between Barack Obama and Rashid Khalidi," said McCain spokesman Michael Goldfarb. *Times* spokeswoman Nancy Sullivan blew Goldfarb off. "As far as we're concerned, the story speaks for itself," she responded. The *Times* would add no details beyond what had appeared in Wallsten's April article.

As for myself, I was less interested in Rashidi's relationship with Obama than I was in his relationship with Ayers. Khalidi does not shy from admitting the latter. He begins the acknowledgment section of his 2004 book, *Resurrecting Empire*, with an eye-popping tribute to his own literary muse.

"First, chronologically and in other ways," writes Khalidi, "comes Bill Ayers." Unlike the calculating Obama, Khalidi had no reason to be coy about this relationship. He elaborates: "Bill was particularly generous in letting me use his family's dining room table to do some writing for the project." Khalidi did not need the table. He had one of his own. He needed help from the one neighbor who obviously could and would provide it.

Chicago's Hyde Park was home to a tight, influential radical community at whose center was the charismatic Ayers and wife Bernardine Dohrn. Remnick calls them collectively "the Elsa Maxwell of Hyde Park." In this world, the couple's terrorist rap sheet only heightened their reputation. With all due respect to Sarah Palin, Obama likely saw them less as "pals" than as surrogate parents. Dohrn and Obama's mother, Ann Dunham, were born the same year, 1942. The couple had given up revolution in 1980 for the long, slow march through the institutions. By 1994, if not earlier, Ayers apparently saw a way to quicken that march.

In October 2008, after reading the Rashidi acknowledgment, I imagined how Ayers and Obama might have proceeded. "I believe that after failing to finish his book on time, and after forfeiting his advance from Simon & Schuster," I wrote, "Obama brought his sprawling, messy, sophomoric manuscript to the famed dining room table of Bill Ayers and said, 'Help.' "

In his book *Barack and Michelle*, Christopher Andersen contends that Obama was allowed to keep the advance, but otherwise describes what happened much as I had imagined. His level of detail suggests a source very close to the scene. (When I asked, he would not tell me who.) Noting that Obama had already taped interviews with many of his relatives, both African and American, Andersen elaborates: "These oral histories, along with his partial manuscript and a trunkload of notes were given to Ayers."

For mentors, Obama consistently chose men like Bill Ayers, the Reverend Jeremiah Wright, Edward Said, Rashid Khalidi, and, before them, the communist poet Frank Marshall Davis. They shared their wisdom, and Obama reciprocated as best he could. In 1997, for instance, Obama reviewed Ayers's *A Kind and Just Parent*, calling it "a searing and timely account of the juvenile court system, and the courageous individuals who rescue hope from despair." In 2003, as mentioned, Obama publicly thanked Khalidi for expanding his worldview.

Khalidi, in turn, publicly thanked Ayers in the acknowledgments section of *Resurrecting Empire*. When Ayers published his memoir *Fugitive Days* in 2001, Said was happy to provide a blurb. "For anyone who cares about the sorry mess we are in," wrote Said, "this book is essential, indeed necessary reading." To complete this cluster back scratch, in his 1997 book, *A Kind and Just Parent*, Bill Ayers walks the reader through his Hyde Park neighborhood and identifies the notable residents therein. Among them are Muhammad Ali, "Minister" Louis Farrakhan (of whom he writes fondly), "former mayor" Eugene Sawyer, "poets" Gwendolyn Brooks and Elizabeth Alexander, and "writer" Barack Obama.

In 1997, Obama was an obscure state senator, whose one book had netted little acclaim and lesser sales. In terms of identity, he had more in common with Mayor Sawyer than poet Brooks. The "writer" identification seems forced and purposefully so, a signal perhaps to those in the know of a persona in the making that Ayers had himself helped forge.

The question was often asked during the campaign why Obama would associate with Ayers. The more appropriate question is why the ever-resourceful Ayers would associate with the then-irrelevant Obama. Before Obama's ascendancy, it was Ayers who had the connections, the clout, and the street cred. He saw the potential in Obama and chose to mold it. As history will record, his creation got away from him.

REFORMERS

If Bill Ayers did help Barack Obama write *Dreams from My Father*, surely a major investment of time and energy, the question has to be asked, why would he do so? The answer may well be found in a 1994 essay by Ayers, whose title befits a former merchant seaman: "Navigating a restless sea: The continuing struggle to achieve a decent education for African American youngsters in Chicago."

In "Navigating," Ayers and his nominal co-author, former New Communist Movement leader Michael Klonsky, offer a detailed analysis of the Chicago school system and a discussion of potential reforms. Curiously, Obama does the same in *Dreams*. What makes his educational excursion curious is that he had little interest in education. In *Dreams*, he admits to spending only a few months working on school issues and then while his mind was "elsewhere." Ayers, however, had been keen on teaching kids even before he started blowing up buildings. In the mid-1990s, his passion for reform inspired him to engineer the rise of a proxy of color who could address problems in ways that he and fellow paleface Klonsky could not.

It should surprise no one that the analysis offered in *Dreams* echoes that of "Navigating." It stands to reason. Each was authored in the same year, 1994. Ayers was clearly the dominant partner in the essay and likely the dominant partner on the book. I found this essay after the November election. I wish I had found it sooner. The parallels are striking. The particular value Obama brought to the partnership, however, can be found not in the many points on which Ayers and the Obama of *Dreams* agree, but rather on the one in which they at least seem to differ.

First, the areas of agreement. *Dreams* tells us that Chicago's schools "remained in a state of perpetual crisis." "Navigating" describes the situation as a "perpetual state of conflict, paralysis, and stagnation." *Dreams* describes a "bloated bureaucracy" as one source of the problem and "a teachers' union that went out on strike at least once every two years" as another. "Navigating" affirms that the "bureaucracy has grown steadily in the past decade" and confirms *Dreams'* math, citing a "ninth walkout in 18 years."

"Self-interest" is at the heart of the bureaucratic mess described in *Dreams*. "Navigating" clarifies that "survivalist bureaucracies" struggle for power "to protect their narrow, self-interested positions against any common, public purpose." In *Dreams*, educators "defend the status quo" and blame problems on "impossible" children and their "bad parents." In "Navigating," an educator serves as "apologist for the status quo" and "place[s] the blame for school failure on children and families."

Another challenge cited in *Dreams* is "an indifferent state legislature." Ayers cites an "unwillingness on [the legislature's] part to adequately fund Chicago schools."

In *Dreams*, "school reform" is the only solution that Obama envisions. In "Navigating," Ayers has no greater passion than "reforming Chicago's schools." In fact, in that same year this article was written,

1994, the ambitious Ayers co-authored the proposal that would win for Chicago a $49.2 million Annenberg Challenge grant.

In *Dreams*, all deeper thoughts on educational reform are channeled through the soulful voices of two older African Americans. The first is "Frank," the young Obama's mentor in Hawaii, the real-life poet, editor, and fellow traveler Frank Marshall Davis. In *Dreams*, Frank makes a spirited distinction between education and training that perfectly mirrors Ayers's own sentiments. More on this shortly.

The second goes by the phonied-up name "Asante Moran," likely an homage to the Afrocentric educator Molefi Kete Asante. In *Dreams*, Moran lectures Obama and his pal "Johnnie" on the nature of public education:

> "The first thing you have to realize," he said, looking at Johnnie and me in turn, "is that the public school system is not about educating black children. Never has been. Inner-city schools are about social control. Period."

Not surprisingly, Moran's take on public education aligns perfectly with Ayers's own. "In an authoritarian system," he insists, "the entire system is twisted towards mystification and geared towards control." Ayers, by the way, frets not just about "control," but about "social control."

"The message to Black people was that at any moment and for any reason whatsoever your life or the lives of your loved ones could be randomly snuffed out," he writes in the full flowering of his paranoid fervor. "The intention was social control through random intimidation and unpredictable violence."

In *Dreams*, Moran elaborates on the fate of the black student: "From day one, what's he learning about? Someone else's history. Someone else's culture. Not only that, this culture he's supposed to learn is the same culture that's systematically rejected him, denied his humanity."

Precociously Afrocentric, especially for a white guy, Ayers has been making the same case since he first got involved in education. In 1968, as the twenty-three-year-old director of an alternative school in Ann Arbor, Michigan, he told the *Toledo Blade*:

> The public schools' idea of integration is racist. They put Negro children into school and demand that they give up their Negro culture. Negro children are forced to speak, behave, and react according to middle-class standards.

In "Navigating," Ayers echoes the apocryphal Moran, claiming that students who do not meet the idealized "white, working-class, well-fed, able-bodied, English-speaking" model are "met with indifference or even hostility and are deemed 'unteachable.' "

By 1994, Ayers had been preaching educational reform for nearly thirty years. Ever since his days in Ann Arbor, he had been promoting "decentralized, flexible, multicultural, small schools." If his theories remained utopian, his tactics had become hardball Chicago, but not quite hardball enough. One major force still intimidated him: Chicago's sluggish and self-interested educational bureaucracy.

Over the years, this bureaucracy had morphed, as Ayers notes in "Navigating," from being a bastion of "White political patronage and racism" to being "a source of Black professional jobs, contracts, and, yes, patronage." For reasons both ideological and practical, Ayers wilts in the face of this bureaucracy.

In none of his writing, in fact, can Ayers bring himself to suggest even the slightest flaw in black culture. Everything, of course, is the white man's fault. In "Navigating" he seems to echo the black activists who gripe that white assaults on a largely black bureaucracy were based not "on hopes for educational change, but on simple Chicago race politics." As to the culprits in the city's race politics, Ayers cites everyone but the black bureaucrats: Mayor Richard Daley, Jr., white businessmen, unnamed "professionals," Reagan education secretary William Bennett, even "right-wing academic Chester Finn."

On this racially tender issue, not so strangely, *Dreams* tells a different story. Obama openly chides the black "teachers, principals, and district superintendents" who "knew too much" to send their own children to public school. "The biggest source of resistance was rarely talked about," Obama continues, namely that these educators "would defend the status quo with the same skill and vigor as their white counterparts of two decades before." As to the claims of these educators, affirmed in "Navigating," that "cutbacks in the bureaucracy were part of a white effort to wrest back control," the author of *Dreams* says teasingly, "not so true."

"Not so true"? In these three words one can anticipate Obama's potential return on Ayers's investment. Simply put, as an African American, Obama could address sensitive racial issues in ways Ayers could not. Ayers surely recognized this. To advance Obama's career, it seems, Ayers finished up *Dreams*, got Obama appointed chair of the Chicago Annenberg Challenge grant, and held a fund-raiser for his state senate run in his Chicago home, all in 1995.

The political calculus behind that ambition helped shape *Dreams*. This was a careful book written to launch the career of a deeply indebted and highly malleable Chicago politician, maybe even a mayor, one who saw the world through white eyes, as Ayers did, but one who could articulate the city's real problems in words that Ayers could not—at least not publicly.

RUSH

In early October 2008, I expanded my publishing format to include the *American Thinker*. Although the audience for the latter was smaller than *WND*'s, the publisher, Thomas Lifson, allowed for longer "think" pieces, and the more words I could assemble in one place, the more convincingly I could make my case.

Lifson has the kind of background more welcome in the blogosphere than in a conventional newsroom. Raised in a liberal household in progressive, good-government Minnesota, he rounded into an antiwar activist in late '60s Harvard. His eclectic graduate studies included sociology, business, and modern Japan. It was in Japan, as Ralph Nader's personal ambassador, that Lifson began to question his own political identity. "I got to know some real leftists over there," Lifson told me. "They were scoundrels."

Off and on, Lifson would spend nineteen years at Harvard, acquiring three graduate degrees and teaching in the Harvard Business School, as well as in the sociology department. In Cambridge, the issue that caused him to recalculate his politics was rent control. "It was so counterproductive," says Lifson. "It was the first time I realized the left could be pathological." The fall of the Berlin Wall, the dissolution of Eastern Europe, and the opening of the Soviet archives showed him just how intrinsic that pathology was.

Still, Lifson could not imagine himself as a right-winger, let alone a Republican. "I was in academia," he laughs, "so I could not be a conservative. It was unthinkable." As a semi-joke, his wife bought him a copy of *National Review*. He read it from cover to cover and agreed with everything he read. "That's when I knew," he says.

As a consultant, usually on matters Japanese with major companies throughout the world, Lifson had saved enough to launch the *American Thinker* in 2003. He has doubled its audience virtually every year since. Although he publishes only about a half-dozen articles a day, the site attracts more than 120,000 daily visitors. As I discovered, if your article is on top, you will get most of that audience, including, occasionally, radio powerhouse Rush Limbaugh.

On October 9, 2008, Lifson ran my first extended piece. In 3,700 words, I was able to present most of what I had learned to date: the publishing history, the lack of any prior quality work by Obama, the parallels in imagery and style, and the state of existing science. Although other publications would shy from the subject, Lifson had no qualms. Living in Berkeley, California, as a near hermit, he did not worry about being snubbed at Georgetown cocktail parties. His gut told him that Obama was "an obvious phony, a con man." The evidence seemed to confirm his gut. In presenting the wealth of evidence then available, I summarized the state of the inquiry:

> Shy of a confession by those involved, I will not be able to prove conclusively that Obama did not write this book. As shall be seen, however, there are only two real possibilities: one is that Obama experienced a near miraculous turnaround in his literary abilities; the second is that he had major editorial help, up to and including a ghost-

writer. The weight of the evidence overwhelmingly favors the latter conclusion and strongly suggests who that ghostwriter is.

David Remnick cannot control his elitist imp in discussing what happened next. "Cashill's assertions might well have remained a mere twinkling in the Web's farthest lunatic orbit had it not been for the fact that more powerful voices hoped to give his theory wider currency." None would be more powerful than that of Limbaugh, a man who haunts the liberal imagination the way Kong did Skull Island.

Having done talk radio for a few years in Kansas City—at a station that had once fired Limbaugh—I have a healthy appreciation for the job Limbaugh does, and no one does it better. Although an obvious partisan, Limbaugh is analytically astute, authoritative, and very rarely wrong. I listen whenever I get the chance.

On October 10 of that year, at noontime, I had touched down from my "lunatic orbit" to moderate a meeting of corporate attorneys in my part-time role as executive editor of *Ingram's*, a regional business magazine. The meeting was intense. We were discussing the end of the financial world as we knew it, and the role of the attorney in sorting through the rubble.

During a break in the action, I checked my voice messages only to discover my inbox was full. This was unprecedented. I feared something had happened to one of my children. The first voice mail explained it all: "Are you listening? Rush is talking about you." (Point of interest: anyone who says "Limbaugh" is not a fan.) I could not tune in. I had to get back to my meeting.

Later, I listened to the podcast. Limbaugh was playing audio excerpts from *Dreams* and commenting on them. The one that triggered my name was this: "A steady attack on the White race, the constant recitation of black people's brutal experience in this country served as the ballast that could prevent the ideas of personal responsibility. . . ."

"Stop the tape," said Rush. "What is this? Ballast? He doesn't talk this way. You know, there are stories out there, he may not have written this book. There's a guy named Jack Cashill. . . ."

Observes Remnick, whose chief hobby seems to be imputing racism to people who live west of Tenth Avenue, "This may not have been Limbaugh's most racist insinuation of the campaign." He cites others he liked less, but he concludes that our collective "libel about Obama's memoir—the denial of literacy, the denial of authorship—had a particularly ugly pedigree."

If asked, I would have traced the "denial of authorship" pedigree to the publication of Friedrich August Wolf's *Prolegomena ad Homerum* in 1795. The brave Mr. Wolf challenged, with good cause, Homer's unique authorship of the *Iliad* and the *Odyssey* and, in so doing, shook the literary world to its core. So unsettled was Elizabeth Barrett Browning by the challenge to this "literary divinity" that she wrote a poem about that "kissing Judas/Wolf."

An 1852 entry by an anonymous author in *Chambers's Edinburgh Journal* took on the most divinely inspired author of them all. Titled "Who Wrote Shakespeare," the article opened a spanking new literary territory, and critics as diverse as Mark Twain, Sigmund Freud, and Helen Keller rushed in as though it were Oklahoma circa 1889. To this day, investigators continue to question the authorship of the plays that bear Shakespeare's name, but not one such investigator—and there are thousands—makes a case for Bacon or Oxford or whomever nearly as convincing as I had made for Bill Ayers's role in *Dreams* by October 2008.

On the off chance that Remnick had spotted a latent bias in my attribution research, I went back and checked *Hoodwinked*. In the book, I document roughly a score of major literary and intellectual frauds in 20th century America. I calculated their ethnic mix and found that three of my subjects were black—almost precisely their percentage in the population. I also covered prominent white women like Margaret Mead and Rachel Carson, the ersatz Indian Ward Churchill, the aforementioned Palestinian wannabe Edward Said, the bisexual Alfred Kinsey, and a bunch of presumably heterosexual white guys. Is there not some kind of diversity award for such multicultural debunking?

The literary fraud that sheds the most light on what Obama can expect, if ever busted, was the brainchild of another black icon, the late Alex Haley. When *Roots: The Saga of an American Family* was first published in 1976, it sold millions of copies and won Haley a special nonfiction Pulitzer Prize. The *Roots* miniseries attracted more viewers than any series before or since. Obama knows the book well and identifies with it. "Would this trip to Kenya finally fill that emptiness?" he wonders in *Dreams* about his upcoming "pilgrimage" to Africa. "The folks back in Chicago thought so. It'll be just like *Roots*, Will had said at my going-away party."

Although rarely discussed, *Roots* gave progressives an entertaining way to instruct their less enlightened brethren in the quiet horrors of American culture. Haley makes his protagonist, the young enslaved Kunta Kinte, a Muslim. Kinte, predictably, sees Christianity as crude and hypocritical. Coming of age during the revolutionary period in Virginia, he sees the American founding as inherently fraudulent as well.

The real fraud, alas, was Haley's. He had ripped off huge chunks of his book from a novel titled *The African*, written by a white guy, Harold Courlander. In 1978, Courlander sued Haley in U.S. district court in New York for copyright infringement. Midway through the trial, not wanting to attract undue attention, the judge counseled the dissembling Haley to settle with Courlander or face a perjury charge. Haley did just that to the tune of $650,000, or more than $2 million by today's standards.

The media paid as little attention to the settlement as they would to the black dead at Waco. In the press, only the *Washington Post* gave the case any ink of note, and even then it used a local hook— "Bethesda Author Settles 'Roots' Suit for $500,000"—to justify its coverage. No one in the media dared to explore the dark heart of the scandal: namely that the author of a Pulitzer Prize–winning work of "nonfiction" plagiarized from a fictional one.

In 1993, literary detective Philip Nobile thought he had busted the fraud wide open in a deeply researched *Village Voice* exposé. "There was no Kunta Kinte," says Nobile bluntly, and he proved as much in compelling detail. Although the European media gave his research huge play, Nobile was either shunned or ignored in the United States. I would not have heard about his work had I not been in Ireland at the time. Despite the lawsuit and Nobile's efforts, *Roots* remains a staple in history classes across America. And the Pulitzer remains in Haley's trophy case.

In a quirky historical footnote, John F. Kennedy, Jr., helped with the *Post* article cited above. As it happens, his father had also been involved in a dustup not unlike Haley's or Obama's, specifically in regard to the book for which he won the 1956 Pulitzer Prize, *Profiles in Courage*. Soon after the award, Kennedy was accused of having had more than a little help in the writing of the book. Short of libeling the accusers as racist, Kennedy supporters reacted to this charge with much the same dumb fury Obama supporters would fifty years later.

One particular accuser, however, had a little more clout than I. That would be the legendary muckraker Drew Pearson. He also had a more formidable platform, namely Mike Wallace's show on ABC. As is evident, the media took their responsibilities to the truth more seriously back in the day.

Understanding full well what a "fraud" label would do to JFK's presidential ambitions, the Kennedys used the servile family retainer Ted Sorensen to force a retraction from Pearson and Wallace. Under oath, Sorensen would testify, "I did not write the book for Senator Kennedy." Had the presumed collaborator on *Profiles* been a figure of comparable disrepute to Bill Ayers—say, Alger Hiss or Julius Rosenberg—Sorensen's prevarications could not have dampened what would surely have been a media firestorm.

In his 2008 book, *Counselor*, Sorensen would finally admit what he had been leaking since the book was first published, that, yes, he "did a first draft of most chapters." He had also received half the book's royalties before being bought out of his contract. Still uneasy more than fifty years later about his testimony before Pearson, Sorensen insists, "I took my oath seriously." He convinces no one, including himself.

Sorensen sums up his sophistry with a question meant to be rhetorical: "Is the author the person who did much of the research and helped choose the words in many of the sentences, or is the author the person who decided the substance, structure, and the theme of the book?" Sorry, Ted, Pulitzers usually go to the guy who put the words on the page. That would not be JFK.

Andersen reports that Obama, unaware of JFK's chicanery, hoped to launch his own political career with a book just like *Profiles in Courage*. He may have succeeded in ways he did not anticipate. In an even quirkier footnote, Ted Sorensen helped Obama with some of his speeches.

Although Remnick would take me to the progressive woodshed for my "libel" of Obama, he and those others who scolded me in 2008 never acknowledged my frequent caveats about the limits of my knowledge or accepted the challenge to prove or disprove my theory. "In that this remains something of a work in progress," I wrote in the October 9 article that sparked Limbaugh's interest, "I am willing to test my hypothesis against any standard of proof and appreciate any and all good leads."

To his credit, Remnick understands just how newsworthy that revelation should have been. "This was a charge," he writes of the fraud accusation, "that if ever proved true, or believed to be true among enough voters, could have been the end of the candidacy."

Four weeks before the election I was confident enough in my thesis to submit it to any test. If proved right, it would have undermined the foundational myth of Obama as genius, confirmed his intimate relationship with an unrepentant terrorist, and, perhaps most damningly, established this still-untested candidate as a liar of consequence. In short, it could have turned the election. I waited for some news operation with more resources and credibility to put my theory to the test. And I waited, and I waited, and I waited.

CHANNELING BILLY

In mid-October 2008, I began to receive emails from a fellow named Ryan Geiser. They were sharp, literate, and on the money. Ryan had been plumbing not just *Fugitive Days* but Ayers's other books, most notably the 1993 *To Teach* and the 1997 *A Kind and Just Parent*.

Geiser would send me emails that began thus: "I've been busy with work and kids lately, but I did have a little time this weekend to glance over some of Ayer's [*sic*] work. The similarities seem to me to be inarguable." He would then casually make an observation about some parallel stunning enough to build an article around.

A week after the Joe the Plumber incident, I asked him if I could give him public credit for his good work. He demurred. "With the left wing media more than happy to attack the messenger rather than analyze the message," he wrote, "there is no reason to give them anything other than the facts to focus on."

When I asked him if I could at least share his credentials with the audience to help me win over critics, he suggested that those critics would not be impressed. His simple bio, however, reminded me what a great country this really is: "My name is Ryan Geiser, I am 39 years old. Married to Shari Geiser, 3 kids, Christian 11, Peyton (a girl) 8, and Jacob 1½. I own a construction company with 20–25 employees. We live in Kearney, Nebraska." In the past month, when not busy with work and family, he had done more meaningful research than most literary critics do in a lifetime.

I contacted Geiser in the course of writing this book, and he consented to let me tell his story. He represents the kind of American the left fails to understand and thus deeply underestimates. Geiser grew up in the tiny town of Arnold, in central Nebraska, population 630 when last calculated. "Be our ambassador," asks the town's modest economic development website. "Spread the word. Ask the kids to come live back home. Tell the pharmacist; the nearly-but-not-quite-ready-to-retire attorney; the baker; the artist seeking nature's inspiration; the young man who dreams of horses, cows, and corn; the woman wanting a safe and healthy place for herself or her children—tell 'em all about Arnold."

Growing up, Geiser lived in a home that had very little in the way of resources. His mother, however, insisted that he read, and Geiser obliged her. He did well in school and won a Regents scholarship that allowed him to attend the University of Nebraska. Stretched for money after his first year, Geiser could not resist the lure of an $18-an-hour construction job that took him across the country. Although he regrets not finishing his education, he was able to save enough to start his own construction business, settle down, and raise a family. Today he does most of his reading on the Internet, mostly at news and financial sites, although he has recently found time to *reread* all 1,368 pages of Ayn Rand's *Atlas Shrugged*.

When Geiser read my first article on *WND*, he checked Ayers's vita, saw that Ayers had written other books, and ordered them through Amazon. "I wanted to see if there is any truth to what you were saying," he told me. Geiser was blown away by what he found. He felt like one of the first guys into the river at Sutter's Mill. There were exposed nuggets everywhere. "It's the most fun I've ever had doing research," said Geiser. What made it fun was that virtually every distinctive word or story he found in one of Ayers's books he could find a parallel for in *Dreams*. And this he was doing with highlighter and hard copies.

Although critics would accuse me of being "obsessed" with Obama, I too was doing my research on the side. No one was paying me for what I was doing. That fall, I was editing my business magazine and working on any number of projects, most notably the preproduction for the documentary *Thine Eyes*, which we would shoot in January, on the subject of the annual March for Life. One Saturday, as I was busily digging away, my wife reminded me that the city leaf collectors were coming on Monday, and that there was much bagging left to do. "Joan," I said, "I am busy trying to save Western civilization." The funny thing is that I meant it, but I still had to bag the leaves.

What Geiser and I worked out that frenzied October were a series of parallel stories and experiences, any one of which should have spurred the media to at least look at what I was writing. For those unmoved by authorship studies, timelines, parallel themes, matching metaphors, Ayers's role as neighborhood editor, or Obama's overnight transformation from struggling hack to literary superstar, Obama's apparent channeling of the thoughts and experiences of Bill Ayers should have been, at the least, legitimate grounds for discussion.

In his 1993 book, *To Teach*, for instance, Ayers tells the story of an adventurous teacher who would take her students out to the streets of New York to learn interesting life lessons about the culture and history of the city. As Ayers tells it, the students were fascinated by the Hudson River nearby and asked to see it. When they got to the river's edge, one student said, "Look, the river is flowing up." A second student said, "No, it has to flow south-down." Upon further research, the teacher discovered "that the Hudson River is a tidal river, that it flows both north and south, and they had visited the exact spot where the tide stops its northward push."

In his 1995 *Dreams*, Obama shares a jarringly similar story from his own brief New York sojourn. As Obama tells it, he takes an unlikely detour to the exact spot on the parallel East River where the north-flowing tide meets the south-flowing river. There, improbably, a young black boy approaches this strange man and asks, "You know why sometimes the river runs that way and then sometimes it goes this way?" Obama tells the boy it "had to do with the tides." The seeming indecisiveness of this tidal river is used here as a metaphor for Obama's own. Immediately afterward, he chooses to drift no more and lights out for Chicago.

In his 1997 book, *A Kind and Just Parent*, Ayers tells of a useful reading assignment from the 1992 book *The Kind of Light That Shines on Texas*, by black author Reginald McKnight. The passage in question deals with the travails of a boy named "Clint." The first black student in a newly integrated school, Clint tries to distance himself from Marvin, the only other black boy in the school.

"Can you believe that guy?" Clint tells a white student. "He's like a pig or something. Makes me sick." Upon reflection, Clint thinks, "I was ashamed. Ashamed for not defending Marvin and ashamed that Marvin even existed."

In *Dreams*, Obama reflects on his own first days as a ten-year-old at his Hawaiian prep school, a transition complicated by the presence of "Coretta," the only other black student in the class. When the other students accuse Obama of having a girlfriend, Obama shoves Coretta and insists that she leave him alone. Although "his act of betrayal" buys him a reprieve from the other students, Obama, like Clint, understands that he "had been tested and found wanting."

In fact, there was a little black girl at Punahou whom Remnick identifies as "Joella Edwards." The difference, Remnick admits without reflection, is that "Barry never rejected Joella." Au contraire, as Joella gushes, "He was my knight in shining armor." As with the story of the unhappily bleached black people, these little racial melodramas smack of willful contrivance.

"Coretta," by the way, is just one of many names in *Dreams* that show up in Ayers's books. Others include Malik, Freddy (with a *y*), Billy, David, Tim, George, Stan, Sally, Andy, Jimmy, Jeff, John, Joe, Jane, Marcus, Rick, Angela, Linda, "Aunt Sarah," and "the old man." Many of the stories involving these characters in *Dreams* seem as manufactured as their names.

In a third of the parallel stories, the evidence for Ayers's involvement is strongest. As suggested earlier, Ayers has strong opinions about "education" on the one hand and "training" on the other. "Education is for self-activating explorers of life, for those who would challenge fate, for doers and activists, for citizens," he writes in *To Teach*. "Training," on the other hand, "is for slaves, for loyal subjects, for tractable employees, for willing consumers, for obedient soldiers." Adds Ayers, "What we call education is usually no more than training. We are so busy operating schools that we have lost sight of learning."

In *Dreams*, written two years later, these sentiments find colloquial expression in the person of "Frank," as in Frank Marshall Davis. "Understand something, boy," Frank tells the college-bound Obama. "You're not going to college to get educated. You're going there to get trained." Frank shares Ayers's distaste for training. "They'll train you to forget what it is that you already know," Frank tells Obama. "They'll train you so good, you'll start believing what they tell you about equal opportunity and the American way and all that shit."

Just as Ayers makes the case that students are often stripped of their ethnic identity and "taught to be like whites," Frank argues that university expectations include "leaving your race at the door." The skeptics who insist that these ideas are progressive boilerplate and thus coincidental have not read the memoir Davis wrote in the early 1970s and amended at decade's end, *Livin' the Blues*. Neither apparently did Ayers or Obama. The folk wisdom that "Frank" mouths in *Dreams* does not at all jibe with the experience Frank Marshall Davis recounts in his memoir.

Davis loved college! He was the rare African American to get a college education in the 1920s, and he savored every minute of it. The years he spent at Kansas State University proved particularly rewarding. The campus was "beautiful," the students "usually agreeable," and his journalism department "excellent." It was here that he discovered his gift for poetry, a gift that was praised and nurtured by his uniformly white professors. In fact, he dedicated his second book of poetry to Charles Elkin Rogers, the department head with whom he shared "a fine friendship."

Throughout his memoir, Davis meets fellow black writers and cites their college backgrounds approvingly. He also meets open-minded white college students, whom he sees as the hope for America's racial future. His college poetry-reading tours on the mainland in 1973 and 1974 are huge successes. They fill him with hope and confidence. Obama visits Davis a few years after these tours while he is living in Waikiki's "Jungle," a neighborhood overflowing with students from the University of Hawaii. In his memoir, Davis describes his student neighbors as "rebels" and "natural allies of the black revolution." The "Frank" who speaks ill of university life in *Dreams* is pure sock puppet. As to who was doing the puppetry, Ayers makes an excellent suspect, the only one, really.

There was some speculation, though no confirmation, that Ayers had met Obama earlier in the decade during their overlapping years on the Columbia University campus in New York. Whether or not they had met in New York, Obama relates an experience at Columbia with the kind of insight and regret that one would expect from a veteran of internecine left-wing warfare.

As Obama tells it, he goes to hear the black activist formerly known as Stokely Carmichael speak at Columbia. Upon leaving, he watches dolefully as "two Marxists" scream insults at each other over minor sectarian differences. "It was like a bad dream," thinks Obama. "The movement had died years ago, shattered into a thousand fragments."

These insights into "the movement" seem much too knowing and weighty for a twenty-year-old bodysurfer just in from Hawaii and L.A. They sound perfectly natural, however, coming from a radical nearly twice that age emerging from a futile decade underground. In an interview for the book *Sixties Radicals, Then and Now*, Ayers makes the same point. "When the war ended," he says, "our differences surfaced. We ended up in typical left-wing fashion: We ate each other . . . cannibalism." Ayers would likely have gone to see Carmichael. He knew him personally and writes about him favorably both in *To Teach* and in the recent *Race Course*.

After leaving Columbia, Obama went to work for what he describes in *Dreams* as "a consulting house to multinational corporations." He observes, "As far as I could tell I was the only black man in the company." He does not boast of his racial uniqueness. Rather, in full grievance mode, he considers it "a source of shame."

As early as July 2005, however, former co-worker and current Obama fan Dan Armstrong revealed Obama's whole account to be a "serious exaggeration." Obama did not work at a multinational corporation, but a "small company that published newsletters." He was not the only black person who worked there. He did not, as claimed, have his own office, wear a jacket and tie, interview international businessmen, or write articles. He mostly just copyedited business items and slipped them into a three-ring binder for the company's customers.

When this discrepancy surfaced years later, pundits in either camp were confused as to why Obama would lie about such seemingly irrelevant details. There are two good, nonexclusive possibilities. For one, the exaggeration enables the reader to see Obama as he would like to see himself—"a spy behind enemy lines." For another, Ayers once again took the framework of Obama's life and roughed in the details.

In *Fugitive Days*, Ayers uses the phrase "behind enemy lines" almost literally to describe his and his comrades' quiet infiltration of the opponent's position. Dohrn has said the same in public. When the Weather Underground declared its state of war with the United States in May 1970, she warned that people fighting "Amerikan imperialism" all over the world "look to Amerika's youth to use our strategic position behind enemy lines to join forces in the destruction of the empire."

Ayers and his radical friends were obsessed with Vietnam. The war there defined them and still does. To reflect their radical savvy, they tend toward the knowing phrase. In *Fugitive Days*, for instance, when conjuring up an image of Vietnam, Ayers envisions "a patrol in the Mekong Delta." When mourning "a hamlet called My Lai," Bernardine Dohrn locates it "in the middle of the Mekong Delta," never mind that the two places are hundreds of miles apart. Similarly, when the young Obama pontificates about "angry young men," he places them "in Soweto or Detroit or the Mekong Delta."

Ayers had a much deeper connection than Obama to "Detroit" as well. Its historic riot took place shortly before Obama's sixth birthday. Ayers lived in Detroit the year after the riot and experienced its meltdown firsthand. In 2007, on his blog, he chose to "commemorate" the fortieth anniversary of what he predictably calls the "Detroit Rebellion."

For obvious reasons, the media and the Obama camp have held Obama blameless for knowing anything about anything before 1970. "Why is John McCain talking about the sixties?" one Obama ad asked. "McCain knows Obama denounced Bill Ayers' crimes committed when Obama was just eight years old."

In reality, Ayers and pals went underground in early 1970 and planted their first bomb in May of that year. Although Obama and his handlers never wearied of this petty deception, false advertising is not the issue. What is at issue is whether Obama maintained an intimate working relationship with a self-described communist whose acts of violence the candidate denounced only to win an election. In the fall of 2008, this would seem to have mattered.

SPACE LIMITATIONS

In the great campaign books of yore—Theodore White's come to mind—the authors made an effort to present the campaigns of both parties with similar detail and a semblance of balance. In the two major books on the 2008 campaign so far released—*The Bridge* by David Remnick and *Game Change* by John Heilemann and Mark Halperin—the authors simply don't know how.

These scribes do to Republicans quite what Edward Said believes Western writers do to "Orientals"—they judge them by their own standards. To paraphrase Said, these efforts can never be "veridic"— meaning genuine. They tend to tell us more about the people doing the judging than those who are being judged.

Despite his postmodern obtuseness, Said may be on to something. In one comic example, Remnick talks about the "pitiable" plight of John McCain having to stump for votes among "right-wing evangelists, free-market absolutists, and other conservatives." Without meaning to, Remnick just described—in the pejorative—the entire Republican Party. Who else is there?

Remnick's myopia surfaces in his discussion of the "wider currency" the conservative media provided my research. He cites Limbaugh as mentioned and a writer for *National Review*'s blog. That writer, un-named by Remnick, was Andy McCarthy, who posted a piece on October 11 describing my work as "thorough, thoughtful, and alarming." Remnick cites these two examples as though they typified the established right's response. I wish they had. In reality, they were rare exceptions. McCarthy was writing against the *National Review*'s grain.

To be sure, not one single major media outlet stepped up to commission a university study or even test the evidence that I had gathered. If my hypothesis were true, and those paying attention may have feared it was, they simply did not want to know.

As to the bloggers, in vintage left-wing style scores of them slashed away profanely without having read anything by either Ayers or Obama. One rather typical young progressive attacked me as an "Internet hobo" (huh?) and interpreted my theory to mean, "Obama didn't write a fucking word in the whole book." Her respondents were less generous still. Wrote one, "Well there are 48 striking similarities between Cashill's chromosomes and a fucking chimp's." Wrote another, "The best part about this whole conspiracy theory isn't how spectacularly wrong it is (and it's completely fucking incorrect), it's the fact that, were it true, it would be the most completely inconsequential conspiracy in fucking history." Wrote a third, "What the fuck is wrong with those people? Can we cure them with savage beatings? As a heathen I suggest we use Science to study the effects of beatings on wingnuts." I read somewhere that profanity shows up nineteen times more often in left-wing blogs than in right-wing ones. When I read it, I thought, "Only nineteen?" In the era of universal self-esteem, dull people seemed not at all shy about expressing sharp opinions.

This collective shrug from the major media did not surprise me.

Their ignorance had a logic. Real knowledge might just have undermined their commitment to a philosophy so evasive—"Yes, we can?"—that they themselves would be at a loss to describe it. Their ideological house of cards required vigilant security guards. That much I got.

What I did not get was why the "respectable" conservative media (RCM), those with a serious and sober presence in New York and/or Washington, were mimicking the turtle-like defenses of their mainstream peers. My thesis involved no eyewitnesses or radar data or ballistics tests. No one would have to leave his or her D.C. desk. All the evidence lay between the covers of a half-dozen or so books, two ostensibly by Obama and the rest by Ayers. I was not asking them to buy my thesis sight unseen but to kick the tires and take it for a test drive. Yet even so simple a literary review proved a task too daunting.

I am not sure I know why. There are good, smart, sincere people in the RCM. But for whatever reason, they had become cautious to the point of cowardly. Phantom beavers had all but dammed up the Clinton-era "communication stream of conspiracy commerce." By the time of the 2008 campaign, it had slowed to such a trickle that the major media could have sold at least half of the American people just about anyone for president, and "just about anyone" is what they sold.

After much back and forth, *Human Events* punted on my research. The *National Review* did, too. The Fox producers downstairs showed interest, but the suits upstairs did not. The managing editor of the *Weekly Standard* referred me to the magazine's literary editor, whose response echoed the others: "An interesting piece, but I'm rather oversubscribed at the moment, the length is considerable, and cutting would not do it justice. (Also, we had a long, rather critical, piece on Obama's oeuvre not too long ago.) So permit me to decline with thanks for allowing me to take a look."

For all my bellyaching, the *Weekly Standard* remains my favorite magazine. I subscribe. Still, a cover story that read "Who Wrote *Dreams from My Father*?" could have shaken up the election, maybe even turned it. Yet not a single conservative writer in the power corridor bothered to do what Nebraskan Ryan Geiser was routinely doing after a busy day framing and drywalling—namely, reviewing the relevant books. That simple. Dang those space limitations!

After the election, the respectable conservative media remained mute or worse. In February 2009, as the evidence of Obama's limitations grew painfully obvious by the day, James Taranto, editor of the *Wall Street Journal*'s online editorial page, rushed once more into the breach.

Taranto singled me out by name as among those of his fellow conservatives who "engaged in irresponsible rumor-mongering and conspiracy-theorizing" for daring to suggest that "Ayers might have ghostwritten Obama's acclaimed autobiography."

I had to respond. "James, There I was, reading my most recent The American Spectator," I began my email to Taranto, "starting with my favorite columnists, James Taranto high among them, and I find myself on the unflattering end of one of your observations." I sent along an op-ed for the *Journal*, a process he does not control.

"Jack—I'm afraid I still find the Ayers-ghostwrote-Dreams idea too far out to take seriously," he wrote back. In a sentence, he summed up the problem with my thesis—it just seemed too perfect. A few months later, the *National Review*'s Jonah Goldberg would protest in a similar vein: "I think trying to claim some sort of literary conspiracy is a bridge too far." In 1994, however, Ayers's help would have seemed no more conspiratorial than if an electrician neighbor had helped Obama rewire his house.

Pre-election, the still-vital forces in the conservative media—the Internet and AM radio, with a particular nod to Rusty Humphries and his producer, Rich Davis—were trying to push the story downstream, but the RCM had closed the locks. This effectively dried up Rush's commentary, and the major media scarcely had to trouble themselves with the controversy at all.

I remember sitting at my office desk late on a Friday afternoon, October 17, eighteen days before the election, E minus 18, humming a Randy Travis tune about the media, "Is it still over / Are we still through / Since my phone still ain't ringing / I assume it still ain't you." In the week since Limbaugh talked about my thesis, I had not received a single call from anyone in the print or television media—right, left, or center—despite my efforts to prime the pump.

It was then that the inimitable Bob Fox called. Although I had never met Fox, still haven't, we would exchange at least two dozen phone calls in the next few weeks. A California businessman, not quite fifty, Bob had recently returned from an extensive health-care consulting gig in Russia. His "ru" email exchange would lend an air of mystery to our correspondence.

Fox had recently received an email from one of his sisters alerting him to the work I had been doing in *WND* and *American Thinker*. A student of languages—he also speaks Russian, German, and French—Fox saw the merit in my thesis and alerted the husband of another sister, Utah congressman Chris Cannon. After six terms, Cannon had lost a primary challenge due to his perceived weakness on the illegal immigration issue. At this stage, he had nothing to lose.

Cannon had been paying closer attention to the Obama phenomenon than most of his Washington peers. "He understood what Obama was from the beginning," said Fox.

After our exchange, Fox had me call Cannon. Even before the weekend was out, Fox and Cannon had contracted to have writing samples from Ayers and Obama tested through a university-based authorship program and arranged a conference call early in the following week with some people of influence on the right. I went back to my leaf-raking that weekend with at least some of the burden lifted from my shoulders.

That Saturday I received a boost from another, unexpected source, namely a classics professor at *the* Ohio State University, Bruce Heiden. Heiden, whom I would later meet over breakfast at his Columbus home, had come a long way from his natural habitat. He had grown up in Coney Island, gone to high school in Brighton Beach, college at

Columbia, and graduate school at Cornell. This was as total a liberal immersion as any American has ever had to endure. Before Ohio, he may have never even seen a Republican in the wild.

For Heiden, the subject that sparked his discontent with the left was public education. The people whose politics he shared argued for a pedagogy that struck him as very nearly perverse. Once Heiden started questioning progressive wisdom on one subject, he started to question that wisdom on a host of subjects, most notably communism. He took to reading Solzhenitsyn, then Whittaker Chambers, and from there it was just a matter of time.

When I met Heiden, he looked as unassuming and professorial as he had when he voted Democratic, and his home—all bookcases and exposed wood—looked like a professor's home. It is just that Heiden no longer thought the way one expected a humanities professor to think. In 2008, the fifty-something prof would cast his first-ever vote for a Republican in a presidential election. In the weeks leading up to that election, the fearless Heiden weighed in on his blog, the Postliberal, with the fascinating assertion that Obama "agrees with Cashill on one important point," namely that Obama himself "didn't write [Dreams]."

Heiden's nearly five-thousand-word argument is observant, amusing, and, for a university professor in the dawning age of Obama, mighty bold. Tenure does have its uses. Heiden analyzes *Dreams'* original 1995 introduction and compares it to the preface affixed in 2004. Absurdities abound. The essay deserves to be read in full, but for practical purposes let me reproduce Heiden's summary:

> According to this analysis, Barack Obama's Introduction to *Dreams from My Father* and his 2004 Preface offer an obfuscated, self-contradictory, and unbelievable representation of his authorship that, upon close reading, proves vacant. As Obama tells it, his authorship of *Dreams* was miraculous, because although he *lacked* the writing skill to be the author of anything, and he didn't *want* to be the author of

a memoir, and he *resisted* becoming the author of a memoir, and he *tried in vain* to become the author of a different kind of book, and he never *had an idea* of being the author of anything until one or several publishers had the idea first and he agreed to *accept the opportunity* they offered to be an author, and even then he only considered himself an author as long as his *publisher* was selling his book, after which he *reverted back* to a complete non-author, reverted so completely that he *wasn't even moved* to reread his book when political opponents were using it against him—because, in short, despite all the reasons Obama gives why he *couldn't* have written a book like *Dreams from My Father*, and despite the fact that, according to Obama's account, he *didn't* write *Dreams from My Father*, nevertheless *Dreams from My Father* somehow "found its way" onto the page with Barack Obama's name under the title as the author. That's a miracle. It couldn't have happened.

As example of Obama's passivity, Heiden offers an oddly truthful passage from the 1995 introduction that speaks to the genesis of the book:

At some point, then, in spite of a stubborn desire to protect myself from scrutiny, in spite of the periodic impulse to abandon the entire project, what has found its way onto these pages is a record of a personal, interior journey—

The subject of this sentence—after the "in spite of" clauses—should rightly have been "I," as in "I wrote this book." Obama has shown no reluctance to use the "I" word elsewhere. Instead, whoever wrote this sentence gives Obama no credit for writing *Dreams*. Yes, Obama's story has "found its way onto these pages." No one questions that.

The 1995 introduction makes the claim, likely true, that Obama had originally intended to write a book "about the current state of race relations" and had agreed to take a year off after graduation to "put thoughts to paper." Somewhere along the way, however, he found his "mind pulled" toward writing a family history despite his desire to protect himself from scrutiny.

The 2004 preface, however, tells a different story. "I received an advance from a publisher," writes Obama, "and went to work with the belief that the story of my family . . . might speak in some way to the fissures of race that have characterized the American experience." In this version of events, which follows immediately after the 1995 introduction in the 2004 paperback, Obama jumps directly into the family history, advance in hand.

Among other curious revelations in the 2004 preface is Obama's claim to have pulled out a copy of *Dreams* "for the first time in many years" and read a few chapters. He does so not to examine the contents for potentially embarrassing revelations but to "see how much my voice may have changed over time." In that he has written nothing of the slightest consequence in the last ten years, it is hard to imagine that his voice would have changed at all or that anyone would notice if it had. Still, he confesses to wincing at the occasional ill-chosen word or phrase and feels the urge "to cut the book by fifty pages or so."

In fact, the book is 150 pages or so too long. *Dreams* serves up several windy accounts of events and conversations, especially in Chicago and Kenya, that just take up space. My interpretation of this unlikely apology varies a bit from Heiden's. I believe Ayers largely wrote the 2004 preface and overlooked the transition from a book on race relations to a family history. I also believe, and this is purely speculative, that he was telling those in the know that he could have done better with *Dreams*, that perhaps he allowed the nominal author too much leeway in what remained in the book. Ayers has an ego. All real writers do.

Obama's ascendancy as a literary superstar had to irritate Ayers at least a little. The spectacular mistiming of his own 2001 memoir, *Fugitive Days*, doomed the book to short-term infamy and long-term obscurity. Now he was playing the deformed Cyrano to Obama's hunky

Christian, and it was Christian who was winning the heart of Roxanne/ America.

To be sure, Heiden's support from within the academy did not change the debate, but it did make me feel a little less crazy. There were times in October 2008 that I could identify with Dr. Miles Bennell, the small-town doctor and seeming madman who desperately tries to convince the local shrinks that giant seed pods of a communist bent have indeed taken over Santa Mira, in the film classic *Invasion of the Body Snatchers*. I still identify.

SWIFTBOATING

Bob Fox and I were in constant contact the week of October 20. Two friendly university professors had signed on to the authorship project, and they were throwing their best science at the various books of Ayers and Obama. Fox kept me continuously updated on their progress.

In the meantime, Congressman Cannon had arranged a conference call among several key members of the "vast right-wing conspiracy." On the line, if I remember right, were Jed Babbin, editor of *Human Events*, direct-mail pioneer Richard Viguerie, leading conservative publicist Craig Shirley, Cannon, myself, and a few others.

After a given electoral defeat, the left consoles itself with the illusion that a cabal of this nature would have contrived the lowest, slimiest smear it could have hoped to get away with, found some moneybags to fund it, snuck it into the public debate, and swayed the weak-minded. The two classic cases of such imagined mischief are that of Willie Horton and the Swiftboaters.

The left's reimagining of the Willie Horton incident reached its demented apogee in Michael Moore's Academy Award–winning *Bowling for Columbine*. While scolding whites for their fear of the black man, Moore shows an ad that he attributes to the 1988 George H. W. Bush campaign. The *Bowling* version of the ad features the scary mug shot of Willie Horton, an African American, and the caption "Willie Horton released. Then kills again."

The real ad, like this one, had focused on what Horton had done—robbed a seventeen-year-old gas station attendant, fatally stabbed him nineteen times, and dumped him in a trash can to die. Twelve years later, despite a life term without parole, Horton received a weekend furlough, during which he knifed, blinded, and gagged a man in Maryland, raped his fiancée, and stole their car.

The real ad, the one produced by the Bush campaign, did *not* show or name Willie Horton. It showed prisoners passing through a revolving door while viewers were told how liberal Massachusetts governor Michael Dukakis had supported this insane furlough program as a form of criminal rehabilitation. Of the thirty prisoners shown in the Bush ad, only three were black. For that matter, it was Al Gore who had first raised the furlough issue during the primaries.

Before the election, few in the media knew exactly who Willie Horton was. Most had never heard the name or seen the photo. After the election, however, Democratic operatives unearthed an ad featuring Horton's mug shot that an independent group had run in New England for two weeks. In the subsequent months and years, in order to paint the new president and his cronies as racist dirty tricksters, a bitter punditry would repeatedly show the Horton ad and attribute it to Bush.

The bait and switch worked. More than fifteen years after the election Moore could show the ad in his movie and expect his audience to assume it was Bush's. A sloppy propagandist, Moore inserted the "Willie Horton released. Then kills again" caption into the ad indifferent to the fact that Horton did not kill upon his infamous weekend leave. Moore assumed, as did the media, that the Bush ad worked by playing on America's chronic anxiety about the black man. The impli-cation, of course, is that the public would have welcomed Dukakis's furlough program had it freed only white killers to rape and plunder.

The media response to the 2004 Swiftboat campaign was equally self-deluding. During the Vietnam War, John Kerry had served in a small area called An Thoi, Coastal Division 11. Of the twenty-three officers he served with in that area, four supported him for president, two took no position, but an astounding seventeen of the twenty-three were willing to publicly condemn him as unfit for command, based on an undeniable history of fabricating slurs against his fellow soldiers and lying about his own war record.

John O'Neill, the former Swiftboater who organized Swift Boat Veterans For Truth, had voted for Al Gore in 2000 and Ross Perot in the two previous elections. When he and his fellow vets held a news conference at the National Press Club in early May 2004 to air their grievances, the media pretended not to notice.

In late May 2004, I was approached by Cleveland talk-show host Paul Schiffer to see if I could produce a video for the Swifties. At that time, they had no money and few connections. The fact that they were talking to me at this point shows how utterly unconnected they were. When I read their material, I was overwhelmed by the consistently damning testimony of so many of Kerry's fellow officers. I suggested a book and played a small role in helping O'Neill and co-author Jerome Corsi find a publisher.

As I watched the campaign unfold that summer, I found it hard to believe that the Democrats were doing nothing to immunize Kerry against the charges that were soon to resurface. In fact, they set Kerry up for a fall by having him boat across Boston Harbor and mount the podium at the FleetCenter as if he were at a VFW convention and de-clare, "I'm John Kerry and I'm reporting for duty."

Like Barack Obama, who had given his keynote speech the night before, Kerry was building a political persona on a precarious foun-dation. "I defended this country as a young man and I will defend it as president," swore Kerry. Obama would make a similarly dubious claim on the campaign trail in 2008. "I've written two books," Obama told a crowd of teachers in Virginia. "I actually wrote them myself." In reality, Kerry was to fighting what Obama was to writing: they both dabbled. Boasting about one's imagined exploits, however, had the potential of playing into the opposition's hands.

Democrats still attribute Kerry's loss to the fact that he would not fight back against the Swifties. They refuse to accept the reality that he could not. The Swifties had the truth on their side. Kerry chose the strategically wiser route—step aside and let the media smear the opposition. Indeed, given the liberals' control of the airwaves and the academy, they have managed to turn *swiftboat* into a verb meaning "a strong pejorative description of some kind of attack that the speaker considers unfair or untrue—for example, an ad hominem attack or a smear campaign." Recall Maureen Dowd's earlier citation of the Swiftboat campaign as a symptom of "our long national slide into untruth."

Republicans have a much keener sense of the way the media work than do Democrats. During the teleconference two weeks before the election, those on the line understood that the moment they went public with the accusation that Obama needed major help from Bill Ayers to complete *Dreams*, the most powerful forces in the media— the *New York Times*, the *Washington Post, Time, Newsweek,* CNN, ABC, NBC, CBS—would, if they could not ignore the accusers, turn their collective wrath upon them.

In that I had no reputation in Washington to protect—dwelling, as I did, "in the Web's farthest lunatic orbit"—I was prepared to move forward. By this time, my confidence in the soundness of my theory was approaching 100 percent. My new telephonic colleagues, however, were understandably more hesitant. They needed a confidence builder. Despite my cautions about the limits of literary science, they hoped to see some hard data. Cannon told them it was on the way.

In a manner of speaking, it was. Two days later, October 22, E minus 13, the two university professors sent us a summary of their authorship study, and the results were encouraging. The study did, however, have a few, well, limitations. The first is that no one could understand it. The report began with the following explanation:

> Our study was based on the well known Chi Square test. This test is run by applying a formula to observed data to compute a Q value. Given the number of degrees of freedom and the desired confidence level, a threshold is looked up in a table or, as in our case, computed using a function built in to a software package. The outcome of the test depends on the Q value in relation to the threshold.

This was the easy part. It got more complicated from there. The professors had done their job well, but we had hoped to present the media with a document that spoke for itself. This one would require actual work from media that did not want to be bothered in the first place. A second limitation was that, in writing at least, the professors did not want to overstate their case lest their prudence be doubted. Although they were more openly supportive over the phone, in print they felt obliged to pull their punches. The result was this:

> The Q values in the Dreams-Dreams comparisons had the same magnitude as the Q values in the Dreams-Fugitive comparisons. This means that the Dreams text fit the Fugitive text as well as it fit other sections of the Dreams text. This fact alone is not sufficient to conclude that there is a common author, but it does raise serious questions. Why are these writings so similar? If Obama wrote Dreams, why does it match so well the writings of another author? In some cases, the fit of Dreams to Fugitive was better than the fit of Dreams to other portions of the Dreams text.

Had the date been E minus 113, the results might have prodded some media outlet on the right to throw some resources at the study, but on E minus 13, this was too little, too complicated, too late. And, as feared, there was a third problem. Valuing their futures in academe, the professors would not put their names on the work, let alone their mugs on TV. This all but negated the work's value. I could hardly blame the profs. In the face of a likely Republican defeat, a futile tilt at the Obama windmill could have cost them their heads.

As a last stab at gathering media attention, I asked the anonymous profs to summarize their results for easy consumption in one hundred words or less. Here are the 119 words I got back:

> The fundamental principle of stylometric analysis is that the frequency of occurrence of function words in a written document is an identifying characteristic of the author. We compared word frequency counts of Dreams From My Father with Fugitive Days and about ten other randomly selected texts. Goodness of fit between different documents was obtained by computing the so called Q value from the standard chi-square hypothesis test. The documents were divided into segments so that both within text and between text comparisons could be made. Under the Q-value statistic, segments of Dreams consistently compared as well with Fugitive segments as it did with other segments of Dreams itself. In contrast, Dreams compared poorly with other documents.

Clear enough? I should add a fourth limitation with the study. Computer-driven authorship studies have the persuasive power of a polygraph, not a DNA analysis. At the end of the day, even O.J. could find a polygrapher willing to prove him innocent. If we went forward with our proof, I had no doubt but that our wily opponents could locate someone willing to contrive a contrary proof. And they owned the academy, not us. We were lucky to find the guys we did.

Truth be told, I could make a better public case for Ayers's involvement by a discussion of the word *ballast* than I could by sharing these results. But who was I? Even to the pundits on our own side, I was just one of those "Internet zanies" mucking up the debate. On the other side of the aisle, the pundits were far less f***ing generous.

VICHY

Bob Fox, just back from Russia, dug in like the Soviets at Stalingrad. The Obama machine would roll on triumphantly, he feared, unless HQ gave us the go-ahead to fire away. The word Fox was getting from the movers and shakers on the right, however, was that there would be no moving or shaking without an imprimatur from the academy. Not one to give up, even if just twelve days shy of the election, he continued looking for a university-based scientist who had the will to do an authorship study and the brass to stand up and defend it.

As it happened, I knew one such guy. Andrew Longman had first started corresponding with me in 2005 when I was reporting for *WorldNetDaily* on the search for WMDs. Longman knew something about the subject. He holds a patent, along with his co-inventors, on a network concept for detecting hidden terrorist nuclear weapons in an urban environment. At the time we were corresponding, he was working contractually with Purdue University, my and his alma mater. His work historically had been a mix of science, scientific instrumentation, computing, and consulting engineering. I figured if you couldn't trust a Boilermaker, whom could you trust?

An evangelical Christian, and a large, goateed one at that, Longman had made the *Drudge Report* earlier in the year when he confronted Chelsea Clinton, who was on campus to stump for her mom. Longman had attended the event and, when called upon, asked a seriously impertinent question.

The House of Representatives impeached William Jefferson Clinton on counts of perjury and obstruction of justice. He was held in contempt of a federal court, was fined and disbarred from practicing law in Arkansas, and resigned rather than be disbarred before the Supreme Court. All of these were a consequence of his blatant lies under oath to a federal grand jury. Miss Clinton, your mother apologized, covered up, and lied for the lies that the President told under oath. How then can the Hillary campaign say the Monica Lewinsky affair was just a personal matter, when candidate Clinton covered up perjury and committed obstruction of justice for the President of the United States?

Chelsea's answer, if any, was lost amidst the hisses and boos raining down on the imperturbable Longman's head. This was a guy I was pretty sure I could count on, and I was right. He gallantly took up the challenge. He did not, however, shy from sharing his handicaps, namely that no one had ever heard of him and to the degree that anyone had it was as the hulking partisan bully who beat up on poor Chelsea. Still, he was capable of doing the science, and he proceeded to do just that. With Longman on board, I now counted Mormons, Catholics, Jews, evangelicals, and agnostics among my ecumenical crew.

At about this same time, I turned to a fascinating character who had recently written to *American Thinker* to disagree with the conclusions of Duquesne's Patrick Juola. A friend had forwarded him a copy of an article in which I had reported Juola's conclusion, namely the belief that "the accuracy simply isn't there" to do a fully reliable authorship analysis. Wrote Chris Yavelow, "I'm sorry to disagree with Mr. Juola. . . . I have developed software that can detect if works are written by the same author, or, given samples of two authors' work, detect within a reasonable doubt, who wrote a third work."

Yavelow, a composer who had helped pioneer the marriage of music and computers, had turned his attention to what he called "computational corpus linguistics" some years earlier. In 2005, he had started marketing software called Fiction Fixer. He clarified: "Don't be concerned with the focus on novels at the website. The software is equally effective with biographies and autobiographies." Yavelow insisted that if he had adequate samples of Obama's and Ayers's writing, he could tell who wrote that. "Please pass this information along to Mr. Cashill," he concluded. "I believe that this would be an important project." Yes, "important" sounded just about right. I was not sure what to expect from Yavelow, but I sent him some relevant materials and promptly forgot about him. In truth I did not expect much.

On Sunday morning, October 26, E minus 9, I heard back from Longman. He had downloaded Patrick Juola's JGAAP software and was running the relevant writing samples through it. As he explained, there were fourteen tests, and fourteen analytic methods, for a total of 196 combinations.

"Right now I am running some trial runs," he wrote, "using the sample writing fragments made available in the program, and firing up other computers to run at the same time."

In the interim Longman had been examining the work of the two anonymous university-based scientists. "They did a very good job," he wrote. "Any engineer or scientist familiar with confidence level statistics will be satisfied that the basic method is reasonable." He phrased his analysis of their work artfully:

The Ayers-Obama matching shows a measurable and substantial effect. It is easily and objectively distinguishable from comparison to a third document. These results achieved through good methodology should readily stimulate scientists skilled in the particular relevant fields to construct their own tests, place objective metrics on the correlation between the Ayers-Obama documents, and publish results. We strongly think this bears immediate investigation by the academic community at large as the initial data presented is highly suggestive that these two documents share large portions of authorship.

That much said, Longman understood that for such a test to be conclusive, or close to it, he would have to run twenty or so comparable memoirs through the software and establish that the Obama-Ayers correlation was stronger than that for Obama–anyone else. He had little doubt that it would be, but "little doubt" did not equal confirmation.

Still, Longman's analysis was enough for Bob Fox to persuade Chris Cannon to hold a press conference in Washington on Tuesday afternoon, E minus 7. Mark Hyman of Sinclair Broadcasting, a Washington insider who had been following our work and supporting it, agreed to come, as did Bruce Heiden of Ohio State. The classics professor, blithely indifferent to his colleagues' Obamamania, was having fun with the project.

Longman chose not to come to D.C. "I have no fear," he said, but he did not have the credentials, either. "Me trying to be a credible spokesman, cross-discipline, and on such short notice, stretches not only my ability to perform, but my public credibility," he explained. "For your success, I don't evaluate it as a good calculus." At first, I tried to change Longman's mind. "The future of the Republic is at stake," I wrote Longman, "and the weird thing is I am not kidding." The more I thought about it, though, the more sense his decision made.

On Monday, October 27, E minus 8, I got a pleasant surprise. Yavelow weighed in. "Upon cursory examination," he wrote, "it's relatively certain that *Dreams From my Father* and *Audacity of Hope* were not written by the same person." He added, "Many aspects of *Fugitive Days* are too close to *Dreams* to be a coincidence (I'm talking about structural things here). I am preparing a report about this which I should be able to email you tomorrow."

At 11 P.M. that same night I received another email from Yavelow. "I'm getting close to finishing the report and it's quite amazing. I am convinced Ayers had a hand in *Dreams From My Father*, and probably wrote the entire thing (excluding dialog which he probably received as cassettes or notes from BHO)." At five the next morning, October 28, E minus 7, Yavelow sent the finished report. "I've put a note on it not to distribute without permission," he wrote. "That's because, with such little sleep I'm starting to imagine repercussions about me having done this—for example, if someone were to feel that I contributed to BHO not winning the election. Perhaps if we talk about this a bit, you can reassure me that such things don't happen in America."

The report ran twenty-seven pages and impressed me immediately with its logic and lucidity. What the report did was compare *Dreams* with *Fugitive Days* on any number of variables. The first one, for instance, Yavelow describes as "attributions," meaning the verb used to introduce a quote or a sentiment, such as he "said" or she "responded." As he observed, some authors get by with as few as three such attributions and many with fewer than twenty.

His Fiction Fixer program tracks 106 possible attributions. Of these, 36 appear in *Dreams* and 34 in *Fugitive Days*. "The remarkable thing," writes Yavelow, "is that these subsets differ by only 4 words, and of these 4, three are relegated to the 'only to be used once' category." His program diagnosed any number of other variables: characters per word, syllables per word, sentence length, structure, flow, paragraph length, readability, verb use, modifiers, contractions, redundancies, and more.

The similarity between the two books on nondialogue sentences was striking. The average number of words per sentence in one book was 17.62 and in the other 17.61. The average number of syllables per sentence was 26.48 in one and 26.27 in the other. *Dreams* averaged 1.44 syllables per word, *Fugitive Days* 1.47. The sentences using dialogue, however, showed no particular correlation, which suggests that these were largely left unedited in *Dreams*.

Yavelow also tracked the use of clichés. "Striking to observe," he writes, "is that out of 3,072 clichés, one of these books uses 5% of the available list while the other uses 7% of the list. Nonetheless, they have 62% of the clichés they use in common! And, not only in common, but often in a nearly corresponding position on the distribution list." For instance, at the top of each list was the phrase "first time." In second place in one and third in the other was "of course." Fifth in one, sixth in the other was "handful," and so on.

Another categorization that struck me as interesting was "sensory triggers," words that relate to the use of the five senses. For sight sensory triggers, the six most frequently used such words in *Dreams*—*black, see, looked, seemed, look, saw*—are also the six most frequently used such words in *Fugitive Days*. The other senses tracked comparably.

Indeed, in no category was there a variation that caused Yavelow to doubt the validity of my thesis. He summed up his findings:

> There is a strong possibility that the author of *Fugitive Days* ghost wrote *Dreams From My Father* using recordings of dialog (either tape recordings or notes). Alternatively, another scenario might be possible: Ayers might have served as a "book doctor" for Obama and given extreme license to edit and rewrite.

In September 2009, remember, Christopher Andersen would note that Obama had indeed given Ayers recordings of dialogue as well as "a partial manuscript and a trunkload of notes." Obama also seems to have given Ayers license to rewrite as he saw fit. Yavelow had beaten Andersen to this conclusion by a year.

Just a few hours after I received Yavelow's report I boarded a plane for Baltimore-Washington International Thurgood Marshall Airport. As we taxied to the gate at BWI, we were greeted by a cold, nasty rain. The weather proved rather an omen. When I checked my phone messages, the first one was from Bob Fox. It said something to the effect of "Don't bother to come today. The press conference has been called off." Heiden had gotten the message before he left and stayed home. For better or worse, I was here.

I called Fox, and he danced around the reason for the cancellation. I think Cannon had chosen not to squander his legacy on some whack job from Kansas City, and Fox was too loyal to say so. In any case, he arranged for Cannon to meet me at 5 P.M. in the office building that bears the name of an earlier Cannon, Joseph Gurney Cannon, the Republican House speaker who opened the building exactly a century earlier.

On the good-news side, as Fox saw it, he had contacted a professor at Oxford University, as in England, who was prepared to do an authorship study. All Fox had to do was raise ten thousand dollars in the next day or two. This demand came not from the professor but from the university. Fox figured that at this late stage, E minus 7, nothing that Longman or Yavelow could say would make a difference. Only an Oxford endorsement could generate an October surprise capable of surprising anyone who mattered.

Having rented a car, I looked for someplace suburban to hole up and ended up, entirely by accident, at the Bowie Town Center, on the road to Annapolis. As I was pulling in, I heard on the radio the audio of an Obama interview from 2001 so ominous that I remember exactly where I was when I heard it.

In this interview, Obama lamented the fact that "the Supreme Court never ventured into the issues of redistribution of wealth and the more basic issues of political and economic justice in this society." He went on to say that the Warren Court failed to "break free from the essential constraints that were placed by the Founding Fathers and the Constitution." Scarier still, he expressed confidence that he "could come up with a rationale for bringing about economic change through the courts."

The Constitution, especially the Bill of Rights, protects the citizen from the government, and here was our would-be president wanting to tear down that wall. Yikes! If I had any doubts about what I was doing in D.C., or why I had invested so much time in what seemed to so many a fool's errand, I doubted no more. The image that Obama had been crafting as a congenial centrist first with *Dreams*, and even more so with *Audacity*, seemed something of a trick on America. Especially vulnerable were our civic baby seals, those well-meaning citizens so anxious to atone for the nation's racial sins that they would vote away the Constitution.

I knew then what Remnick would later affirm, namely that my theory, "if ever proved true, or believed to be true among enough voters, could have been the end of [Obama's] candidacy." I knew too that we had all but run out of time, a fact that just about everyone had come to accept other than the relentless Bob Fox.

I met with Cannon later that afternoon. Although pleasant enough, he took the meeting as a courtesy. His heart was no longer quite in it. Staffers were packing up and taking plaques off the wall as we spoke. He suggested a few people I might meet with in the next few days but beyond that he had little to offer. He had already resigned himself to defeat.

So had just about all of Republican Washington. It felt like Paris, May 1940. "I remember it clearly: You wore blue, the Germans wore gray." Some were planning to flee, others to collaborate. Few were prepared to fight. Back in Missouri, a battleground state, *la résistance* was still slugging it out in the hills and dales as though victory were possible. Partisans in flyover country took their inspiration from one particular person, Sarah Palin. It was she who gave them reason to believe that the McCain campaign was worth the fight. McCain would never have carried Missouri—and any number of other states—without her.

They didn't get this in Washington. They didn't get Sarah Palin. Truth be told, they didn't get America. The bluing of conservative bloodlines could be traced through the Buckley family. Whereas William would surely have resisted, son Christopher chose to collaborate. "I've read Obama's books, and they are first-rate," he wrote in endorsing Obama weeks before the election. "He is that *rara avis*, the politician who writes his own books. Imagine." Yes, Christopher, but even a rare bird can poop on your head.

David Brooks, who had graduated from the *Weekly Standard* to the *New York Times* in 2003, proved no more red-blooded. "I remember distinctly an image of—we were sitting on his couches, and I was looking at his pant leg and his perfectly creased pant," Brooks wrote, "and I'm thinking, a) he's going to be president and b) he'll be a very good president." In the immediate wake of the release of *The Audacity of Hope*, Brooks published an unmanly *Times* column headlined "Run, Barack, Run."

Despite Mark Hyman's best efforts, I could not get on the agenda of Grover Norquist's highly influential Wednesday morning meeting. (When I did get on some months later and explained my project, I heard at least a few boos from the Vichyites in the cheap seats.) Nor was I able to get any D.C. media attention save from the tireless G. Gordon Liddy, who, at eighty-something, could still sense a con when he saw one. A twenty-something reporter from the *Washington Times* called because someone told her to, but she had no idea what the story was about. I referred her to my website and asked her to call me back. She never did.

LONDON FOG

No later than Thursday morning, E minus 5, I got a surprising and welcome call from the London *Times*. The reporter, Sarah Baxter, sounded sympathetic and interested, and for a moment at least, she gave me cause to believe that Bob Fox's improbable British strategy might just pay off.

What attracted her to the story was the failure of Fox to raise the ten thousand dollars needed to pay for a study by Oxford professor Peter Millican. As I understood it, the intellectual property guardians at Oxford would not take Fox's down payment and an IOU. I sent a story on the Oxford angle to *WND*, which ran it on Saturday, November 1, E minus 3.

That same morning, I received a long and amiable email from Millican. He humbly corrected my designation of him as "arguably the world's leading authority." (His modesty would prove well justified.) As he related, contractual arrangements had stalled "for no very clear reason." He attributed the breakdown not to Oxford but to "the relevant Republican authorities." In other words, and this Millican may not have known, Bob Fox simply couldn't come up with the dough.

Millican clarified another issue. There was no study to "liberate," as I had suggested in my posting. True, he spent some time "preparing for a detailed study," but he had been unable to commit the time necessary for "a full study." The breakdown in contract negotiations, a heavy teaching load, and his need to prepare a conference paper had kept him from completing the task.

After his initial investigations—"such as they were"—Millican had cautioned Fox on the likely outcome: "I told him that if he was to go ahead he should see it as a gamble: not likely to succeed, but potentially with a huge payoff if it did." I responded promptly to Millican in equally amiable terms:

Peter

> *Yes, sorry for the journalistic shorthand. I know that the difficulty has been on our side of the drink. Bob Fox discovered what I was doing a couple of weeks ago and has done his best to advance it, and he may have gotten ahead of himself. After talking to [Patrick] Juola a month ago, I was skeptical of the value stylometrics bring, but I seemed almost alone in my skepticism. Media people especially kept demanding to see "studies."*
>
> *What worried me from the beginning was exactly what Juola warned against—the power of one study to undo the literary detective work that preceded it, especially given the political leanings of our professoriate. . . . I do not know what heat we can generate in the next few days, but you would probably be better off staying out of it altogether. This is an unusual election, and I fear it could make 2000 seem like a stroll in the park.*

When Millican sent his pleasant email on Saturday he knew what was coming the following day. I had no idea. On Sunday, under Sarah Baxter's byline, the London *Times* ran a blistering front-page story headlined "Republicans try to use Oxford don to smear Barack

Obama." The only Republicans that Baxter identified were Cannon and Fox. Baxter did not quote me at all, and I suspect her headline had been more or less written before she even called me.

In that same day's paper, both in print and online, Millican fleshed out the libel in a lengthy op-ed perversely titled "How they tried to tarnish Barack Obama: Peter Millican reveals how he was drawn into a plot to link the Democrat to a former radical." Good gosh! And I was worried about *our* professoriate. Millican's breathless opening paragraph needs to be read in full:

> Last Sunday I received an urgent call from Bob, a man close to a Republican congressman in the American west. He wanted to enlist my services to prove a scandalous allegation against Barack Obama, which would surely affect his prospects in the forthcoming election. Namely, that his famous 1995 memoir, Dreams from My Father, on which so much of his reputation was built, was in fact written largely by Bill Ayers, a Vietnam-era domestic terrorist.

Millican went on to explain that the studies we had produced were "badly flawed." The problem was not in the execution, but in the lack of effective controls. To do a thorough job, analysts would have had to compare *Dreams* and *Fugitive Days* to multiple contemporary memoirs. Our guys all acknowledged this limitation. None had time or resources to carry out such a study pre-election.

Neither did Millican. Here a certain timeline comes into play. Fox had called Millican on Sunday, likely late in the day given the eight-hour time differential. Sarah Baxter called me no later than Thursday morning to discuss the stalled negotiations. I remember taking the call in my D.C. motel, and I checked out on Thursday morning. I cite this detail because Millican had told me he did not contact the "relevant journalists" until late on Friday. He apparently misremembered.

In the three- or four-day window from late Sunday to early Thursday, days heavy with teaching duties and paper preparation, not to mention contract negotiations, Millican managed to prove that there was "nothing that would give Obama any cause for concern." After a mini-review that allowed no time to even read the books in question, he dismissed the forensic work of three American analysts—one of whom was using Millican's own software—as "completely unsubstantiated." And if my guys were modest about their conclusions, Millican was anything but. He came down from Oxford to the London *Times* as confidently as Moses had come down from the mountain.

In his front-page op-ed, Millican describes Fox as "sincerely interested in getting to the truth," but he has nothing good to say about "the Republicans." He writes, "I was left with the impression that payment for propaganda was fine; but payment for objective research was quite a different matter." What Millican chose not to see is that the "Republicans" in question *were* Bob Fox.

The reader will recall that in a personal email just a day earlier— thank God for Yahoo! Search—Millican had written, "I told [Fox] that if he was to go ahead he should see it as a gamble: not likely to succeed, but potentially with a huge payoff if it did." Fox had put up five thousand dollars of his own money but could get no takers on the other five.

The fact that Fox could not muster another 5K suggests that, as far as "Republican plots" go, this was not exactly Watergate. Working out of San Diego, Fox had little pull in D.C., where Republicans were too busy plotting survival strategies to pay attention. If Millican were dangling a "huge payoff" even with slim odds, and Fox had any connections beyond the preoccupied Cannon, money would not have been an issue.

"Maybe one day I'll go back and do the analysis in detail, but I doubt it," writes Millican in conclusion. "I would rather spend my time on serious research questions than on improbable theories proposed with negligible support." Needless to say, I fired back quickly, but as my conclusion reveals, a Boilermaker writing for *WorldNetDaily* is at something of a disadvantage against an Oxford don writing for the *Times* of London.

> No, Peter, that is not good enough. Finish your mother-loving study and then let others have at it. It's not quite cricket to use the *London Times* on the eve of the election to establish your "narrative" and then tip-toe off the field.... The evidence of Ayers' involvement overwhelms the dispassionate observer, and you don't have to be an Oxford don to see it.

Millican promptly returned the fire that same Sunday. He posted a piece on PhiloComp.net titled "The Story of an Unlikely Hypothesis (and a Fine Book)," in which he dismissed my theory not just as "unlikely" but as "laughably unsubstantiated." What he posted, however, was so shabby and slapdash that it had me checking Britain's famous libel laws before I was halfway through. The posting has since been scrubbed, and I rely here on my own response posted on *WND* on Monday, November, 3, E minus 1, to remind me of what he had written.

As I observed, Millican seemed to be a man on a mission, reassuring readers on PhiloComp that they would "be pleased to discover that the probable next leader of the free world did not get his impressive first book written by Bill Ayers." After an admittedly cursory analysis, he said of my hypothesis, "I feel totally confident that it is false." The evidence that he advanced to support his assertion, however, would not pass muster in freshman comp.

Millican began by trivializing the parallel stories in Obama's and Ayers's works: "Even if parallel passages were to be found between Obama's [1995] book and Ayers's Fugitive Days of 2001, the charge of plagiarism could only be directed at Ayers. . . ." Let me repeat: I found not just parallel passages but detailed and distinctive parallel stories, at least three of them, all of them embarrassingly obvious.

Millican tried to explain them away by suggesting that Ayers possibly plagiarized *Dreams*, given that *Fugitive Days* was published six years after *Dreams*. If Millican had bothered to read what I had written—or if he had read the books in question—he would have known that two of the parallel stories appear in Ayers's 1993 book, *To Teach*. The third parallel story is cited in Ayers's 1997 book, *A Kind and Just Parent*, but has its origins in a 1992 book by black author Reginald McKnight. Ayers apparently knew enough about this story by 1995 to adapt it to Obama's life.

About my text-based detective work Millican was fully evasive. He failed to explain, for instance, how Obama, whose seagoing was limited to bodysurfing, managed to mimic at least thirty nautical metaphors— some very sophisticated—used by the former merchant seaman Ayers. He failed to say how or why Obama absorbed Ayers's postmodern patter and his weary '60s weltanschauung, almost to the very word. In his hasty analysis, Millican also chose to overlook the most powerful fact of all, namely that Obama was not a writer, but then again, he may not have noticed. Millican is not much of a writer himself.

I had not heard the last from Millican. After he erased his errors and added a few wrinkles to accommodate my charges, he continued to send me chatty emails as though we were engaged in some friendly academic debate. After ignoring them for several days, I responded.

> *My apologies, but you have confused me from the beginning. Please, when you go to the London Times of your own accord and call the work that we had all done to that point "laughably unsubstantiated" forgive me for feeling slimed.*
>
> *When you say of Bob Fox that he left you "with the impression that payment for propaganda was fine; but payment for objective research was quite a different matter," forgive me for feeling slimed by association.*
>
> *Unfortunately, the headline that the Times offered more or less fit the content you provided: Ours was a plot to "tarnish" Obama, based on nothing.*

> *As for [my charge of your work being] "shabby and slapdash," when you publicly say of the parallel stories that "the charge of plagiarism could only be directed at Ayers," when, in fact, all the Ayers' excerpts made it into print before Dreams, I would think "shabby and slapdash" rather fits and only half way compensates for "laughably unsubstantiated."*
>
> *This is a war of words I did not start. When you enter those charges into the public record unsubstantiated via the London Times with the righteous wind of Oxford behind you, and I leave them un-rebutted, your remarks stand. A private email to you after the first salvo accomplishes nothing. Besides, I am not sure whether I will meet the good Dr. Millican that Bob Fox still swears by or the mean one that trashes us in the London Times.*

Although my flight did not leave BWI until Sunday, November 2, by Thursday I had had enough. I packed up and drove to my ancestral homeland. There I spent the weekend with my oldest brother, Bill, a retired and politically simpatico high school principal, who lived in the McCain-friendly wilds of western New Jersey. Although largely asymptomatic, he was dying of an immune disorder. We hiked the Appalachian Trail that weekend, suspecting there would be no such hikes in the future. There were not. Bill was permanently housebound within months and dead a year later. Before the weekend was through, I was relieved that Washington had had nothing more to hold me.

History has duly recorded that our collective effort to call attention to Obama's apparent fraud came to naught. On November 4, Barack Obama was elected the forty-fourth president of the United States, though without the help of Kansas and Missouri or my brother's Warren County. "I began to weep, and felt ashamed, but could not stop myself." No, that was not me weeping, but Obama. At the end of every major section in *Dreams*, he weeps. His and Ayers's characters "sob" a lot, too—on at least four occasions in each of their memoirs. At the end of this major section, I did not have the time for either weeping or sobbing. I still had work to do.

II

The Wilderness Campaign, 2009–2010

MILLI VANILLI

I am sure that I was not the only McCain voter who felt at least a twinge of relief when our man lost. I had envisioned four years of Republican drift and dreary presidential compromise, all exquisitely recorded by a vengeful media. The election had also spared me the burden of saving the republic. Without the pressure of a deadline, I could pursue my detective work recreationally and get back to making a living.

To that end, I arrived in Washington on January 21, the day after the inauguration, to oversee a six-camera shoot of the annual March for Life on the 22nd. Driving in from BWI, I could see that street vendors had turned New York Avenue into an open-air Obama-Mart. My co-producer stopped to buy Obama puppets for his kids. I had to admire the obvious commerce. Like many others, I still retained half a hope that, if nothing else, President Obama could convince the eternally alienated that, yes, they actually could.

On the eloquence front, the new president got off to an unexpectedly slow start those first few months when, for instance, he told Jay Leno his recent effort at bowling resembled "the Special Olympics or something" or when TOTUS—the teleprompter of the United States—apparently rebelled and had the president thanking himself for being invited to the White House on St. Patrick's Day.

On that momentous first day, however, January 20, the president had no teleprompter to blame. There was nothing impromptu about the occasion. And yet, on the National Mall, before some 1.8 million fans, Barack Obama had something of a Milli Vanilli moment. The faithful may have been as oblivious or indifferent to the breakdown as were Fab and Rob's fans on that awful day twenty years earlier when the pair's record skipped, but the more astute observers—even the friendly ones—winced. By all rational accounts, the gap between what an inaugural audience expected and what the president delivered had never been wider.

To be fair, the proverbial "expectations" had been a shade high. As British literary heavyweight Jonathan Raban noted, "No recent inaugural has been as keenly anticipated as Obama's." That anticipation derived from Raban's understanding, a common one among otherwise sophisticated Obama watchers, that Obama was "the best writer to occupy the White House since Lincoln."

Of course, the accepted evidence for Obama's oversized talent could be found only in *Dreams*. This was Obama's "authentic voice," or so Raban declared. Imagine then his dismay at an inaugural address that suffered from "moth-eaten metaphors," "faux-antique dialect," and jarring semantic errors like Obama's use of the word *forbearers* when he meant *forebears*.

"It was so rhetorically flat, so lacking in rhythm and cadence, one almost has to believe he did it on purpose," opined Charles Krauthammer, adding, with just a touch of irony, "Best not to dazzle on Opening Day. Otherwise, they'll expect magic all the time." Other observers were at least as perplexed. "It is simply mysterious how such tired language could sound appropriate to the ear of Obama the writer," wrote Michael Gerson in the *Washington Post*.

"Not one of his greatest," conceded Bill Ayers with a postmodern wink to a *Free Press* reporter. "But I think he intended it that way. I think he was lowering expectations. You know he's not Superman." To find a rationale for the speech's lameness, Raban waxed downright Jesuitical. "What needed to be said had to be phrased in language as well-worn and conventional as possible," he concluded, "to give the illusion of smooth continuity between Obama's speech and those of past presidents."

There was, of course, a much more plausible explanation for the speech's failure, but no one in the major media, friend or foe, dared to suggest it: namely, that after lip-synching texts for his entire public career, Obama decided to voice this one largely on his own. Although a "disconcerted" Raban grudgingly conceded that twenty-seven-year-old video gamer Jon Favreau had served as Obama's chief "ghost" since 2004, he and other true believers refused to probe any further. To even consider the possibility that Obama needed help with *Dreams*, the holy writ of the Obama canon, was fully taboo.

Had Raban been paying attention, he might not have been so surprised. Just a week earlier, Ben Smith posted on the *Politico* blog an article Obama had written in March 1983 while a senior at Columbia. Titled "Breaking the War Mentality," the 1,800-word article had been published in Columbia's weekly newsmagazine, *Sundial*, at the height of the KGB-generated anti-nuke craze. Given its ideological drift, Smith and others focused on its content. They would have more profitably focused on its style. The find represented the clearest sample yet of Obama's literary DNA.

Obama was twenty-one at the time and on the verge of graduating from an Ivy League university. Had he been raised by wolves in an Indonesian cave and then unleashed on the Columbia campus a year earlier, the reader might cut him slack for such low-C tripe. In fact, though, he was completing his fourth year of college after spending eight years at Hawaii's best prep school. His formal training as a writer culminated in this essay. It is unlikely to the point of impossible that he would subsequently improve his skills to the level found in *Dreams* even if he had worked at it, which he did not.

When the article surfaced, most commentators, left and right, focused on its politics. The *New York Times* expressed a sneaky admiration for the piece, to wit, "Barack Obama's journalistic voice was edgy with disdain for what he called 'the relentless, often silent spread of militarism in the country' amid 'the growing threat of war.' "

If, however, the content was no sillier than that generated by the average Columbia senior in 1983, the "journalistic voice" was well below the Ivy norm. This needs to be shown. Forgive me in advance if this exercise seems pedantic, but the problems I cite—such as the five sentences in which the noun and verb do not agree—would have shocked even my mother, and she never got beyond the eighth grade. My comments follow each selected sentence. The italics in all cases are mine.

> The more sensitive among us struggle to extrapolate experience of war from our everyday experience, *discussing* the latest mortality statistics from Guatemala, *sensitizing* ourselves to our parents' wartime memories, or *incorporating* into our framework of reality as depicted by a Mailer or a Coppola.

This is your classic dangling participle: the words *discussing, sensitizing*, and *incorporating* modify the subject, *the more sensitive among us*, but three other nouns stand between the participles and the subject. Also, note that *incorporating* should have an object. It makes no sense as is.

> But the *taste* of war—the sounds and chill, the dead bodies—*are* remote and far removed.

The subject here is *taste*. The predicate should be *is*, not *are*.

We know that wars have occurred, will occur, are occurring, but *bringing* such experience down into our hearts, and *taking* continual, tangible steps to prevent war, *becomes* a difficult task.

Another problem with noun-verb agreement. This time the subject of the "but" clause is plural—*bringing* and *taking*. The verb should be *become*—although *is* would make more sense. The last two commas, both inappropriate, may have confused Obama.

These groups, visualizing the possibilities of destruction and grasping the tendencies of distorted national priorities, *are throwing their weight into shifting America off the dead-end track.*

Here, the participle is placed appropriately, but at sentence's end Obama throws three awkward metaphors, all clichés, into a nearly indecipherable mix. Also, how does one grasp a tendency?

Along with the community Volunteer Service Center, ARA has been Don's primary concern, *coordinating* various working groups of faculty, students, and staff members, while simultaneously seeking the ever elusive funding for programs.

Coordinating is another participle left to dangle.

One wonders whether this *upsurge* stems from young people's penchant for the latest *"happenings"* or from growing awareness of the consequences of nuclear holocaust.

This whole sentence clunks. *Upsurge* is the wrong word. *Happenings* should be singular, but even then it sounds like something Mike Brady would have said to Greg or Marcia ten years earlier.

Generally, the narrow *focus* of the Freeze movement as well as academic discussions of first versus second strike capabilities, *suit* the military-industrial interests, as they continue adding to their *billion dollar erector sets.*

The subject is *focus,* but it is isolated from its predicate by a needless comma, and that predicate should be *suits* in any case. *Erector sets* is another cringe-inducing metaphor.

The very real *advantages* of concentrating on a single issue *is leading* the National Freeze movement to challenge individual missile systems, *while continuing* the broader campaign.

Here is still another problem with agreement. This should read, *advantages . . . are leading* but only if *advantages* could lead. The last phrase dangles.

ARA encourages members *to join buses* to Washington and participate in a March 7–8 rally intended to *push through the Freeze resolution* which is making its *second trip* through the House.

Join buses? This sounds like something you would hear in an ESL class. A rally cannot *push* a resolution through the House. Now on its second *trip?*

An entirely student-run *organization,* SAM casts a *wider net* than ARA, though for the purposes of effectiveness, *they* have tried to lock in on one issue at a time.

Organization is singular, and thus *they* has no antecedent. The *wider net* cliché is lazy.

By organizing and educating the Columbia community, *such activities* lay the foundation for future mobilization against the relentless, often silent spread of militarism in the country.

"People" organize and educate, not *activities.*

The *belief* that *moribund* institutions, rather than individuals are at the root of the problem, *keep* SAM's energies alive.

Again, an agreement issue: This should read, "The belief . . . *keeps* SAM's energies alive." The random use of commas throws everything off. Plus, the word choice sucks all logic out of the sentence. In the previous paragraph, Obama warns his readers about "the relentless, often silent spread of militarism in the country." In this paragraph, the reader is told that these same military institutions are *moribund*—that is "nearly dead." How their debilitated state keeps the *energies* of the Students Against Militarism (SAM) *alive* is not exactly clear.

Regarding Columbia's possible compliance, *one comment* in particular *hit upon* an important point with the Solomon bill.

The subject of *hit upon,* not an apt verb to begin with, should have been a person, not a *comment.*

What members of ARA and SAM try to do is *infuse* what they have learned about the current *situation, bring the words of that formidable roster on the face of Butler Library, names like Thoreau, Jefferson, and Whitman,* to bear on *the twisted logic of which we are today a part.*

I went back and reread the hard copy on this sentence to make sure it had not been deformed when digitized. This, alas, reads as weirdly as written. *Infuse* is the wrong word. One infuses something "into" something else. There should be an *and* after *situation*, not a comma. Obama utterly mangles the "bring to bear" phrase. It should read something like "bring the words of those formidable men on the face of the Butler Library—Thoreau, Jefferson, Whitman—to bear." As to how or whether we are part of a *twisted logic*, I will leave that to the reader's imagination.

In *To Teach*, Bill Ayers includes an essay by his son Zayd, written when he was twelve. It reads considerably better than Obama's Columbia essay. The essays my daughters wrote in high school are dramatically better. Every single article in the Spring 2010 edition of the twenty-page *Purdue Review*, a conservative *Sundial* equivalent, is better written. There is no conceivable way that the author of "Breaking the War Mentality" could have written unaided *Dreams from My Father* ten years or a hundred years later.

After the *Sundial* article, Obama had nothing in print for another five years. Remnick reports that Obama took a stab at a short story or two, but Remnick shares no samples. In *Dreams*, Obama cops to only the occasional journal entry during this period. Not surprisingly, when Obama makes his next serious literary effort, many of the signature failings on display in "Breaking" manage to find their way into his previously cited 1988 essay, "Why Organize?"

> *Facing these realities*, at least three major strands of earlier movements are apparent.

> *Facing these realities* modifies nothing. *Strands* do not "face reality."

> The *election* of Harold Washington in Chicago or of Richard Hatcher in Gary *were* not enough to bring jobs to inner-city neighborhoods.

> Of course, it should read, "The election . . . was."

... neither new nor well-established companies will be willing to base themselves in the inner city and still compete in the international marketplace.

The grammar is passable here. The logic is not. Obama means, I think, "Companies willing to base themselves in the inner city, new or established, will not be able to compete in the international marketplace."

Moreover, such approaches can and have become thinly veiled excuses for cutting back on social programs, which are *anathema* to a conservative *agenda*.

Agendas do not have *anathemas*.

But *organizing* the black community *faces* enormous problems as well . . . and the urban landscape is littered with the *skeletons* of previous *efforts*.

Organizing does not *face*. *Efforts* do not leave *skeletons*.

Obama wrote this essay in 1988, perhaps to pad his résumé for Harvard Law, at which he would enroll that same year. It shows a modest improvement from his Columbia essay five years earlier, which may be due to more vigilant editing, but it exhibits many of the same problems—awkward sentence structure, inappropriate word choice, a weakness for clichés, the continued failure to get verbs and nouns to agree. More troubling for the Obama faithful, this essay shows not a hint of the grace and sophistication of *Dreams*. Two years later, this same writer would be elected president of the *Harvard Law Review* (*HLR*). Soon after the election, he would begin writing his critically acclaimed memoir. Only in Obama's uniquely privileged slice of America could a writer of such modest talent achieve so much.

In 1990, Obama contributed an edited, unsigned student case comment to the *HLR*. This was his third and final published piece before *Dreams*. Granted that an analysis of fetal-maternal tort suits allows little room for soaring rhetoric, but the language one finds here does not even rise above the plain. "Suits by a fetus against third parties provide an additional deterrent to unwanted intrusions on a woman's bodily integrity," reads a typically leaden sentence. As to the note's message, Obama may be the one prominent Democrat on record to argue against the expansion of tort law. Unfortunately, he opposed expansion because of "the dangers such a conceptualization poses to the constitutional rights of women." In other words, if the court allows the unborn to sue their mothers for negligence, they might one day be able to sue abortionists for homicide.

From the publication of *Dreams* in 1995 to its reissue in 2004, Obama had nothing in print beyond a semiregular column in the neighborhood newspaper, the *Hyde Park Herald*. If he wrote a single inspired or imaginative sentence in his many columns, I was not able to find it. More than a few evoke the clumsy, ungrammatical Obama of his Columbia days. Sentences that begin "One of the paradoxes recessions pose . . ." can come to no good end. Worse, virtually every column promised more counterproductive meddling in the life of the community. Such was the petty political yoke to which our literary master had to harness his outsized talent during these fallow years.

The one column that attracted any attention—the January 2000 "Family Duties Took Precedence"—did so for its heart-stopping shamelessness. At the time, state senator Obama had a lot of explaining to do. In late December 1999, while on vacation in Hawaii, he missed a critical vote on a gun control measure. He had missed votes before, but now he was challenging former Black Panther Bobby Rush for his congressional seat. When he caught heat from Rush and the media, Obama used the column to roll out his alibi.

To explain why he had gone to Hawaii, Obama cited the death of his mother, the death of his grandfather, and the subsequent loneliness of his ailing grandmother at Christmastime. To explain why he stayed—"10-footers on the North Shore" would not fly in the hood—he paraded an allegedly flu-ridden baby. "I could not leave my wife alone with my daughter," said Obama, "without knowing the seriousness of the baby's condition and without knowing whether they might be able to get a flight out of Hawaii before New Year's Day." On the plus side he spared the reader any tales of his dog, "Checkers" apparently having stayed behind in Chicago.

This same awkward, uncertain, cliché-happy Obama reemerged in the inaugural address. "Some phrases were just strange," wrote Michael Gerson of the speech at the time. "Recriminations have 'strangled' our politics, as in some 'CSI' episode. We have 'tasted the bitter swill of civil war and segregation.' Yuck, in so many ways."

Two days after the inauguration, I was able to participate in my first-ever March for Life. Among my assignments that day was to escort our spokesperson, actress Jennifer O'Neill, the hearthrob of every male breathing the summer of the *Summer of '42*. It was a tough job, but someone had to do it.

Having a camera on a central rooftop, we were able to estimate the crowd size, which we tabbed at about 350,000. For drama's sake, I assigned our six cameramen to find as many pro-abortion protestors as they could and, if possible, interview them. Although we looked hard, none of us could identify a single such protestor. *USA Today* found a ragtag handful and gave them, incredibly enough, equal photographic billing. The rest of the media ignored the march altogether.

The crowds were roughly the same for the march in 2010, which I also attended, but if anything, the media coverage was even more subversive. Krista Gesaman of *Newsweek* headlined her article "Who's Missing at the 'Roe v. Wade' Anniversary Demonstrations? Young Women." She claimed that "a majority of the participants are in their 60s" and wondered whether the march would soon die off from attrition. In fact, about 75 percent of the marchers were under twenty-five, with more females than males among the young people. Young women were everywhere and unavoidable. They filled every hotel lobby in town. Many of them had spent countless hours on buses to get there.

During the 3 P.M. ET hour of CNN's *Rick's List* on the day of the march, Rick Sanchez acknowledged that it was the thirty-seventh anniversary of *Roe v. Wade*, then asked, "both sides being represented today, but it does appear to me, as I look at these signs that—which side is represented the most. . . . Do we know?"

As Sanchez deliberated, CNN's cameras seemed to have found the same disgruntled crew of pro-abortion protestors that *USA Today* had found the year before. After the commercial break, Sanchez finally conceded that although he had *not* "gone out and counted signs individually," most of the protestors "seem to be anti-abortion activists." In fact, just like the year before, the numbers broke out to be about 350,000 pro-life marchers to about five or so abortion supporters. At least 100,000 of these marchers were young women.

In January 2009, the day after the march, the new U.S. president, apparently to protect "the constitutional rights of women" wherever they might be, quietly ordered his administration to start funding abortion providers overseas. The mist of uncertainty enshrouding the president was already beginning to dissipate.

GENIUS SCHOOL

Among the many questions left unanswered during the election was just how Barack Obama got into Harvard Law School. As the evidence trickled in, it became clearer that Obama never did need a Saudi-led conspiracy to secure a place in Cambridge. He had the one thing it took all along.

Obama surely understood this. David Mendell tells the reader that Obama "won" a full scholarship to Occidental but as a bench-warming, B-minus student Obama had to know what he had done to "win" it. Despite adding considerable information to the record, David Remnick chooses not to know. He tells us that Obama was an "unspectacular" student in his two years at Columbia and at every stop before that, going back to grade school. A Northwestern University prof who wrote a letter of reference for Obama reinforces the point, telling Remnick, "I don't think [Obama] did too well in college." As to Obama's LSAT scores, Jimmy Hoffa's body will be unearthed before those are.

How such an indifferent student got into a law school whose

applicants' LSAT scores typically track between the 98th and 99th percentile and whose GPAs range between 3.80 and 4.00 is a subject Remnick bypasses. Mendell is likewise silent on the mystery admission. This surprises because in stretches he saw more of Obama than Michelle did, and he writes objectively and intimately about Obama's ascendancy.

Mendell traces Obama's sudden itch to become a lawyer to the model of the recently deceased Mayor Washington, but Washington went to Northwestern's very respectable law school in Chicago. The thought doesn't cross Obama's mind. In *Dreams*, he limits his choices to "Harvard, Yale, Stanford." Writes Mendell as casually as if the honor were deserved, "Obama would soon be accepted at the most prestigious law school in the nation."

Michelle Obama's experience shows just how wonderfully accessible Harvard could be. "Told by counselors that her SAT scores and her grades weren't good enough for an Ivy League school," writes Christopher Andersen, "Michelle applied to Princeton and Harvard anyway." Sympathetic biographer Liza Mundy writes, "Michelle frequently deplores the modern reliance on test scores, describing herself as a person who did not test well."

She did not write well, either. She even typed badly. College dropout Ryan Geiser found Michelle's senior thesis at Princeton online and concluded, "I could have written it in sophomore English class." Mundy charitably describes it as "dense and turgid." The less charitable Christopher Hitchens observes, "To describe [the thesis] as hard to read would be a mistake; the thesis cannot be 'read' at all, in the strict sense of the verb. This is because it wasn't written in any known language."

Hitchens exaggerates only a little. The following summary statement by Michelle captures her unfamiliarity with many of the rules of grammar and most of logic:

> The study inquires about the respondents' motivations to benefit him/herself, and the following social groups: the family, the Black com-

munity, the White community, God and church, the U.S. society, the non-White races of the world, and the human species as a whole.

Still, Michelle was admitted to and graduated from Harvard Law. One almost feels sorry for her. She had to have been as anxious as Bart Simpson at Genius School, but Bart at least knew he was in over his head, and he knew why: he had cheated on his IQ test. "It doesn't take a Bart Simpson to figure out that something's wrong," he tells the principal and demands out. Michelle fled inward and, as at Princeton, found refuge in her blackness. The obvious gap between her writing and that of her highly talented colleagues marked her as an affirmative-action admission, and the profs finessed her through.

Obama was sufficiently self-deluding—some would say narcissistic—that he felt little of that anxiety. Later in his book, Remnick lets slip into the record a revealing letter Obama had written while president of the *HLR*. He attempts here to illustrate Obama's maturity on matters racial. In the process, however, he suggests one explanation for how Obama got into Harvard and how he became an editor of the review. Wrote Obama to the *Harvard Law Record*:

> I must say, however, that as someone who has undoubtedly benefited from affirmative action programs during my academic career, and as someone who may have benefited from the Law Review's affirmative action policy when I was selected to join the Review last year, I have not felt stigmatized within the broader law school community or as a staff member of the Review.

As Shelby Steele notes, Obama simply refused to see the implications of affirmative action that were obvious to others. "American universities impose this policy on black students with such totalitarian resolve," he writes, "that even blacks who don't need the lowered standards come away stigmatized by them." Remnick refuses to concede Obama's need for affirmative action, let alone any stigma attached to it. He boasts that this "inner sanctum of the establishment" accepted only the "brightest and most ambitious" first-year students and offers as explanation, "Obama's grades were good."

As he does on many occasions, Remnick chooses not to share with the reader a larger truth. The fact is that Obama did not make the law review the old-fashioned way, the way *HLR*'s first black editor, Charles Houston, did seventy years earlier. To Obama's good fortune, the *HLR* had replaced a meritocracy in which editors were elected based on grades—the president being the student with the highest academic rank—with one in which half the editors were chosen through a writing competition.

This competition, the *New York Times* reported in 1990, was "meant to help insure that minority students became editors of The Law Review." If Obama's entry in the writing competition had begun, "As an angry young black man . . . ," I suspect his odds of being selected editor would have improved considerably.

"By the time Barack got to campus, in 1988," fellow alum Elena Kagan would tell Remnick, "all the talk and the debates were shifting to race." In the same spring 1990 term that he would stand for the presidency of the *HLR*, the law school found itself embroiled in a nasty racial brouhaha. Black firebrand law professor Derrick Bell was demanding that Harvard appoint a black woman to the law faculty. This protest would culminate in vigils and protests by the racially sensitive student body, in the course of which Obama would compare the increasingly absurd Bell to Rosa Parks.

Feeling the pressure, *HLR* editors wanted to elect their first African American president. Obama had an advantage. Spared the legacy of slavery and segregation, and having grown up in a white household, he lacked the hard edge of many of his black colleagues. "Obama cast himself as an eager listener," the *New York Times* reported, "sometimes giving warring classmates the impression that he agreed with all of them at once."

In February 1990, after an ideologically charged all-day affair,

Obama's fellow editors elected him president from among nineteen candidates. As it turned out, Obama prevailed only after the *HLR's* small conservative faction threw him its support. Once elected, Obama contributed not one word to the *HLR* or any other law journal. As Matthew Franck has pointed out in *National Review Online*, "A search of the HeinOnline database of law journals turns up exactly nothing credited to Obama in any law review anywhere at any time." Remnick confirms the same. Of course, that would not stop the deans at the University of Chicago Law School from hinting at tenure for Obama. To put this offer in perspective, imagine the manager of the White Sox hinting at a starter's job for a guy who had not yet gotten a hit, even in the minors.

Bottom line: had Obama's father come from Kentucky, not Kenya, and been named O'Hara, not Obama, there would have been no *Harvard Law Review*, no Harvard, no Columbia, and probably no Punahou. Hillary supporter Geraldine Ferraro made the mistake of saying as much during the primary season. "If Obama was a white man, he would not be in this position," she blundered, forgetting for a moment that the obvious was now verboten.

When attacked, this feisty paisana refused to roll over. "I am livid at this thing," she told the *New York Times*. "Any time you say anything to anybody about the Obama campaign, it immediately becomes a racist attack." She was clearly on to something. Lost in the hubbub following Obama's "More Perfect Union" speech was his comparison of Ferraro's comments to those of Jeremiah "God damn America" Wright.

The irony of all this, of course, is that a process designed to compensate the descendants of slaves has compensated a man whose maternal ancestors were not slaves but slave owners. On the paternal side, the first of Obama's African relatives to have even seen a white man was his grandfather.

When affirmative action quietly morphed into "diversity," and the rationale for unearned glory shifted from compensation to cultural variety, Obama could not provide that, either. Growing up in a white family in the least black state of America without "Dakota" in its name, he contributed less "blackness" to the cultural stew than an everyday white hip-hopper. Still, Obama looked the part, more or less, and appearances proved enough for institutions anxious about their "metrics."

Race alone, however, guaranteed little. It would have won Obama few plaudits from the media if he had taken his wisdom from, say, an Alan Keyes and not a Bill Ayers. This point is critical. Blackness bestows media advantage on the ambitious only to the degree they fulfill progressive expectations. Keyes, a black Republican who ran against Obama in the 2004 U.S. Senate race, cannot even get a *bright* out of Remnick let alone a *brilliant*, despite an earned Ph.D. from Harvard and his unprompted eloquence. To Remnick, Keyes is merely a "demagogic fool."

The case of Supreme Court justice Clarence Thomas is even more instructive. "I'm black," he told Steve Kroft of *60 Minutes*. "So I'm supposed to think a certain way. I'm supposed to have certain opinions. I don't do that." And he has paid the price. Without approving what follows, Kroft summarized with surprising candor Thomas's reputation in liberal circles:

> . . . a man of little accomplishment, an opportunistic black conservative who sold out his race, joined the Republican Party and was ultimately rewarded with an affirmative action appointment to the nation's highest court, a sullen, intellectual lightweight so insecure he rarely opens his mouth in oral arguments.

In his bestseller, *My Grandfather's Son*, Thomas recounts a life that offers some striking parallels to Obama's. He too is abandoned by a deadbeat father. His mother also surrenders him to the care of his grandfather. But the parallels end here. Thomas comes of age in a tough-love home in hardscrabble Jim Crow Georgia, not in the indulgent air of nearly race-blind Hawaii. He never has to question his racial identity. He has it shoved down his throat every time he leaves the house.

None of this, however, has earned Thomas a nickel's worth of praise from media that pride themselves on their racial largesse. Thomas's failure to embrace "the liberal pieties," he writes in *Grandfather*, meant that he "had to be destroyed." Obama embraced those pieties as much out of ambition as principle. Had fashion favored black conservatives, I have no doubt but that he would be one.

The embrace of those pieties secured Obama the protection of an embarrassingly complicit media. *Newsweek's* Jonathan Alter would happily ignore the obvious to conclude in his book *The Promise*, "Obama's faith lay in the cream rising to the top." The reason why: "He himself was a product of the great American postwar meritocracy."

COPYCATS

At Harvard, Barack Obama may have learned a few things about writing that were not exactly featured in the catalogue. And as mentors, he had two masters of the craft. One, Harvard Law professor Laurence Tribe, hired Obama as his research assistant in 1989 and took a powerful liking to the young man. After the 2008 election, Tribe would gush, "His stunning combination of analytical brilliance and personal charisma, openness and maturity, vision and pragmatism, was unmistakable from my very first encounter."

Obama found a second prominent mentor among the Harvard Law faculty in professor Charles Ogletree, an African American. In the run-up to the 2008 election, Ogletree would enthuse, "I'm so excited about this candidacy that I just can't tell you. I'm just overfull with joy." If anything, Ogletree and Tribe should have been overfull with joy in the simple fact that they had hung on to their Harvard jobs.

In August 2004, while Obama was cruising to victory in the U.S.

Senate race, Ogletree was sorting his way through a mess of his own creation. He had been forced to apologize for somehow letting passages from Yale scholar Jack Balkin's book *What Brown v. Board of Education Should Have Said* find their way into his own book *All Deliberate Speed*. At Harvard, given Ogletree's standing, none dared call this plagiarism.

At the Massachusetts School of Law, however, Dean Lawrence Velvel called it exactly what it was, and he did so publicly. Tribe, something of an academic showboat, moved swiftly to defend Ogletree. Although conceding that plagiarism by the prominent had become "a phenomenon of some significance," Tribe questioned the "decency" of those like Velvel who would go public on issues "about which your knowledge is necessarily limited."

Velvel promptly responded. If decency prevented inquiry, he argued, interested parties would have to "depend for criticisms on those who are closest to the situation, who have the most reason not to discuss it lest they or their institution be harmed, and who are least likely to publicly discuss or criticize."

I could understand Velvel's frustration. In the course of my research into *Dreams*, I often ran into similarly stupid defenses. Of course, my knowledge was "limited." How could it not be? I could no more expect a frank admission from the principals involved—the publisher, the editor, the writer(s) of *Dreams*—than Velvel could from Ogletree or Tribe.

In a delightful turn of the paddle wheel, Tribe's showboating caught up with him just a few weeks later. Amazed by the sheer moxie of Tribe's Ogletree defense, an anonymous tipster dropped the proverbial dime on the Harvard sage. As it happens, passages from Henry J. Abraham's 1974 book, *Justices and Presidents*, had somehow found their way into Tribe's 1985 book, *God Save This Honorable Court*. The tipster reported Tribe's heretofore unreported pilfering to conservative scholar Joseph Bottum, who confirmed it and penned a damningly detailed five-thousand-word article for the *Weekly Standard*.

Forced to review the twin cases, the Harvard Law School dean, Elena Kagan, and Harvard's then president, Larry Summers, faced an obvious challenge: Ogletree was a black star on a faculty often criticized for being overly white, and Tribe was *the* superstar of the judicial left. Had the plagiarizers-in-residence not been such sacred cows, Summers and Kagan would have promptly ground them into hamburger. Instead, the administrators dithered strategically in hope that the scandal would somehow fade away.

This dithering made sense. Given the progressive pedigree of both Ogletree and Tribe, the media had little interest in pursuing the story, and the Harvard faculty had even less. So Summers and Kagan let months pass before even announcing they had appointed a committee of inquiry. On this chummy panel were past Harvard president (and future interim president) Derek Bok and two other Harvard insiders.

In April 2005, the committee reported its findings to Summers and Kagan. An actual physical report, if one existed, was never released. Not surprisingly, Ogletree and Tribe were cleared. The transgressions, Summers and Kagan agreed, had surely been the "product of inadvertence." This being so, they thought it time to "consider the matter closed" and move on.

That same April, Velvel reentered the fray, posting a nearly ten-thousand-word analysis on his blog. Writes Velvel of the administrative response, "it *is* a travesty. Its language is misleading, its logic miserable, and its spirit corrupt." What troubled Velvel most was this: Ogletree and Tribe could claim "inadvertence" because both likely had research assistants write chunks of their books for them. Adds Velvel, "Ghostwriting, horribly enough, has become all too prevalent in academia as a general matter."

The fact that Ogletree used ghostwriters, says Velvel, was "widely accepted." The case against Tribe was nearly as strong. The many instances of "copycatting" include a nineteen-word stretch in Tribe's book identical to a nineteen-word stretch in Abraham's earlier book. This struck Velvel as "more like what one would expect of a student than of a Tribe." He points out too that a former Tribe assistant, Ron Klain, had reportedly claimed to have written large sections of Tribe's *God Save This Honorable Court*.

Still, Tribe and Ogletree skated. They may have been taking their cues on stonewalling from historian Doris Kearns Goodwin. A Pulitzer Prize–winning Harvard Ph.D., Goodwin was serving on the university's governing board in 2002 when rightly accused of a word theft so felonious she should have had her Ph.D. recalled, not to mention her Pulitzer.

For her 1987 book, *The Fitzgeralds and the Kennedys*, Goodwin had lifted entire passages without attribution from at least three different sources, most conspicuously Lynne McTaggart's 1983 book, *Kathleen Kennedy: Her Life and Times*. Wrote McTaggart, for example:

Mrs. Gibson gave a tea in her honor to introduce her to some of the other girls—hardly a routine practice for new recruits.

Wrote Goodwin:

Mrs. Harvey Gibson gave a tea in her honor to introduce her to some of the other girls—hardly a routine practice for new recruits.

Goodwin added only the first name "Harvey" and passed the sentence off as her own. She did the same with just the most minimal alterations in scores of other instances as well. When challenged, Goodwin wrote a long-winded and utterly disingenuous apologia in *Time* unintentionally summarized by her phrase "mistakes can happen." These "mistakes" netted McTaggart, in her words, "a substantial monetary settlement."

If caught making the same or even lesser "mistakes," a Harvard student would have had to withdraw from school immediately, stay away from campus for at least two additional semesters, and work satisfactorily at a full-time job for six months before being readmitted.

Even if allowed back on campus, the student would have an "academic dishonesty" mark permanently branded on his record.

When the student editors of the *Harvard Crimson* went after Goodwin, Tribe dependably went after the editors. He scolded them for their "lack of any real sense of proportion or, for that matter, much sense of decency." If his prose was awkward, Tribe's instincts were sound. No liberal has used the "decency" gambit so nimbly since Joseph Welch in the Army-McCarthy hearings.

With support from Tribe and other literati, Goodwin wormed her way out of what should have been a career-killer. Through a combination of dissembling, denial, discreet payoffs to the plagiarized author, and strategic Bush-bashing, she was able to slither back onto network TV and the bestseller lists. So deft was the colonic mix that by 2008 Obama could cite "a wonderful book written by Doris Kearns Goodwin" without the slightest sense of taint.

"That Harvard is setting a very bad example, with all too much of the bad stuff centered in its law school, is all too evident," writes Velvel. One unfortunate consequence of this phenomenon was that the young were watching and learning from the masters. Here is how Velvel imagines their thought process might go:

> On balance, it is *well* worth it, for on the one side lies fame and fortune, and on the other lies only a slap on the wrist. And, especially if I can hide my misdeeds for years (as seems usually to occur), and in the meanwhile *have* become a big deal, I am virtually *assured* of suffering nothing other than a minor slap on the wrist if and when I am finally caught.

One has to wonder whether Obama, when pressed to complete his book, took his cue from his esteemed Harvard mentors. Did one or the other whisper in his ear, "Have someone else write it, we do this all the time"? If so, his appointment of Kagan to the Supreme Court made sense. Her history of whitewashing the sins of the powerful would not have troubled him as it did Velvel, who wanted her fired for helping turn Harvard into a joke:

> Since it is now known that Harvard professors have plagiarized, copy-catted, and pretty certainly have had stuff ghostwritten for them, the bona fides and reputations of nearly everyone at Harvard is called into question, especially people in the law school.

In the years to come, of course, Harvard Law would have no more prominent exemplar of its literary legacy than President Barack Obama.

GREEN PEPPERS

In an ascent shrouded by mystery, no element of that ascent has remained more mysterious than Obama's love life, a love life that has defied even the best of his biographers. In his six-hundred-plus-page biography, David Remnick lays down the baseline of what the mainstream media know about the president—or at least what they want us to know. Where Remnick falls oddly silent—not even to hector the blogosphere—is on the question of Obama's amours.

In his all-consuming search for identity, Obama's romances should surely have been at the heart of the narrative. Whether he dated white women or black women—and what he might have learned from either—matters. Yet Obama gives the reader very close to nothing. "Cosby never got the girl on *I Spy*," he laments in *Dreams*, but in his own retelling, he does not do much better.

Obama spent thirteen not-so-swinging single years on the mainland before he married Michelle in 1992, and ten of those years were before he even met her. Remnick creates a credible picture of him during this stretch as a popular, good-looking man about town. Obama's Chicago mentor Jerry Kellerman tells Remnick that Obama dated various women and "was more than capable of taking care of himself." Another Chicago friend, John Owens, claims, "Barack tends to make a strong impression on women." And Remnick refers specifically to an "old girlfriend" that Obama rather coolly abandoned upon leaving Chicago for Harvard in 1988. Confirms Mendell, likely Remnick's source, "He had a serious girlfriend (and a pet cat), but all three parted amicably when he went to Harvard."

And yet, unless I missed something, despite scores of interviews with Obama acquaintances, never do we actually hear from a woman who dated Barack Obama, either in Remnick's book or Mendell's. Indeed, we learn no more about Obama's Chicago sweetie than we do the cat. The same vacuum is apparent in Christopher Andersen's book. Andersen quotes Obama's New York roommate, Sohale Siddiqi, on the subject of Obama's allure—"I couldn't outcompete him in picking up girls, that's for sure"—but we do not hear from any of the girls he might have picked up or dated. None of them has so much as a name.

In *Dreams*, Obama creates a similarly virile image of himself. At one point, when his half sister Auma visits him in Chicago pre-Michelle, he tells her about a ruptured relationship with a white woman back in New York. He adds, with more than a little calculation, "There are several black ladies out there who've broken my heart just as good," but we do not read as much as a single sentence about any of these ladies. The astute reader wonders whether they exist.

In *Dreams*, in fact, the only lover Obama talks about is the mystery woman in New York. Although he speaks of her briefly and in retrospect, he does so vividly and lovingly. "She was white," he tells Auma. "She had dark hair, and specks of green in her eyes." This is no casual relationship. "We saw each other for almost a year. On the weekends, mostly. Sometimes in her apartment, sometimes in mine. You know how you can fall into your own private world? Just two people, hidden and warm. Your own language. Your own customs. That's how it was."

This nameless young woman had grown up on a sprawling estate in the country. It was during a visit to the country home that Obama began to see the distance between "our two worlds." That distance widened irreparably back in New York when the woman questioned the response of a black audience to a play by an angry black playwright. This led to a "big fight, right in front of the theater," one that undid the relationship. "I pushed her away," Obama tells Auma ruefully.

An interracial romance should have been grist for an aspiring writer's mill, especially a writer as obsessed with racial identity as Obama. Frank Marshall Davis lovingly details his romances in his memoir. So too does Bill Ayers in his. That Obama dedicates only a few paragraphs to this one romance—and these in a flashback—raises questions about its authenticity, not to mention Obama's forthrightness. In real time, Obama hints at only one other liaison, this one in Chicago. When awakened by a loud stereo, Obama protests but only because "on this particular evening I have someone staying over." That's it, "someone."

I am not the only one to have noticed this. One correspondent of mine thinks that Obama modeled his inamorata on Kay Adams, Michael Corleone's wife in *The Godfather*. Nebraskan Ryan Geiser makes a much more convincing case for a more proximate source, Diana Oughton. Ayers was obsessed with Oughton, who died in 1970 in a Greenwich Village bomb factory blast. In *Fugitive Days*, he fixes on her in ways that had to discomfit the Weatherwoman he eventually settled for.

Physically, the woman of Obama's memory with her "dark hair, and specks of green in her eyes" evokes images of Oughton. As her FBI files attest, copies of which Geiser sent me, Oughton had brown hair and green eyes. The two women shared similar family backgrounds as well. In fact, they seemed to have grown up on the very same estate.

"The house was very old, her grandfather's house," Obama writes of his girlfriend's country home. "He had inherited it from his grandfather." Writes Ayers of Oughton in *Fugitive Days*, "She had been to the manor born—the oldest of four sisters, she was raised in rural Illinois, her father a kind of gentleman farmer from a previous age."

Ayers knew this manor from experience. According to a *Time* article written soon after her death, Oughton "brought Bill Ayers and other radicals" to the family homestead in Dwight, Illinois. Oughton's father's grandfather built the main house on the estate, a twenty-room Victorian mansion. Formally known as the John R. Oughton House, it was placed on the national historic register in 1980. In this unlikely setting, Diana and her Weather pals would defend "the revolutionary's approach to social ills" in discussions with her too-tolerant old man.

The carriage house, in which Diana lived as a child, now serves as a public library. It may have already seemed like one when Ayers visited, an impression that finds its way into Obama's words as a library "filled with old books and pictures of the famous people [the grandfather] had known—presidents, diplomats, industrialists."

"It was autumn, beautiful, with woods all around us," Obama writes of his visit to his girlfriend's country home, "and we paddled a canoe across this round, icy lake full of small gold leaves that collected along the shore." As aerial photos of the Oughton estate—103 South Street, Dwight, Illinois, for those who wish to see—confirm, the estate has a small lake and, despite forty years of encroaching development, is still thickly ringed by trees.

"I realized that our two worlds, my friend's and mine, were as distant from each other as Kenya is from Germany," says Obama of his girlfriend. Ayers expressed similar anxieties about Oughton. "She knew other worlds and other languages and I knew nothing," he writes; "she was sophisticated and I was simple, she was untouchable." Although Ayers had come from a family of means himself, Oughton's world intimidated him: "Diana's whole story was written on her face, etched with every advantage, accented with privilege." She awed him as she attracted him. "I adored her the moment I saw her," he writes, "but I knew she was way beyond my reach—too mature, too smart, too experienced."

In projecting Ayers's sentiments, or so it appears, Obama suggests more than a metaphor when he describes how he and his girlfriend fell into their "own private world" where they were "just two people, hidden and warm." Ayers and Oughton shared a literal "hidden world," one that functioned, in Ayers's words, as "a parallel universe somewhere side by side with the open world." Again, Obama seems to be channeling Ayers when he relates how he and his friend developed their "own language," their "own customs." Writes Ayers of Oughton and others in the underground, "We spoke in a language that was meaningless babble to outsiders." He adds, "We invented words; we constructed culture."

"Between the two of us," Obama writes, "I was the one who knew how to live as an outsider." This was a sensation that the fugitive Ayers—"nowhere a stranger but everywhere an outsider"—was fully capable of imagining and imparting. In *Dreams*, Obama worries that his world would inevitably yield to his girlfriend's. "I knew that if we stayed together," he writes, "I'd eventually live in hers." In *Fugitive Days*, Ayers describes how seductive the world of the Oughtons could be: "a perfect marriage, a comfortable career in banking, say, or the law, two golden children, the clubs, the country home."

Despite his obsession with Oughton, Ayers had other lovers, but then again, so did Oughton. This troubled Ayers considerably. He does not say whether this led to their parting, but he was not with her at the end. When Obama says, "I pushed her away," one has to wonder if we are really hearing Ayers. This split with Oughton led one radical feminist in the underground, Jane Alpert, to chastise Ayers publicly "for his callous treatment and abandonment of Diana Oughton before her death." That death continues to haunt Ayers and almost assuredly found an outlet in *Dreams*, written six years before his own memoir.

"Whenever I think back to what my friend said to me, that night outside the theater, it somehow makes me ashamed," an unsmiling Obama tells Auma, while cutting "green peppers." In his 1997 book, *A Kind and Just Parent*, Ayers specifically links "green peppers" with "saltpeter" and other "mysterious drugs in the food" that scare young men with the threat of impotence. Go figure.

Remnick concedes that *Dreams* is not to be taken at face value. On any number of points, all fairly trivial, he attempts to sort out the fact from the fancy. On the subject of this critical relationship, the one and only in *Dreams* before Michelle, Remnick has conspicuously little to say. The reader of *The Bridge* would not know Obama had such a relationship if Remnick had not mentioned it casually in his later discussion of *Dreams* as a book.

Christopher Andersen was more curious but made little headway in confirming the story or identifying the woman. "No one," he writes, "including his roommate and closest friend at the time, Siddiqi, knew of this mysterious lover's existence." Abhorring a vacuum, I have ventured to fill it. Given Remnick's list of the allowable ways to interpret *Dreams*—verifiable fact, recollection, re-creation, invention, and artful shaping—I choose "D" for the mystery woman, "invention." In the absence of any contrary information, best evidence argues for a creation largely of Ayers's contrivance. As to why Obama would need to invent a girlfriend, I will come to that soon enough.

Long before Obama meets Michelle, he meets "Regina" from Chicago's South Side. Obama describes her as "a big, dark woman who wore stockings and dresses that looked homemade." And although Obama has no romantic interest in Regina, Remnick rightly describes her as a "harbinger" of Michelle, more literary device than flesh-and-blood woman. It is she who sets him on his journey to find his inner African American and rather forcefully at that.

"Her voice," Obama writes, "evoked a vision of black life in all its possibility, a vision that filled me with longing—a longing for place, and a fixed and definite history." The home life that Regina describes—"evenings in the kitchen with uncles and cousins and grandparents, the stew of voices bubbling up in laughter"—proves a powerful lure for Obama.

In *Dreams*, it is Regina who convinces Obama to abandon the name Barry. "Do you mind if I call you Barack?" she asks. "Not as long as you say it right," he answers. Coming straight from the motherland, Barack Sr. pronounced his name "BARR-ick," not "buh-ROCK." Barack Sr. himself was known as "Barry" when he was in Hawaii. When Obama visits Africa, well after he has become "Barack," all of his kin call him "Barry." It is Obama who will insist on saying the name wrong, perhaps strategically. This rebranding would actually help pave his way to the presidency.

Not until the very end of *Dreams* does Obama find Michelle and the fulfillment implicit in Regina's vision. As described in *Audacity*, her kitchen sounds suspiciously like Regina's—"uncles and aunts and cousins everywhere, stopping by to sit around the kitchen table and eat until they burst and tell wild stories and listen to Grandpa's old jazz collection and laugh deep into the night."

Like so much in his life, his choice of a church, for instance, Obama's selection of Michelle is fragrant with calculation, not only on an emotional level but also on a political level. Remnick more than hints at this. A black campaign worker in South Carolina tells him that Obama's selection of a black wife, particularly a dark-skinned one, "matters to people here." Princeton political scientist Melissa Harris-Lacewell, a black female who had attended Obama's church, elaborates: "I don't think Obama could have been elected President if he had married a white woman." She adds, "Had he married a white woman, he would have signaled that he had chosen whiteness."

At the height of the Reverend Wright controversy, Obama played his Michelle trump card. "I am married to a black American who carries within her the blood of slaves and slaveowners," he boasted in his bellwether speech on race, "an inheritance we pass on to our two precious daughters."

Dreams culminates in Obama's wedding to Michelle. As with all previous relationships, this tale of courtship is strikingly devoid of any reference to love, sex, or romance. At his most passionate, Obama says of Michelle, "In her eminent practicality and Midwestern attitudes, she reminds me not a little of Toot [his grandmother]." That description must surely have warmed the cockles of Michelle's heart.

In *Audacity*, Obama does not even get the date of their first meeting right. "I met Michelle in the summer of 1988," he writes, "while we were both working at Sidley & Austin." Obama acknowledges he had just finished his first year at law school, but he did not begin Harvard Law until the fall of 1988. As shall be seen, there are some serious date manipulations in the Obama narrative. This is not one of them. This is what happens when other people write your books.

WINE-DARK SEA

I had underestimated Obama's muse. At first glance, I had thought the mystery girlfriend on the large estate a gratuitous imposition. On first reading, I had seen in *Dreams'* many nautical references the muse's sea-stained fingerprints, indifferently applied. And then the lightbulb flicked on. Of course, the muse had taken Obama's ungainly, bloated manuscript and infused it with the structure and spirit of Homer's *Odyssey*. The nautical imagery, the mystery girlfriend, and many more of the book's inventions serve a purpose.

On December 28, 2008, I published a piece in *American Thinker* on this subject. I argued that in *Dreams* Obama "assumes the role of both Telemachus and Odysseus, the son seeking the father, and the father seeking home." Having spent two full years of high school Greek classes reading the *Odyssey*, I wondered, however, if I had not unwittingly wielded "Maslow's hammer." Said psychologist Abraham Maslow some years back, "It is tempting, if the only tool you have is a hammer, to treat everything as if it were a nail."

If I needed validation, I got it three weeks later in the *New York Times*. The paper's Pulitzer Prize–winning literary critic, Michiko Kakutani, described *Dreams* almost exactly as I had: "a quest in which [Obama] cast himself as both a Telemachus in search of his father and an Odysseus in search of a home." I seriously doubt if Ms. Kakutani purloined my thesis, especially given her conclusion that *Dreams* was "the most evocative, lyrical and candid autobiography written by a future president." She apparently inferred the Homeric structure in reading the text, as did I.

The *Dreams* muse leaves scarcely a Homeric trope unturned in his mining of the *Odyssey* to describe Obama's "personal interior journey." Before he completes his heroic cycle, Obama will confront green-eyed seductresses, Sirens, blind seers, lotus-eaters, the "ghosts" of the underworld, the God-guide Hermes, and about a half-dozen sundry "demons." Only when I found a "menacing" one-eyed bald man, however, did I feel confident I had not hammered in vain. *Menacing*, by the way, is one of those words that Ayers likes: he uses it multiple times in every book. Even toy soldiers he describes as "menacing."

Early in *Fugitive Days*, Ayers tips his Homeric hand. "Memory sails out upon a murky sea—wine-dark, opaque, unfathomable," he writes with a knowing wink. "Wine-dark" is quintessential Homer. Bestselling author Thomas Cahill named his book on ancient Greece *Sailing the Wine-Dark Sea*. It did not surprise me to learn that Cahill had attended my high school, but then again so had Weather Underground alum Brian Flanagan, who had taken the same Greek courses I did a year ahead of me. Ayers and pals may have been lunatics— Flanagan seems the sanest of the bunch—but they were literate ones.

Dreams and the *Odyssey* both begin in medias res, a literary technique in which the narrative starts in mid-story and not from the literal beginning. Odysseus's son, Telemachus, is twenty when the *Odyssey* begins. Obama has just turned twenty-one. Each saga begins with the young protagonist receiving an unexpected call that inspires him to seek out his missing father, Telemachus's from Athena, Obama's courtesy of Ma Bell.

The structure of *Dreams* is more naturally chronological than the uneven *Odyssey*. After the opening sequence, Obama takes the reader back to his "Origins." There he tells us that Barack Sr. quit the isle of Hawaii and abandoned his son for Harvard in Obama's third year of life. (In reality, it was his first. More on this later.) Odysseus too had quit the isle of Ithaca and abandoned his son to fight in the Trojan War in Telemachus's first year of life.

As a former merchant seaman, Ayers often thought in terms of charts and maps when plotting life's journey. In *Fugitive Days*, he yearns for a "mariner's chart of the past" to help navigate, but he knows there is no such thing. He and his colleagues must face every day "as free people with neither road maps nor guarantees." In *A Kind and Just Parent*, he writes of a friend, "the geography of his life was mapped around hard work, family and faith."

Obama uses the imagery of maps and charts much as Ayers does. In the introduction of *Dreams*, Obama talks of the book he had originally intended to write, a prosaic analysis of race and law. He describes it as "an intellectual journey that I imagined for myself, complete with maps and restpoints and a strict itinerary." He changed his mind, of course, and settled on "a record of a personal, interior journey— a boy's search for his father, and through that search a workable meaning for his life as a black American."

As Obama becomes aware of his blackness, he begins "to see a new map of the world, one that was frightening in its simplicity, suffocating in its implications." He traces the map's origins back to the day, centuries earlier, when "blind hunger" drove the white man to land on Africa's shores. "That first encounter had redrawn the map of black life," Obama argues. In *Race Course*, Ayers speaks of "the map of my life, already drawn."

When Obama leaves Hawaii for college in Los Angeles, he leaves his white mother and grandparents "at some uncharted border." Aware now of his blackness and their whiteness, he feels "utterly alone," not unlike the "utter loneliness" that Ayers felt upon setting off on his own. From this point on, Obama himself will be responsible for "charting his way through the world." He and Ayers both describe this world as "uncertain." Like Odysseus, he feels himself "unanchored to place." He adds, "What I needed was a community." Obama's effort to locate that community in black Chicago, like Odysseus's effort to regain his troubled Ithaca home, is fraught with peril and temptation, some of it factual, some of it finessed from facts, some of it fully invented.

Obama is not the first writer to see Hawaii as the land of the lotus-eaters. "Junkie. Pothead," he writes in retrospect of the experience. "That's where I'd been headed: the final, fatal role of the young would-be black man." In Los Angeles, change comes slowly. Finding his way as a black man, he resists the allure of his own Calypso figure, the "good-looking" Joyce. This Occidental College co-ed tries to lure him from his quest for black self-fulfillment with the worldly equivalent of immortality, namely assimilation and "multiracial" anonymity. Despite her "honey skin and pouty lips," Obama resists the "gravitational pull" of her postracial promise.

While still in Los Angeles, Obama finds his own private Cyclops in a college library "whose boundaries," Rod Serling might have said, "are that of imagination." The Cyclops in question is actually an Iranian student, an "older balding man with a glass eye." He sits across from Obama and a black friend and, for no good reason, chides them about the failure of American slaves to rebel in any meaningful way. Obama's friend falls strangely mute before the Iranian's "menacing look," but Obama leaps to the slaves' defense.

"They did fight. Nat Turner, Denmark Vescey [*sic*]," snaps Obama. He adds, "Was the collaboration of some slaves any different than the silence of some Iranians who stood by and did nothing as Savak thugs murdered and tortured opponents of the Shah?"

This conversation allegedly takes place in early 1980, a few heated months after fifty-two Americans were taken hostage in the newly Islamic Iran. If Obama were still focusing his anti-Iranian wrath on the Shah and Savak, he was one of only about a half-dozen Americans so inclined. I suspect Ayers inserted the scene to strengthen the Homeric theme and settle an old score with the American-friendly Shah. By the way, in *Fugitive Days* Ayers cites "Nat Turner's uprising, Denmark Vesey's revolt" as positive examples of democratic action. Writing in 2001, three years into the Google era, he even gets the spelling of "Vesey" right.

Obama leaves Los Angeles for Columbia a year later. To make the brooding Telemachus imagery work, Obama had to scrub one person out of the record, Occidental friend Phil Boerner. Boerner transferred with Obama to Columbia and roomed with him his first year in New York. There is no mention of a character anything like him in *Dreams*. A registered Democrat and Obama fan, Boerner conveniently lay low until well after the 2008 election. It seems likely that he was told to. Wrote Boerner in January 2009:

> I remember often eating breakfast with Barack at Tom's Restaurant on Broadway. Occasionally we went to The West End for beers. We enjoyed exploring museums such as the Guggenheim, the Met and the American Museum of Natural History, and browsing in bookstores such as the Strand and the Barnes & Noble opposite Columbia. We both liked taking long walks down Broadway on a Sunday afternoon, and listening to the silence of Central Park after a big snow. I also remember jogging the loop around Central Park with Barack.

What makes Boerner problematic for the Obama narrative is his very normality. This obliging middle-class guy from suburban D.C. makes Obama sound so thoroughly cheerful and *white* that one questions whether the Sturm und Drang of Obama's New York is really Obama's. "Like a tourist, I watched the range of human possibility on display," writes Obama, "trying to trace out my future in the lives of the people I saw, looking for some opening through which I could re-enter." Reenter what? This seems more the reflection of a soon-to-be ex-fugitive than that of a metrosexual happily browsing the Met. Ayers, by the way, uses the phrase "human possibility" twice in *Fugitive Days*.

As might be expected, Manhattan proves more seductive than Hawaii or Los Angeles. Obama finds himself as attracted as he is repelled by "the beauty, the filth, the noise, and the excess" of the city. There was no denying "the city's allure," he writes, nor its consequent power to corrupt. Smitten by the Siren song of the city, Obama feels himself "uncertain of my ability to steer a course of moderation."

The opening scene of *Dreams* unfolds in 1982, Obama's senior year at Columbia, in and around a small New York City apartment with "slanting floors" that he shared with Siddiqi on East Ninety-fourth Street. As the scene unfolds, Obama is making breakfast "with coffee on the stove and two eggs in the skillet." In *Fugitive Days*, Ayers lives in apartments with "sloping floors" and talks about food almost as lovingly as he does bombs. He too uses the Southern regionalism "skillet."

Obama makes an exception to his alleged New York "solitude" for an elderly neighbor, a "stooped" gentleman who wore a "fedora." In *Fugitive Days*, it was Ayers's grandfather who was "stooped" and a helpful stranger who wore a "fedora." One day, Obama finds his neighbor dead, "crumpled up on the third-floor landing, his eyes wide open, his limbs stiff and curled up like a baby's." In *Fugitive Days*, Ayers tells of watching his mother die, "eyes half open, curled up and panting."

After the neighbor's death, the police let themselves into the old man's apartment, and for no good reason Obama finds himself in the apartment as well. On the neighbor's mantelpiece, Obama reports seeing "the faded portrait of a woman with heavy eyebrows and a gentle smile." Obama is the rare writer to fix on eyebrows—heavy ones, bushy ones, wispy ones. There are seven references to "eyebrows" in *Dreams*. There are six references to eyebrows in *Fugitive Days*—bushy ones, flaring ones, arched ones, black ones. This eyebrow fixation is unusual to the point of fetish.

At the climax of *Dreams'* opening sequence, Obama receives the critical phone call. It comes from his aunt Jane in Nairobi. "Listen, Barry, your father is dead," she tells him. Obama has a hard time understanding. "Can you hear me?" she repeats. "I say, your father is dead." The line is cut, and the conversation ends abruptly.

Apparently, Ayers so liked the dramatic structure of the *Dreams* opening sequence that he mimicked it in *Fugitive Days*, which also opens in medias res with a dramatic phone call. The call comes from Dohrn. Ayers learns that Oughton has been killed in a Greenwich Village bomb blast. "Diana is dead," says Dohrn. Ayers has a hard time understanding. "Diana is dead," she "repeats slowly." Ayers drops the line, and the conversation ends abruptly.

It is in Manhattan too that Obama meets his Circe, the aforementioned Oughton-like figure. "Her voice sounded like a wind chime," he would later tell Auma. "We saw each other for almost a year." Odysseus too shares the temptress Circe's bed for a year. Like Obama's unnamed girlfriend, Circe lives in a "splendid house" on "spacious grounds." She likewise wants her lover to stay forever, but Odysseus's mates warn him off: "You god-driven man, now the time has come to think about your native land once more, if you are fated to be saved and reach your high-roofed home and your own country."

Ultimately, Obama steels himself against New York's Sirens, rejects Circe, and manages to find his way to Chicago and an adventure as a community organizer. What he still lacks, however, is a "guide that might show me how to join this troubled world." He still feels the "incompleteness" of his identity as a black American. Thinking Kenya might make him whole, Obama leaves on his African pilgrimage immediately after his weepy first visit to Reverend Wright's church and just before he begins Harvard in fall 1988.

Structurally, this timing works. Its accuracy is another question. Africa.com traced his first visit to Kenya to 1983, the summer after college graduation, "when he had come to mourn his late father." In that Barack Sr. died in late 1982, this makes sense. Mendell also puts this first visit in 1983. Britain's *Independent* and Obama's uncle Sayid specify 1987 for the first trip, as does Obama himself when speaking at a Kenyan university at 2006. Remnick sticks to the official version, 1988, the year that Obama suggests in *Dreams*.

Which account, if any, is correct I cannot say, and the answer is not terribly relevant in itself, save that this level of uncertainty haunts the entire Obama story as told and retold. Obama, for instance, first hears from his half sister Auma in 1983 when she calls to tell him his half brother David was killed in a motorbike accident, but David was not killed until 1987. Barack Sr. apparently lost both legs in car accidents, but in *Dreams* he has both legs until the last accident kills him. Almost nothing can be taken at face value, including, as shall be seen, the date of Obama's birth.

One trip that Obama does not even allude to in *Dreams* or *Audacity* is his 1981 trip to Pakistan. In fact, it was not until April 2008 at a San Francisco fund-raiser that Obama casually let it be known that he had traveled to Pakistan at all. Two weeks before the Pakistani admission, someone had improperly accessed Obama's passport on three occasions. The CNN lead suggests a major story in the making: "The CEO of a company whose employee is accused of improperly looking at the passport files of presidential candidates is a consultant to the Barack Obama campaign, a source said Saturday." That consultant was John Brennan, a former CIA operative then advising Obama.

The story predictably went nowhere despite the fact that Obama would later appoint Brennan deputy national security adviser. The most likely explanation is that Team Obama was doing oppositional research on its own candidate—and possibly the other candidates as well—and that Obama outed himself on a questionable trip to a Muslim country before the opposition could. Whatever the motive, a caper like this, once discovered, might have cost a less charmed candidate his career.

About his African pilgrimage Obama is much less shy. As told in *Dreams*, he spends eight weeks on this journey, an inexplicable luxury for a chronically broke young man no matter what the year. His first stop is allegedly Europe. I say "allegedly" because most of the specifics sound like they were pulled from a Michelin Guide. The one exception is a sojourn to the Spanish boondocks that even Remnick concedes is "not an especially convincing sequence." Its details sound like they were pulled from Ayers's memory.

After a couple of weeks wandering around Paris's Luxembourg Garden and other tourist hot spots, Obama finds himself awaiting the night bus at "a roadside tavern about halfway between Madrid and Barcelona." While waiting, he shoots pool at what might be the only pool table in any bar in Europe.

Here, emerging "out of nowhere," is a classic Homeric guide-god in the guise of a Senegalese traveler. This man is "somehow making the same journey"—that is, the journey of all dispossessed third-worlders struggling to find their way home, to their own Penelopes. The traveler shows Obama a photo of his young wife, with whom he would reunite as soon as he saved the money. Home, he seems to be telling Obama—in Spanish no less—is where a man and his wife make it to be. Need I mention that in *Fugitive Days* Ayers tells us he was a pool player who, during his merchant seaman days, frequented roughneck bars in this part of the world?

Whether he actually went to Europe or not, Obama realizes that this side trip was a "mistake." Although beautiful, Europe wasn't his. "I began to suspect," writes Obama, "that my European stop was just one more means of delay, one more attempt to avoid coming to terms with the Old Man." Like Odysseus, he knows he has to find his way back home. Obama hopes to find that home in Kenya. He will not. Despite the rush of "freedom that comes from not feeling watched," he soon realizes how much he still looks and thinks like an American. Africa is not Obama's home. It is his Hades.

Needing to consult the blind prophet Teiresias, Odysseus makes a long and difficult journey to "Hades' murky home," specifically a stream called Acheron, which branches off the river Styx. There he is instructed to pour libations to the deceased. Once he does, he is swarmed by the many and sundry "shades of the dead." Once in Kenya, Obama makes a similarly difficult journey of several days' duration by train, bus, jalopy, and finally on foot to "a wide chocolate-brown river," besides which rests the grave of Obama's great-great-grandfather in the heart of "Obama Land."

His trip to the interior serves the same purpose that Odysseus's trip to the underworld serves, a chance to reconcile with the spirits of the past. "The Old Man's here," Obama thinks, "although he doesn't say anything to me. He's here, asking me to understand." Here Obama meets, among other relatives, a blind great-uncle who pours him his own home-brewed libation. The night passes for Obama as in a dream. Men come and go, drinking "ceremoniously," perhaps six men, perhaps ten. Obama is not quite sure. They "merge with the shadows of corn."

If the blind seer Teiresias gives Odysseus involved instructions on how to return home, Obama's great-uncle cuts to the chase. He tells Obama that many men have been lost to the "white man's country," including his own son. "Such men are like ghosts," he says, adding that if Obama hears of his son, "You should tell him that he should come home." Obama leaves the land of his ancestors—after some prerequisite weeping—wiser than when he came, his great-uncle's "blind eyes staring out into the darkness." He knows that he too will become ghostlike unless he finds his own home.

What Obama pulls from his African experience, in a sequence that feels heavily indebted to his muse and largely contrived after the fact, is that home is where the heart is. Cultural "authenticity" is an illusion, and there is "no shame in confusion." There was shame only in the silence that leads the individual to try to form an identity without help from a community of others.

From Africa, the book passes at warp speed through Obama's

Harvard experience and culminates with his wedding to Michelle. Just as the *Odyssey* ends with Odysseus reuniting with his wife, Penelope, Obama rounds his circle by marrying into the African American culture that has beguiled him all his life. Michelle is "a daughter of the South Side," the real McCoy. "I am married to a black American who carries within her the blood of slaves," Obama would remind America during his briefly celebrated Philadelphia race speech.

With the promise of fatherhood implicit in marriage, the abandoned son claims the potential to be a father, and the father of authentic African Americans at that. The penultimate paragraph of the book has Obama describing his older half brother Roy, who now calls himself "Abongo." (Had Obama called himself "Abongo Obama," he would not have won a state senate seat, let alone the presidency.) The alert reader hears in Obama's description of his brother, especially its first sentence, a mischievous muse describing Obama:

> The words he speaks are not fully his own, and in his transition he can sometimes sound stilted and dogmatic. But the magic of his laughter remains, and we can disagree without rancor. His conversion has given him solid ground to stand on, a pride in his place in the world. From that base I see his confidence building; he begins to venture out and ask harder questions; he starts to slough off the formulas and slogans and decides what works best for him. He can't help himself in this process, for his heart is too generous and full of good humor, his attitude toward people too gentle and forgiving, to find simple solutions to the puzzle of being a black man.

In *Dreams*, as in the *Odyssey*, almost nothing can be taken at face value. This is why Stephen Maturin, one of the two protagonists of Patrick O'Brian's masterful sea novels, did not much like Odysseus. "He lied excessively, it seems to be," observes Maturin in *The Far Side of the World*, "and if a man lies beyond a certain point a certain sad falseness enters into him and he is no longer amiable."

HOG BUTCHER

In the spring and summer of 2009 I had little opportunity to pursue authorship issues. I had entered a contract to write a book on the economy, eventually called *Popes and Bankers: A Cultural History of Credit and Debit from Aristotle to AIG*, and I labored under the antique notion that once you sign a contract and accept an advance, you have a moral obligation to honor that contract. Thus, when I saw a message in my AOL inbox whose subject heading was "759 striking similarities between *Dreams* and Ayers' works," I at first ignored it. The claim seemed too outsized to take seriously. When I was unable to open the documents, I emailed the sender, asked him to reformat, and then forgot about the email. He resent his documents a few days later.

This time I was able to open them, and I was duly impressed. The analysis was systematic, comprehensive, and utterly, totally, damning. Of the 759 matches, none were frivolous. From the 759 I culled out 180 that deserved the term *striking*. Some of them I had already reported. Others I was holding in reserve, waiting for a long-form opportunity to present, but many others I had not yet noticed.

As a control, I tested these words and phrases against those in my own 2006 book, *Sucker Punch*, like *Dreams* and *Fugitive Days* a memoir that deals extensively with race. In that I am closer to Ayers in age, race, education, and family and cultural background than is Obama, our styles should have had more chance of matching. They don't. Of the 180 examples, I matched, strictly speaking, on six. Even by the most generous standard, I matched on only sixteen.

For this new source of meticulously indexed data I had, in no small part, Emanuel Swedenborg to thank. The 18th century scientist and Christian mystic wrote some eighteen theological works, the best known of which was a treatise called, in its English translation, *Heaven and Its Wonders and Hell from Things Heard and Seen*. In the book, Swedenborg offers a meticulous, detailed account of the afterlife, which he claims to have experienced firsthand.

In the centuries that followed, Swedenborg attracted any number of followers, many of them influential, like Ralph Waldo Emerson and William Butler Yeats, and some obscure, like the fellow who contacted me, a forty-something surveyor, ski resort jack-of-all-trades, and mathematician, who prefers the anonymity of "Mr. Southwest." Working for several hours a day for several months, he had compiled this amazingly detailed compendium in his spare time. He attributes his discipline to his daily reading of Swedenborg.

It was altogether serendipitous that Mr. Southwest stumbled onto this issue. Largely apolitical, he had voted for the Democratic presidential candidate in the previous three elections. After he had acquired a satellite radio, he found himself listening to Sean Hannity and Rusty Humphries and began to think that maybe they made some sense. In September 2008, he heard me on Rusty Humphries. This inspired him to do some digging on his own. The pickings were ripe. He sent me some early discoveries and when I sent him back a thankful email, he was "psyched" and started burrowing in seriously. He did his research using the interlibrary loan service at the college from which he had graduated with a math degree.

In isolation, none of the 759 similarities was enough to indict. So when critics attacked my research they tended to single out one or two specific parallels and mocked them. For instance, both Ayers and Obama not only quote the "hog butcher" phrase from Carl Sandburg's poem "Chicago," but they also misquote it the same way as "hog butcher to the world." It should read, "Hog Butcher *for* the World." (Sandburg liked caps.) When I wrote about the research of Mr. Southwest and Nebraskan Ryan Geiser—"Mr. West" and "Mr. Midwest" in my online postings—any number of critics isolated this reference and assailed me for daring to infer anything from it. "Not an uncommon slip-up," *Washington Post* blogger Steven Levingston assured his readers.

Levingston underestimates the degree of difficulty. To slip up in the same way, Obama and Ayers must make a series of identical choices. First, they have to refer to the Sandburg poem. For Ayers, this would be natural. He grew up in Chicago in an era when students were still expected to memorize poems. Obama, however, uses the "hog butcher" line before he moves to Chicago. Still, he uses the exact same phrase from that poem that Ayers does. "What do you know about Chicago anyway?" Obama is asked. "I thought a moment. 'Hog butcher to the world,' I said finally."

Like Ayers, Obama uses only those five words in isolation and no others. Like Ayers, he gets the third word wrong and no other and chooses, like Ayers, not to use capital letters the way Sandburg does. Finally, Obama could have adapted any number of noted phrases from the poem, "City of the Big Shoulders" for instance, or "Player with Railroads." In *Livin' the Blues*, Frank Marshall Davis, whose favorite poet was Sandburg, paraphrases the former, referring to Chicago as that "broad-shouldered brute of a burgh."

"If I were writing a book that was supposed to endear me to the voters of Chicago, and I wanted to insert a line from a poem about the city, I would probably quote it accurately," wrote Geiser about the genesis of the Sandburg glitch. "Ayers likely misquotes Sandberg from memory." In a similar vein, when both authors misspell Frantz Fanon's first name as "Franz" and incorrectly refer to the South African city of "Sharpeville" in the possessive as "Sharpsville" (*Dreams*) and "Sharpesville" (*Race Course*), they have to make multiple choices to make the same mistake.

Of similar note, both Obama and Ayers use the phrase "pie-in-the-sky." Although I have used the phrase myself, I have always used it the way most people do, as an adjective. Both Obama and Ayers use it as a noun, as in "gray beards preaching pie-in-the-sky."

Apparently, somewhere along the way Ayers and Obama shared a menagerie. In addition to hogs, both also fix on the water buffalo. At a war protest in the 1960s, Ayers sees a photo of "small boys with bamboo sticks perched upon their backs." Curiously, in *Dreams*, Obama also remembers seeing a boy sitting "on the back of a dumb-faced water buffalo, whipping its haunch with a stick of bamboo." Note that these boys whip the beast not just with sticks, but with bamboo sticks. As it happens, each also talks about birds of paradise, yellow dogs, ducks, hippos, chickens, Cheshire cats, and an African boy's need to "kill a lion" to prove himself a man.

Working from Mr. Southwest's documentation, I wrote that Ayers was fixated with faces, especially eyes. He writes of "sparkling" eyes, "shining" eyes, "laughing" eyes, "twinkling" eyes, eyes "like ice," and people who are "wide-eyed" and "dark-eyed." As it happens, Obama was also fixated with faces, especially eyes. He too writes of "sparkling" eyes, "shining" eyes, "laughing" eyes, "twinkling" eyes, and uses the phrases "wide-eyed" and "dark-eyed." Obama adds "smoldering eyes," *smoldering* being a word that he and Ayers inject repeatedly. Obama also uses the highly distinctive phrases "like ice," in his case to describe the glistening of the stars. To counter this, Levingston comforted *Post* readers with the notion that "eyes have mesmerized writers throughout history."

Remnick does much the same in his book. He repeated this non-sense when he was the in-studio guest on a Chicago radio show. Although I was a call-in guest on the same show, he casually reduced my work to the "notion that [Obama] uses the word *eyes* a lot." I had already written twenty thousand or so words on the subject. He had read enough of them to slime me in his book, and still he was able to ratchet up the silliness with me listening in. Mr. Remnick, Hath not a Boilermaker ears?

What amuses in retrospect are the parallels in my first article on Mr. Southwest's research that Levingston—and Remnick for that matter—saw but chose not to reveal. Both Obama and Ayers, for instance, use "Mekong Delta" as a synecdoche for Vietnam. Both have scenes in which clueless "State Department" officials—plural—link Indonesia with the march of communism through the archaic, colonial-sounding "Indochina." Both talk of the West's "imperial culture." Both use the phrase "perfectly American" ironically, if not bitterly.

Isolate any one of these matches, and it means nothing. Multiply it by 759 or even 180, and the evidence overwhelms. *Washington Post* readers were told none of this.

Levingston summed up my argument thus: "The book [*Dreams*] is beautifully written and yet, in Cashill's opinion, Obama is—and always was—a crappy writer." I would never use the word *crappy*, but I must give Levingston credit for so nicely summarizing my thesis even if he does dismiss it—ouch!—as "the stink that fills the detective's nose."

AUDACITY

In his 2006 book, *The Audacity of Hope*, Barack Obama presumed to tell the world just who he was and what he believed. One challenge he knew he would face—especially after September 11—was convincing America that he was one of its own.

Despite his professed Christianity, there has been much talk about Obama's Muslim roots, and that talk is not without some merit. Obama did, in fact, register in his Indonesian school as a Muslim and occasionally attended prayer services with his Indonesian stepfather, Lolo Soetoro. "Barry was a Muslim," his third-grade teacher told the *Los Angeles Times* in 2007, but this was a rare acknowledgment by the media. In general, they approached the issue in damage-control mode.

Even such fundamental questions as whether Soetoro ever adopted Obama have gone unasked. In fact, it is Obama's murky status as Soetoro's stepson that has caused many soi-disant "birthers" to question his citizenship. The best known of those is Philip Berg, the Hillary Clinton supporter who filed suit against Obama challenging his "Constitutional qualifications" to serve as president. What Berg contends is that when Obama returned to Hawaii at age ten, he did so as "Barry Soetoro" on an Indonesian passport and has never legally changed his name back to Obama.

The fact that Obama was listed on his mother's 1968 passport renewal application as "Barack Hussein Obama (Soebarkah)"—with the unexplained "Soebarkah" in parentheses on the application—or that Ann Dunham's 1965 passport application and any that might have preceded it were inexplicably destroyed has done little to still birther discontent.

In *Dreams*, Obama takes pains to distance himself from his Muslim roots, particularly during his Indonesian phase. Obama tells the reader he "made faces" during Koranic studies and was scolded for it. And that is it for him and Islam. There is no mention in *Dreams* or *Audacity* of his 1981 trip to Pakistan and little mention of his close Pakistani friends and roommates.

Obama is more elusive still about his relatives. Yes, Lolo Soetoro was a Muslim, but he practiced a kind of half-baked hybrid. Yes, his grandfather was a Muslim, but he converted because Islam better reflected his mercilessness. But no, Barack Sr. was not a Muslim. On one occasion in *Dreams*, a Chicago barber asks, "Barack, huh. You a Muslim?" Obama replies evasively, "Grandfather was." If he conceded that his father was a Muslim, he would have had to deny his father to erase his Muslim roots, and that would have worked against the plotline.

In reality, Barack Sr. lived his early life as a Muslim. In *Dreams*, Obama's half brother Roy suggests that he died one as well. "The government wanted a Christian burial," Roy tells Obama. "The family wanted a Muslim burial." By 2006, knowing how toxic a Muslim heritage would be to an aspiring presidential candidate, Obama would write in *Audacity*, "Although my father had been raised a Muslim, by the time he met my mother he was a confirmed atheist." During the campaign, the Obama press office declared that Obama Sr. was simply "an atheist" and did not mention his Muslim upbringing. An atheism-friendly media accepted this line uncritically.

In September 2008, in a conversation with George Stephanopoulos set up to quell such rumors, Obama slipped up and referred to "my Muslim faith," before quickly correcting himself. Slip-up or no, he found it "deeply offensive" that the Republican camp was suggesting "that perhaps I'm not who I say I am when it comes to my faith."

In *Audacity*, Obama hoped to establish "who I say I am." The very title of the book, however, gives the wary reader pause. Obama names it—misnames it actually—after the life-changing sermon by Jeremiah Wright, "Audacity *to* Hope." In *Dreams*, Obama recounts the sermon approvingly and in some detail. He cites classic Wright pearls like "White folks' greed runs a world in need" as if they actually made sense. And this, he boasts, is the sermon that set him on the road to Christianity or something like it.

To those paying attention, Obama's conversion seemed as calculated as his choice of wife. Mendell notes that in 2004 "Obama, without fail, would mention his church and his Christian faith when he was campaigning in black churches and more socially conservative downstate Illinois communities." Yet when Mendell tried to talk to Obama about his faith and his "ever present bible," Obama proved "uncharacteristically short" in his responses. When Mendell persisted, Obama claimed that he was drawn to Christianity because "many of the impulses that I had carried with me and were propelling me forward were the same impulses that express themselves through the church." In other words, Jesus thought pretty much along the same progressive lines as Obama did.

In *Audacity*, Obama is even more ambiguous about his politics than he is about his faith. That, I believe, was as intended. The book seems to have been planned and written by committee, and the final product shows it. In October 2006, when *Audacity* hit the bookstores, it did not get the raves *Dreams* had. The *New York Times'* Michiko Kakutani describes *Audacity* "as much more of a political document. Portions of the volume read like outtakes from a stump speech." Still, despite the book's "flabby platitudes," she assures her readers that "enough of the narrative voice in this volume is recognizably similar to the one in *Dreams From My Father*."

The question that must first be asked is who provided that narrative voice. In the way of recap, after being elected senator in November 2004, Obama replaced his loyal agent Jane Dystel and her 15 percent cut with a powerful D.C. attorney who charged only by the hour. Some time before his swearing-in as senator, Obama signed a two-book deal with Crown for somewhere in the neighborhood of $2 million and pocketed the $300,000 that would have otherwise gone to Dystel.

Despite the onerous workload of a freshman senator, Obama found time to write a 431-page book without any acknowledged writing help in what was roughly an eighteen-month window. This was the same writer who blew a six-figure advance because he was unable to produce a book during three much less hectic years, the same writer who between his 1995 masterpiece and *Audacity* had written nothing deeper than an occasional lame column for a community newsletter.

In reality, the window was much less than eighteen months. "He procrastinated for a long time," concedes Remnick. It is understandable why Obama might have. His schedule was ridiculous. He would typically fly into D.C. on Monday evenings and out on Thursday evenings. In addition to a daily trip to the gym and occasional lunches and dinners with friends, Obama's D.C. workdays were packed, in his own retelling, with "committee markups, votes, caucus lunches, floor statements, speeches, photos with interns, evening fund-raisers, returning phone calls, writing correspondence, reviewing legislation, drafting op-eds, recording podcasts, receiving policy briefings, hosting constituent coffees, and attending an endless series of meetings."

When home, in that first year alone, Obama hosted eighty-nine town-hall meetings throughout the state of Illinois. He traveled abroad to Russia, Eastern Europe, Israel, and Iraq. "Like a traditional pol," admits Remnick, "he spent hours making cajoling calls" to fill the coffers of his political-action committee. Given his high profile, he hit the campaign trail to raise money for his colleagues. All business aside, the fatherless Obama also worked hard to be a good father to his daughters and a good husband to Michelle. Accordingly, he set aside Sundays for his family and as much other time as he could squeeze in.

"There was another inkblot on this sketch," writes Mendell. "Writing a book is a full-time job in itself." Somehow Obama managed to moonlight a book project in the wake of a day job that always ran overtime. "I usually wrote at night after my Senate day was over, and after my family was asleep—from 9:30 p.m. or so until 1 a.m.," he told interviewer Daphne Durham of Amazon. Once he got started, Obama wrote his initial draft in longhand.

"His best writing time comes late at night when he's all alone, scribbling on yellow legal pads," confirmed the embarrassingly credulous Jay Newton-Small in *Time* two months before the November 2008 election. "This is how he wrote both of his two best selling books—*Dreams from My Father* and *The Audacity of Hope*—staying up after Michelle and his two young daughters had long gone to bed, reveling in the late night quiet."

Time was apparently shorthanded on fact checkers. As to *Dreams*, Obama's oldest daughter was born in 1998, three years after the book was published. As to *Audacity*, his family may have gone to bed early, but that was in Chicago. Obama was in D.C. He came home most weekends, but I cannot imagine the Obamas abandoning their Twelve Oaks social life for book writing. The late-night story line may have been based on Obama's habits but was surely inflated to accommodate his casual completion of a task that would have sent Hercules looking for his union rep.

Although he had dissed Christopher Andersen on Chicago radio for using "unnamed sources," Remnick relies on a person known only as an "aide" to explain how a slow writer, off to a late start, using 19th century technology, could pen (literally) a well-researched, 431-

page book in the face of an absurd work schedule. "He was punching the clock during the day and then coming alive at night to write the book," says the "aide." That was enough to satisfy Remnick. He adds that facing his deadline, Obama wrote "nearly a chapter a week." The chapters are on average nearly fifty pages long. Remnick is a writer. He should know better. Obama had to be taking a page out of the Tribe-Ogletree playbook.

In the acknowledgments section of *Audacity*—*Dreams* does not have one—Obama lists an astonishing twenty-four people who provided "invaluable suggestions" in reading or fact-checking the book prior to publication. These include David Axelrod, Cassandra Butts, Forrest Claypool, Julius Genachowski, Scott Gration, Robert Fisher, Michael Froman, Donald Gips, John Kupper, Anthony Lake, Susan Rice, Gene Sperling, Cass Sunstein, Jim Wallis, Peter Rouse, Karen Kornbluh, Mike Strautmanis, Jon Favreau, Mark Lippert, Joshua DuBois, Robert Gibbs, Chris Lu, Madhuri Kommareddi, and Hillary Schrenell. As a point of comparison, other than the publisher's people, my English professor wife is the only one who reads my books before publication. None of the twenty-four above is a publisher person. They are all Obama people.

Although Obama singles out Gibbs and Lu, if there is a muse in chief among this crowd, it is almost assuredly speechwriting wunderkind Jon Favreau. Favreau first met up with Obama at the 2004 Democratic National Convention and although he had just turned twenty-three, he did not hesitate to offer advice on Obama's keynote speech. Obama interviewed Favreau on his first day in the Senate in 2005 and promptly hired him. And there is the rub. Favreau is one of eight people who, Obama carefully notes, "read the manuscript on their own time." As a paid Senate staffer, Favreau would have had to do book writing on his "own time." So would have Obama, for that matter.

No writer was closer to Obama or more trusted than Favreau. While getting to know the senator, he carried *Dreams* around and committed it to memory. His goal, reports Ashley Parker of the *New York Times*, was "to master Mr. Obama's voice," meaning the voice of *Dreams*. Continues Parker: "Now, he said, when he sits down to write, he just channels Mr. Obama—his ideas, his sentences, his phrases."

Mendell got to see Favreau in action before he became a minor celebrity. "In crafting a speech," Mendell writes, "Favreau grabs his laptop and sits with Obama for about twenty minutes, listening to his boss throw out chunks of ideas. Favreau then assembles these thoughts into political prose." Although I cannot prove that *Audacity* was assembled in the same fashion, I can confirm that portions of *Audacity* sound like "outtakes from a stump speech" precisely because they were, in fact, outtakes from a stump speech.

Kudos to Mr. Southwest for his work on this. He found thirty-eight passages from Obama speeches delivered in 2005 or 2006 that appear virtually word for word as ordinary text in *Audacity*. The first example comes from a speech Obama gave on October 25, 2005:

. . . those who work in the field know what reforms really work: a more challenging and rigorous curriculum with emphasis on math, science, and literacy skills. Longer hours and more days to give kids the time and attention they need to learn.

This second excerpt comes from *Audacity:*

And in fact we already have hard evidence of reforms that work: a more challenging and rigorous curriculum with emphasis on math, science, and literacy skills; longer hours and more days to give children the time and sustained attention they need to learn.

By June 2006, with a deadline imminent, Obama appears to have been either inserting whole speeches word for word into the manuscript or lifting passages from the manuscript to use as speeches. The first example comes from a June 28, 2006, speech:

Indeed, the single biggest "gap" in party affiliation among white Americans today is not between men and women, or those who reside in so-called Red States and those who reside in Blue, but between those who attend church regularly and those who don't.

This second excerpt comes from *Audacity:*

The single biggest gap in party affiliation among white Americans is not between men and women, or between those who reside in so-called red states and those who reside in blue states, but between those who attend church regularly and those who don't.

Of course, all that this proves is that whoever wrote Obama's speeches wrote large sections of *Audacity*, perhaps all of it, and this is an issue only if someone other than Obama wrote his speeches. As we are seeing, though, illusions of genius are not easily sustainable. When senior editor Rachel Klayman of Crown pulled *Dreams* from the vaults and put it back into circulation, she unknowingly set in motion a series of compounding untruths, beginning with the foundational myth that Obama is a literary lion. To sustain that myth, Obama's enablers had to make us believe that he also wrote *Audacity* by himself, as well as most of his speeches, staying up until the wee hours each night to do so.

The public flowering of Favreau after Obama's election to the presidency—the *Washington Post* first discovered him and his laptop in a D.C. Starbucks—complicated this scenario. So lost in Obama worship was British writer Jonathan Raban that he confessed to being "disconcerted" to learn that Obama used speechwriters at all. He felt even more "let down" when he discovered that the Philadelphia "More Perfect Union" speech was "a joint Obama/Favreau production."

Of the thirty-eight speech passages from 2005 to 2006 that found their way into *Audacity*, the Obama faithful are forced to believe that Obama wrote all of them. If he did not, then he did not write *Audacity* by himself, and if he lied about that, then he was also capable of lying about his unique authorship of *Dreams*. It seems much more likely that Favreau wrote most of these speeches, if not all. Yes, Obama may have dictated his thoughts or written down notes in longhand, but why would he not have given those notes to his gifted, government-issue speechwriter to put into prose?

Here is what I believe happened. Obama knew he had a problem on his hands when *Dreams* was republished in 2004. He recruited Ayers to write the distinctly postmodernist preface to the 2004 edition, but once he was elected to the U.S. Senate they both knew that Ayers was poison. To achieve continuity, Ayers was asked to write the prologue to *Audacity* and the final pages of the epilogue, but no more.

Although not one word or phrase reaches smoking-gun status, I was able to match every distinctive phrase and concept from this last thousand-word stretch of *Audacity* to a comparable one from Ayers's work—with one interesting exception. This extraordinary parallelism suggests a certain haste on Ayers's part as he seemed to be mining his own clichés.

Many of the words and phrases in the *Audacity* epilogue can be found in the Ayers books, often multiple times. These include words like *contingent, obscurity, torrent, inherently, satisfying, glimpse, fleeting, demonstrable, calculation, petty, nameless, faceless,* as well as *narrow* and *landscape* used metaphorically, *thousand* used hyperbolically, and *labor* used as a verb.

Telling too are the phrases: "my heart," "filled with," "measure of," "sense of," "what matters," "the path to." Again, none of these is significant in itself. It is just that every phrase I searched in *Audacity* I found in Ayers, again often multiple times. I do not believe Favreau was that good a mimic.

More than the word matches, it was the conceptual parallelism that convinced me of Ayers's involvement. For instance, Obama tells us that "satisfaction is not to be found in the glare of television cameras." Ayers is equally disdainful of "the sinister glare of celebrity." Obama talks about our "collective dreams." Ayers uses the word *collective* more often and in more ways than even Marx did. Speaking of Marx, Obama uses the concept of "process" in a consciously dialectic sense, as does Ayers.

In *Audacity*'s epilogue, Obama tells the reader that he strives "to help people live their lives with some measure of dignity." Ayers too sees the need "to validate the dignity and worth of students," to honor "the full measure of their humanity," and to make efforts "to achieve and extend human dignity."

In the epilogue's most dramatic moment, Obama relates a conversation he had had nearly twenty years earlier with an older friend of his, an academic who offered Obama advice on law school and a political career beyond. "Both law and politics required compromise," the man tells Obama, adding that he himself had thought about going into politics but was unwilling to compromise.

Ayers likely put his words in this poor man's mouth. In *Fugitive Days*, for instance, he tells us that he and his comrades were eager to "combat the culture of compromise." Looking back, Obama concedes that he was "perhaps more tolerant of compromise" than this older friend was. Curiously, *tolerant* is the one key word I could not find in any of Ayers's books. Apparently, he had no particular use for that concept.

Other than the epilogue and the prologue, the voice and style of *Audacity* are fairly workmanlike and consistent. As with *Dreams*, Obama surely contributed, especially in the personal reminiscences, but there is no way he could have actually written the body of the book without substantial help. That help seems to have come from one key individual. Of all the writers in Washington, only Favreau could have had the private time with Obama to pull this off without attracting attention. If, say, Ted Sorensen had stopped by daily to powwow with Obama, someone surely would have caught wind of it, even if Obama did not name the book *Son of Profiles in Courage*.

At this point, Favreau is just about the only real suspect. If I am correct, Favreau labored to make *Audacity* sound like *Dreams*, but he simply does not write as knowingly or maturely as the *Dreams* muse does. Consider this passage from *Audacity*:

> But travel a few blocks farther in any direction and you will also experience a different side of Mac's world: the throngs of young men on corners casting furtive glances up and down the street; the sound of sirens blending with the periodic thump of car stereos turned up full blast; the dark, boarded-up buildings and hastily scrawled gang signs; the rubbish everywhere, swirling in winter winds.

This is the kind of stretch that Kakutani rightly describes as "recognizably similar" to the "narrative voice" of *Dreams*. It reads, however, like a description of a generic ghetto street that could have been imagined from the comfort of a D.C. Starbucks, not the real Chicago so vividly described in this passage from *Dreams*:

> . . . during my very first days in Chicago I had seen the knots of young men, fifteen or sixteen, hanging out on the corners of Michigan or Halsted, their hoods up, their sneakers unlaced, stomping the ground in a desultory rhythm during the colder months, stripped down to T-shirts in the summer, answering their beepers on the corner pay phones: a knot that unraveled, soon to reform, whenever the police cars passed by in their barracuda silence.

It takes a seaman to know how silently a barracuda passes. Now, compare the above to an excerpt from Ayers's *A Kind and Just Parent*: "Here a knot of young men stand around a stoop talking and passing a bottle." In *Race Course*, there is more of the same: "Knots of men collected on corners and in the vacant lot next to our building, smoking, passing a bottle, or a skinny joint." Not all authors assemble their young men into "knots."

More to the point, consider the way each of the two muses uses the telling word *ballast*. In *Dreams* the word is used with an understanding of what the word actually means, namely a weight that stabilizes a boat and prevents it from capsizing:

> A steady attack on the white race . . . served as the ballast that could prevent the ideas of personal and communal responsibility from tipping into an ocean of despair.

In *Audacity*, the word is flat-out misused:

> . . . one is tempted to assume that the impact of faith on politics is largely salutary, a check on personal ambition, a ballast against the buffeting winds of today's headlines and political expediency.

No one in the know uses the phrase "ballast against" in reference to a ship. Then too there is the unnatural linking of "headlines" and "expediency" as metaphorical "winds." The *Audacity* muse appears to be channeling the Obama of *Dreams*, right down to the nautical metaphors, but not quite getting it right.

One Republican who has voiced his suspicions about *Audacity* is Bush adviser Karl Rove. He tells of running into Obama soon after *Audacity* was published. "Hey, I understand you got me in your book," said Rove. "I don't think so," Obama replied. Rove continued, "I think you got me in your book saying, 'we're a Christian nation.' " Said Obama, "Where'd I say that?" Rove showed him.

THE PLAN

Whether or not Barack Obama actually wrote *Audacity of Hope*, the content of the book matters. Those millions of Americans who read it or read about it had good reason to think of it as Obama's governing blueprint. After two years of the Obama presidency, however, the reader can see the book more clearly for what it is—a masterful strategic feint.

One senses the guiding hand of David Axelrod. The repositioning of Obama took an insider's understanding of the way the media work—Axelrod started as a *Chicago Tribune* reporter—and some serious chutzpah. Axelrod saw in "Obama" a product that would have excellent shelf appeal if properly repackaged, and he used the fall 2006 release of *Audacity* to roll that product out.

Although the media chose not to see, there was no mistaking the nature of the core product, Obama himself. As a boy in Indonesia, his secular humanist mother would say of less enlightened Americans,

"They are not my people," and Obama got the message. As a teen in Hawaii, communist Frank Marshall Davis nudged him further to the left. Upon hitting the mainland, Obama immersed himself in a deeply leftist milieu. After college, he rejected a corporate life to community organize Saul Alinsky–style. At Harvard, he found mentors like Tribe and Ogletree. After Harvard, when he could have had any job he wanted, he returned to Chicago and civil rights law. For a pastor, he chose the most radical one in Chicago. For pals, he turned to people like Ayers, Dohrn, and Khalidi. As a state senator, he proved himself, in Mendell's words, an "unabashed liberal." In the U.S. Senate, the *National Journal* cited him as "the most liberal." And yet *Audacity* would all but institutionalize Obama's position as "a healer, not a divider." This repositioning was chapter one, verse one in what "Ax" and Obama called "The Plan."

Axelrod could not have accomplished this with just any candidate. From his childhood on, the multicultural Obama had shown the ability to blend Zelig-like into a range of environments. Although this trait could be useful, even endearing, it could also be irritating. At Harvard, for instance, he pitched the small conservative bloc to get himself elected president of the law review. The maneuver left at least a few of them thinking Obama "somewhat two-faced" and "all things to all people." One of his black congressional opponents in 2000 called him what many others in the community felt, a "white man in blackface." The Clinton camp wrote him off as a "politically calculating chameleon."

The media, of course, chose not to read the fine print on the Obama package. With the help of what even David Remnick concedes was "generally adoring press coverage," Obama was reborn as a centrist. At the start of his Senate career in 2005, *Newsweek* made Obama its cover boy under the heading "The Color Purple." This represented a full media buy-in to the conceit Obama had advanced in his God-fearing, flag-waving convention keynote speech. There he ceremoniously rejected the blue state–red state dichotomy and insisted that "there's not a liberal America and a conservative America; there's the United States of America."

Audacity gave new meaning to the phrase "purple prose." Writing from the left, Michael Tomasky neatly summarizes the gist of the book in his critique for the *Saturday Review of Books*:

> The chapters boil down to a pattern: here's what the right believes about subject X, and here's what the left believes; and while I basically side with the left, I think the right has a point or two that we should consider, and the left can sometimes get a little carried away.

In his otherwise flattering review, *Time* magazine's Joe Klein had less patience still with this presidential two-step. Klein counted no fewer than fifty instances of "excruciatingly judicious on-the-one-hand-on-the-other-handedness" in *Audacity*. He calls the tendency "so pronounced that it almost seems an obsessive-compulsive tic." More generously, Remnick calls *Audacity* "a shrewd candidate's book."

One sign of that shrewdness was Obama's professed respect for Ronald Reagan. "Reagan spoke to America's longing for order," writes Obama, "our need to believe that we are not simply subject to blind, impersonal forces but that we can shape our individual and collective destinies, so long as we rediscover the traditional virtues of hard work, patriotism, personal responsibility, optimism, and faith." Nor does he, unlike so many on the left, dismiss Reagan as merely an effective, if deceptive, communicator. His appeal "spoke to the failures of liberal government." That government, according to Obama in words that now do cartwheels across the page, "had become too cavalier about spending taxpayer money."

Between these words of praise, Obama offers a critique of Reagan and his policies so gentle as to leave the impression that the Reagan revolution merely needs a little tweaking. *Audacity* is pure seduction. With an eye on 2008, Obama had cast his sauciest come-hither look at Reagan Democrats and Republicans of unsteady resolve.

Lest his seeming moderation alienate his party's hotheads, Obama sent out the appropriate smoke signals to keep them on the reservation. Nowhere is this more evident than in his treatment of gay marriage. The inclusion of a gay marriage amendment on the Ohio ballot in 2004 may have cost Kerry the election. It was a losing issue. Accordingly, during his 2004 Senate race and the 2008 presidential race for that matter, the crafty Obama opposed same-sex marriage.

In *Audacity*, he tells the story of how one of his lesbian supporters phoned him to express her dismay at his position. The call reminded him that he had to remain "open to the possibility that my unwillingness to support gay marriage is misguided," that perhaps he "had been infected with society's prejudices and predilections and attributed them to God." Translation: he was prepared to change positions as soon as God and/or David Axelrod gave him the sign. The base got the message.

Although the left's shift in self-designation seems awfully coy, for Obama the label "progressive" fits much better than "liberal." A liberal can have a fixed set of values, much as conservatives do. But a progressive, by definition, is always progressing. Like a great white, if one stops moving, it dies. Obama's fellow progressives, the party's base, understand that the long march through the institutions will have many strategic stalls, perhaps even a few reversals, but the march inevitably continues forward. In crafting *Audacity*, Axelrod was confident that party activists would see why Obama was marching in place. Their almost universal support for Obama in 2008 suggests that they did.

For all his strategic legerdemain, Axelrod is no Svengali. Obama has none. From the beginning of Obama's political career, his critics, myself included, have been looking for the man behind the curtain, but

I am now convinced that if there is a wizard, it is Obama himself. He may be a "bound man," forced to operate within narrow constraints, but he provides the drive. Fueling that drive, writes David Mendell, is "an internal conceit that formed in his character after being treated as a special human being as far back as childhood."

Occidental is not good enough for Obama, so he transfers to Columbia. He wearies of community organizing and limits his law school choices to "Harvard, Yale, Stanford." Civil rights law proves small beer, and he runs for office. The state senate is beneath him, and so he runs for Congress. His opponent, Bobby Rush, calls him "a tool of the white liberals," but if anything, the white liberals are his tool.

Undeterred by his loss to Rush, Obama runs for the U.S. Senate. Incredibly, even the U.S. Senate is infra dig. "He was so bored being a senator," says one aide. "The job was too small for him," writes Remnick with a straight face. "He's been bored to death his whole life," summarizes confidante Valerie Jarrett. "He's just too talented to do what ordinary people do."

Such uncommon people often find their way into the progressive camp because it encourages their deep-thought thinking and allows for the accumulation of power. Jonathan Alter openly marvels at the "many extraordinarily smart men and women" who have grouped themselves around Obama, not the "legion of second-raters" whom Bush attracted. (Yes, he actually writes this.) Like their president, they believe that "human beings don't always do what's in their rational best interest . . . but with the proper government rules and incentives, society could be dramatically improved." Alter thinks of Obama as the most extraordinary of all these "brilliant policy mandarins."

Alter's view of Obama conforms to Obama's youthful view of himself. College friend John Drew contends that in his Occidental days Obama saw himself as "part of an intelligent, radical vanguard that was leading the way towards this revolution and towards this new society." Obama may have sublimated his radicalism but not so his self-esteem. In 2008, he was still capable of confusing his capture of the Democratic nomination with "the moment when the rise of the oceans began to slow and our planet began to heal."

Throughout his career, Obama has attached himself to people more powerful than he, but as with the Chicago liberals, it is not they who have used him, but he who has used them. Given this pattern, it seems likely that it was Obama who sought out the help of Khalid al-Mansour and through him that of Percy Sutton, and when they had served their purpose, he moved on.

Obama found his way to Jeremiah Wright precisely because Wright had power and influence that Obama did not. When Ayers advanced Obama's career in the mid-1990s, it was Ayers who had the clout and Obama who had the cunning to profit from it. It was Jane Dystel who had the connections in the publishing world that Obama needed, and it was he who exploited them until he did not need them or her anymore. At the end of the day, Obama would disown all of these people and others as well. "I think he's an arrogant, self-absorbed, ungrateful jerk," said one former Chicago ally. "He walked away from his friends."

The Alice Palmer drama set something of a pattern. A popular state senator, Palmer chose to run for U.S. Congress when a sexual assault and child pornography *conviction*—the indictment did not deter voters in 1994—derailed the career plans of seat holder Mel Reynolds. In the interim, Palmer helped prep Obama to run for her state senate seat. When Palmer got beat in the primary by Jesse Jackson, Jr., she asked Obama to step aside so she could run for reelection as state senator. Not only did Obama refuse, which was understandable, but he challenged—successfully—the signatures Palmer had gathered to get back on the ballot. In anyone's book, this was dirty pool.

Obama's treatment of Jeremiah Wright leaves one almost feeling sorry for Wright. Unwittingly, the Obama campaign had transformed one of Chicago's most respected and influential preachers—however berserk—into everyone's idiot uncle. To undo the harm the Wright videos had done to the campaign, Obama and Favreau concocted a five-thousand-word stemwinder to distance Obama from the man without exactly disowning him.

Obama delivered the speech, titled "A More Perfect Union," in Philadelphia in March 2008. Its central trope was pure soap opera. "I can no more disown him," said Obama of his pastor, "than I can disown the black community." Obama proceeded to compare Wright to his cryptoracist Hawaii grandma and promised to abandon neither. In the course of the speech, however, Obama condemned "in unequivocal terms" many of the comments that Wright had been making for the last thirty-six years. As Obama would soon learn, the pastor did not exactly cotton to a public spanking by a protégé.

At the time, the speech proved to be something of a hit. MSNBC's cheaply thrilled Chris Matthews would describe it as "one of the great speeches in American history" and the *New York Times*' feckless Frank Rich would call it "the most remarkable utterance on the subject by a public figure in modern memory." Indeed, so effusive was the gushing that several of the more prominent gushes were collected into a book called *The Speech*.

For a speech to be anything like "great," however, the speaker should at least mean what he says. As soon became clear, Obama did not. A few weeks afterward, Wright went public once again. Holding forth at the National Press Club, he pulled out a few paranoid goodies from his oldies collection, including the one that the United States invented the HIV virus to kill off the black population and another that U.S. terrorism inspired September 11. Wright might have gotten away with these claims—the Associated Press called them "colorful"—had he not also challenged Obama's authenticity.

"If Senator Obama did not say what he said, he would never get elected," Wright said of the Philadelphia speech. "Politicians say what they say and do what they do based on electability, based on sound bites, based on polls." In revenge mode, Wright had knowingly stuck his knife under the heel plate of Obama's moderate façade and twisted.

Long before *The Speech* reached the bookstores, Obama had already invalidated its central premise. In other words, Wright *could* be disowned and unceremoniously was. The announcement of the same was swift and public. Obama called Wright's latest remarks so inexcusably "divisive and destructive" that he had to denounce the man this time—not just his comments—and resign from his church.

Not since Molotov-Ribbentrop have so many progressives casually ignored so major a flip-flop. Most of the media bought in as well. Charles Krauthammer, a conservative columnist for the *Washington Post*, was one of the few to see Obama's series of equivalences for "the cheap rhetorical tricks they always were." Added Krauthammer, "Obama has now decided that the man he simply could not banish because he had become part of Obama himself is, *mirabile dictu*, surgically excised."

Obama had been listening to Wright's comments for the last twenty years. What really bugged Obama about the good reverend's press club bitch-slap was Wright's failure to accommodate himself to "The Plan." Obama just about said as much. "And what I think particularly angered me," Obama fumed at an impromptu press briefing, "was his suggestion somehow that my previous denunciation of his remarks were [*sic*] somehow political posturing." On his own, Obama still had problems with noun-verb agreement, let alone the truth.

Wright's street-sharpened senses told him who inevitably had to be behind "The Plan," a revelation he shared with a reporter from the *Daily-Press* of Newport News, Virginia, in June 2009. "Them Jews ain't going to let [Obama] talk to me," Wright confided. Obama was duly shocked, as he had never once heard Wright "talk about any ethnic group in derogatory terms"—or so he had assured us in Philadelphia.

Obama treated Bill Ayers very nearly as shabbily as he had the Reverend Wright. After denouncing Ayers's past in the ABC debate, Obama responded to pressure from McCain and Palin by recalibrating his denunciation. "When Ayers committed crimes in the sixties, Obama was eight years old," said one radio ad. "Obama condemned those despicable acts. Ayers has had no role in Obama's campaign, and will have no role in his administration." What was once "detestable" had been upgraded to "despicable." Obama, however, remained permanently eight years old even though he was of voting age when Ayers walked away—"Guilty as hell. Free as a bird"—from his increasingly irrelevant *1970s* career as underground warrior.

One did not have to be a weatherman to sense that Ayers would quickly blow cold on the Obama presidency. A lifelong radical, he had little patience with the progressives' "long march"—a phrase Obama actually used in the Philadelphia speech—even if he and they were marching in the same direction. Still, the speed and the severity of Ayers's criticism, let alone the medium for doing so, shocked even veteran Ayers watchers.

In late February 2009, less than five weeks into the Obama era, Ayers blasted Obama's decision to send additional troops to Afghanistan. "We've seen this happen before," Ayers told Sean Hannity's guest host Alan Colmes on *Hannity*, a show held in deep contempt even among the shallow left. "We've seen a hopeful presidency, Lyndon Johnson's presidency, burn up in the furnace of war."

Ayers referred to Obama's Afghanistan decision as a "colossal mistake." He uses the word *colossal* when something truly irks him. Consider the following unsubtle passage from *Fugitive Days:* "The Pentagon was ground zero for war and conquest, organizing headquarters of a gang of murdering thieves, a colossal stain on the planet, a hated symbol everywhere around the world."

Ayers has so much emotional equity invested in hating America that nothing Obama could have done short of letting Hugo Chávez set defense policy and Perez Hilton design new army uniforms would have appeased him. Ayers's pique would not matter much were he really just a "guy who lives in my neighborhood" long since outgrown. As Obama understands, Ayers is much more than that. He is the potential extortionist in the neighborhood. Ayers served Obama a reminder of the same shortly after Christopher Andersen's book *Barack and Michelle: Portrait of an American Marriage* was published in September 2009.

To repeat, it was not as if Andersen confirmed Ayers's role in *Dreams* in passing. He spends six pages on this revelation. It is not as if Andersen had a bone to pick with the president. He seems to love the guy. It is not as if Andersen has a reputation for reckless journalism. Just the opposite. He is a pro with a proven track record. Bizarrely, his book proved a bigger story in Zaire, whose major media covered it fairly, than in New York or Washington.

Thanks to the work of intrepid journalist Hanspeter Born, one other country where the story got traction was Switzerland. Fluent in English, Born serves as chief foreign correspondent for the influential Zurich-based weekly *Die Weltwoche* and has covered the last eight American presidential elections. In the 2008 cycle he was one of Obama's early admirers, and even before the Iowa voters caucused in early January, Born was predicting an Obama victory in November. "Watching him in Iowa," he tells me, "I was very impressed and thought he was a new kind of politician who could put an end to the deep cultural divisions in America."

That Obama wrote his own books impressed Born all the more. When, however, journalists contacted people who had known the young Obama, and their memories contradicted his, Born became suspicious. Having actually investigated the Swiftboaters' accusations and found them to be true, he wondered whether Obama might just be another dissembler like John Kerry. The more he saw of Obama the more disillusioned Born became. "I came to think of him as narcissistic, intellectually arrogant, thin-skinned and in the thrall of post-1960s left wing illusions," he says.

Born has been interested in questions of attribution ever since he did his Ph.D. dissertation on Shakespeare's involvement in an anonymous Elizabethan play. An informed observer, he became convinced that Ayers was "the main author of the book" and weighed in with a four-thousand-word article on the same for *Weltwoche*. What amazed him about the American media—"Remnick is typical"—was that not one journalist other than Andersen bothered to investigate an attribution issue of this magnitude. "Why don't people want to know the truth?" asks Born. "Surely, it does not take rocket science to establish the facts."

Closer to home, truth still mattered to bloggers like Chicagoan Anne Leary, a Harvard grad and the chief cook and bottle washer at BackyardConservative.com. In early October 2009, Leary was heading back to the Midwest when she ran into Ayers in the Starbucks at Reagan National Airport. (What is it with Obama collaborators and Starbucks?) To prove the encounter, Leary shot a picture of Ayers on her BlackBerry and posted it. "An instant blight," she would write. "Scruffy, thinning beard, dippy earring, and the wire rims."

"What are you doing in D.C., Mr. Ayers?" she asked respectfully. Ayers told her he was giving a lecture in Arlington to a Renaissance group on education. The theme, by the way, was "A Time for Reflection, Celebration and Rebirth." Writes Leary, "How touching. At best, useless, at worst, so wrong." U.S. secretary of education Arne Duncan was also in attendance. Trying to assess her sympathies, Ayers continued, "You shouldn't believe everything you hear about me. You know nothing about me."

"I know plenty," said the admirably brazen Leary. "I'm from Chicago, a conservative blogger, and I'll post this." At this point, the encounter turned weird. Out of the blue, Ayers said to Leary, "I wrote *Dreams From My Father*."

"Oh," Leary replied. "So you admit it."

"Michelle asked me to," he answered with a straight face. "Stop pulling my leg," said Leary, then thinking to herself, "What a horrible thought," the leg pulling, that is.

"I really wrote it," he insisted.

"I believe you probably heavily edited it," Leary countered, but when he continued to insist that he wrote it, she said, "Why would I believe you? You're a liar." At this point, Ayers turned and walked off, suggesting as he did that she prove he wrote *Dreams* so he could split the proceeds with the Obamas.

That same weekend Ayers had played a similar game with reporter Will Englund from the *National Journal*. "Here's what I'm going to say," said the mischievous Ayers when asked about the authorship issue. "This is my quote. Be sure to write it down: 'Yes, I wrote *Dreams From My Father*. I ghostwrote the whole thing. I met with the president three or four times, and then I wrote the entire book. And now I would like the royalties.'"

"Ayers is messing with conservatives," wrote faux conservative David Weigel, then writing for the *Washington Independent* before his self-immolation at the *Washington Post*. This was the standard bromide with which the media eased their initially uneasy stomachs. But before her encounter with Ayers, Leary, like most conservatives, had paid little attention to the authorship of *Dreams*. Even after Andersen's book was published, most respectable conservatives shied away from the issue, and those like myself who pursued it weren't worth messing with.

The fact that Ayers had volunteered all this information surprised Leary. There was obviously irony in the air, but I suspect a double level of irony on Ayers's part: he says what is *true* as a way of throwing doubt on what is, in fact, true. I talked to Leary, however, and she was not at all convinced that Ayers was being ironic at all. If his intended audience was the White House, he may not have been.

NOBEL LAUREATE

The very same week that Ayers was protesting Obama's "insane" warmongering in Chicago, Obama was giving his Nobel Peace Prize acceptance speech in Oslo. Given that Obama had been in office less than two weeks when the nominations closed, the Nobel selectors would seem to have been inspired more by Obama's oratory on the stump than by any actions taken in those first ten days on the job.

"Clearly, the award was an aspirational award," said Bill Ayers knowingly. "They were making a comment on the war-like presidency of George Bush, wishing Obama would repudiate that and declare himself a peace president."

This was not the first time the Nobel Committee had chosen its winner to embarrass the United States. Nor was Obama the Peace Prize's most absurd recipient. Hell, Al Gore had won just two years earlier for his global warming gimcrackery, but even Gore was not the most fraudulent of winners. That honor falls to one Rigoberta Menchú.

When the Nobel Peace Prize committee met to award its 1992 prize, the choices were many and good. With the collapse of the Soviet Union in 1991 and the fall of the Berlin Wall two years before, committee members might have chosen any of the architects of that empire's demise—Ronald Reagan, for instance, or Margaret Thatcher or Pope John Paul II or Solidarity or the Soviet dissidents. But no, this being 1992, the five-hundredth anniversary of Columbus's "discovery" of the Americas, the committee took the opportunity to rub its thumb in America's eye by awarding the prize to the aforementioned Menchú, a Guatemalan *indigena*.

Her autobiography, *I, Rigoberta Menchú: An Indian Woman in Guatemala*, earned her the prize. It had sold well, and to many of the same easily deceived people who would soon buy *Dreams*. The *Chronicle of Higher Education* accurately described the book "as a cornerstone of the multicultural canon."

That cornerstone was about to crumble. A few years before the award was given, a young Stanford scholar named David Stoll was researching the anthropology of civil war for his Ph.D. dissertation. He had read Menchú's book and was sympathetic with her people and her cause. It was hard not to be. Menchú describes in heartbreaking detail how the right-wing ruling class stole the land of her father and other native peoples and used the army to suppress dissent in some seriously nasty ways.

In the book's most dramatic scene, the army hauls more than a score of dissidents to the square of the little Maya town of Chajul, among them Rigoberta's teenage brother. The soldiers then did what right-wingers are wont to do when feeling their repressive oats: they poured gasoline on the prisoners, set them ablaze one by one, and celebrated while the dissidents toasted. One more thing—they forced the family members to watch. "I just wanted to do something," remembers Rigoberta, "even kill a soldier."

After much heroic resistance, Rigoberta fled the country. In 1982, while in Paris, she told her story to feminist Elisabeth Burgos-Debray. Elisabeth borrowed the "Debray" monicker from her ex-husband, the famed international gadabout and Che Guevara pal Régis Debray, the Bill Ayers of France. Do we see something of a pattern here?

In 1989, Stoll found himself in the infamous town of Chajul. When he asked an elderly gent about the public burning, the man answered, "The army burned prisoners alive? Not here." When Stoll expressed disbelief, the man insisted that the burning of a whole parcel of people in the town square is something he would likely have remembered. No one else in town could recall the incident either. This was the first of many major discrepancies that Stoll discovered.

Stoll knew he had a problem on his hands. The postmodern, postcolonial era was in full flower. A white male gringo judged an *indigena*'s "narrative" at his own risk. For the very act of judging, any number of academics stood ready to roast him for cultural imperialism, if not racism. Says Stoll, "We have an unfortunate tendency to idolize native voices that serve our own political and moral needs, as opposed to others that do not." He was not talking about *Dreams*, but he might as well have been.

By creating what Stoll calls "mythologies of purity," academics could blind themselves to reality often at the expense of the people they were mythologizing. Stoll was convinced that this willful blindness was hurting Guatemala, and in 1993 he published a book to deconstruct the narrative that Rigoberta and Elisabeth had constructed. Other than Rigoberta's age, just about every other contention in Menchú's book proved false, often spectacularly so.

I, Rigoberta Menchú, Stoll argues, "protected revolutionary sympathizers from the knowledge that the revolutionary movement was a bloody failure." In fact, Stoll believes that the book firmed up international support for the insurgency and helped keep the revolution alive after it had lost most of its internal political support.

Appealing as it was to feminists, Marxists, multiculturalists, and supporters of indigenous rights—in other words, just about everybody in academia—*I, Rigoberta Menchú* had become nearly as sacred a text as *Dreams*. "Rigoberta's story of oppression is analogous to a preacher reminding listeners that they are sinners," observes Stoll. "Then her story of joining the left and learning that not all outsiders are evil makes it possible for the audience to be on her side, providing a sense of absolution." In very similar words, one could describe the salutary effect of *Dreams* on the liberal reader.

Stoll's book and subsequent articles whipped up a firestorm in the academic community. That community's bible, the *Chronicle of Higher Education*, interviewed numerous academics across the country and came to a bizarrely predictable conclusion about most professors who taught the book: "They say it doesn't matter if the facts in the book are wrong, because they believe Ms. Menchu's story speaks to a greater truth about the oppression of poor people in Central America."

Happily for Rigoberta and later for Obama, the Nobel Prize committee cared more about the *pravda* than the *istina*. In progressive circles, big truth trumps little facts when the outcome matters. Rigoberta got to keep her award. "All autobiographies embellish to a greater or lesser extent," Geir Lundestad, director of the Norwegian Nobel Institute, told the *New York Times*. In Oslo, the president was among friends.

Unfortunately, the Norwegians were subverting Team Obama's "Color Purple" strategy with a gesture so leftist and phony that even Obama-friendly comedians felt compelled to mock it. Said Bill Maher with some accuracy, "The Nobel committee said he won for creating a new climate for international politics, which sounds so much nicer than 'In your face, George Bush, you cowboy asshole.' "

Jibed Erick Erickson, "Obama is becoming Jimmy Carter faster than Jimmy Carter became Jimmy Carter." Erickson's joke reflected a certain reality. Obama had not been in office three months when he told an eager audience in Strasbourg, France, that America has "shown arrogance and been dismissive, even derisive" toward its allies. Said

Britain's *Telegraph* approvingly, "His speech in Strasbourg went further than any United States president in history in criticising his own country's actions while standing on foreign soil." It was with speeches like these that Obama had won over the Nobel Committee.

It was for speeches like those that Jimmy Carter had won the Nobel Peace Prize in 2002. Axelrod and company did not like the comparison. As they knew well, in a center-right America the Carter brand did not have sufficient shelf appeal to earn a second term. So Obama went to Oslo and delivered a speech that George Bush's speechwriters could have written. "The United States of America has helped underwrite global security for more than six decades with the blood of our citizens and the strength of our arms," he trumpeted. The Norwegians likely did not understand English well enough to know that they too had become part of "The Plan."

GOING ROGUE

In the fall of 2009, Sarah Palin's memoir, *Going Rogue*, hit the bookstores and bestseller lists simultaneously. Unlike Barack Obama, who did not even have an acknowledgments section in *Dreams*, Palin gave credit where it was due. Specifically, she thanked writer Lynn Vincent for "her indispensable help in getting the words on paper." And yet the story is told honestly and sincerely in Palin's voice. There is no artifice, no postmodern mumbo jumbo, and not a sentence in the book Palin could not have written herself. My personal favorite: "I love meat." I suspect that, unaided, journalism major and former reporter Palin is the better writer than Obama.

Hardball host Chris Matthews thought otherwise. He had shown the silly depths of this animus when he had earlier learned of Palin's book deal. "Sarah Palin—now don't laugh—is writing a book," sniffed Matthews. "Not just reading a book, writing a book." Unspoken, of course, was the assumption that Obama wrote his own books. "Actually in the words of the publisher she's 'collaborating' on a book,"

Matthews continued. "What an embarrassment! It's one of these 'I told you' books that jocks do."

If the media were no more likely to fact-check *Dreams* or *Audacity of Hope* than they were the Koran, they swarmed all over *Going Rogue*. The Associated Press alone dispatched eleven reporters to review Palin's book. Others did not need to fact-check or even read the book. They knew all they needed to know in advance.

In the week of *Going Rogue*'s release, the *New York Times* house conservative David Brooks would call Palin "a joke." Dick Cavett, the Norma Desmond of TV talk, would dismiss her as a "know-nothing." Ex-con Dem fund-raiser Martha Stewart would brand Palin "a dangerous person." And thousands of lesser liberal lights would deride her as "stupid," an "idiot," or a "moron" (8.5 million Google hits for "Palin moron").

How the literary/media establishment responded to the respective memoirs of these two political figures revealed far less about the authenticity, honesty, and quality of the tales the authors tell than it did about the collective mind-set of that establishment.

From a classical perspective, Palin's is the more compelling narrative. The obstacles that she must overcome to fulfill her destiny are many, varied, and real. Raised in the frozen outback by a schoolteacher father and a school secretary mom, Palin accomplishes nothing without a good deal of work, often under difficult physical circumstances.

Palin takes a semester or two off to pay for college. She works at a diner over the summer. She enters the Miss Alaska contest to help pay tuition and is awarded second runner-up and "Miss Congeniality." She interns in other summers to become a sports reporter. After college, Palin joins fiancé Todd on his Bristol Bay salmon boat. During slow salmon runs, she works "messy, obscure seafood jobs" until she can find a job as a sports reporter, and even then she keeps returning to Bristol Bay when the salmon are in season.

Back in Hawaii, Obama spends grades five through twelve at Hawaii's poshest prep school. Like Palin, he too plays basketball, but while she is leading her school to the state championship, he is a second-stringer on a team whose wins and losses go unremarked, even though it too wins a state championship. The only scores Obama shares, in fact, are the imagined racial ones that need to be settled.

Obama admits to "marginal report cards" in prep school, but the diversity bean-counters keep his dreams alive. After two druggy, uninspired years at Occidental College, Obama transfers to the Ivy League, Columbia to be precise, for some drug-free mediocrity. In *Dreams*, Obama dedicates one half of a sentence to a summer job on a construction site. Otherwise he is silent on work and how his tuition might have been paid. As to his grades and SAT scores, it would be easier to pry North Korea's nuclear secrets out of Kim Jong Il.

After several years as a low-paid community organizer in Chicago, Obama decides to return to law school. Despite a lack of resources and a lackluster performance at Columbia—he does not graduate with honors—Obama heads off for Harvard. He had absorbed the diversity zeitgeist deeply enough to see success as an entitlement.

In the spring of 1989, during Obama's first year at Harvard Law, Palin's "life truly began" with the birth of her oldest son, Track. That summer, with Todd working a blue-collar job on the North Slope oil fields, Palin, her father, and their Eskimo partner work Todd's commercial fishing boat in Bristol Bay. Palin's mother meanwhile babysits the ten-week-old Track.

In 1992, while an anxious Obama dithers in an office that the University of Chicago had given him to write *Dreams*, half of his $125,000-plus advance already cashed, Palin is pulling her babies, Track and Bristol, along on a sled as she goes door to door seeking votes in her run for Wasilla City Council.

Not surprisingly, Palin's tenacity makes her enemies among those who had cashed in their Republican heritage for the perks and power of office. Her perseverance in the face of this resistance makes for compelling political drama. That she is a woman challenging the good old boys of backroom Alaska heightens the tension. Yet despite pushing the boundaries of female accomplishment throughout her career—as sports reporter, as commercial fisherman, as councilwoman, as mayor, as oil and gas commissioner, as governor, as vice presidential candidate—Palin never loses her sense of the feminine.

Having five children surely helps. So does living in an environment where manly virtues still matter. An exchange with the larger-than-life Todd helps clarify Alaskan reality. Todd is a four-time winner of the Iron Dog competition, a 2,200-mile snowmobiling marathon. One night, Sarah expresses interest in competing. Says Todd:

> "Can you get the back end of a six-hundred-pound machine unstuck by yourself with open water up to your thighs, then change out an engine at forty below in the pitch black on a frozen river and replace thrashed shocks and jury rig a suspension using tree limbs along the trail?"

When Sarah answers "Nope," Todd replies, "Then go back to sleep, Sarah." Todd lives his Eskimo heritage. He does not just dream about it, let alone exploit it.

While Palin is slugging through Alaska's political morass like a determined Iditarod musher, Obama is cruising through Illinois politics on skids greased by his Chicago cronies. The combination of his black genes and white demeanor makes the famously "articulate and bright and clean" Obama an irresistible choice to keynote the race-conscious 2004 Democratic convention. "I mean, that's a storybook, man," adds the inimitable Joe Biden.

Now if only the story Obama told had been true.

GRAMPS

Kansas City keeps a person grounded. Those inclined to take themselves too seriously here do so at their own risk because no one else will. Unlike, say, California, where the rich and famous can buy themselves boats and views and Lakers tickets and even better weather—L.A. suburb Malibu is twenty-five degrees cooler in July than L.A. suburb Riverside—the rich and (slightly) famous here can buy only bigger houses, but many of them are discreet enough not to.

Every lunch hour when the weather is tolerable, I sit out on the open portico of a small eatery and watch the world go by. Inevitably some of the world stops by: Dave, the UPS guy, who talks politics and investment strategy well enough to have his own show on CNBC; Paul, the banker, who details the havoc Washington is wreaking on his industry; Hank and Jerry, the cops, who confide in me, the son of a cop, how political correctness is killing the people it is supposed to protect; Floyd, the barber—no, just kidding. Yet a hint of Mayberry lingers in Kansas City. People here are saner, more centered, and better informed than the Alters and Remnicks of the world could begin to comprehend.

Fittingly, it was on this same portico on a lovely day in May 2010 that Don Wilkie and I applied Occam's razor to the sphinx that is Barack Obama. For those who find comfort in credentials, fifty-something Wilkie will disappoint. His are admittedly no better than Ryan Geiser's or Mr. Southwest's. He runs a small business in Michigan that bears his name and has as its motto the bluntly functional "Your 'ONE STOP' cost saving Conveyor Chain supplier." He prepared for the conveyor chain business by earning a B.A. in sociology from Bill Ayers's alma mater, the University of Michigan.

The fact is I had lost interest in credentials a long time ago. In charge of hiring copywriters at the ad agency where I worked in the 1980s, I quickly discovered that portfolios told me little about a person's talent, and résumés told me nothing at all. Unlike a law school, however, we could not afford a bad hire. So I took to testing: one hour, one marketing problem, solve it in an ad. "I don't work well under pressure," one woman told me, expecting a break. "Sorry, hon, but you're in the wrong business." A fellow shared with me in advance that he was good but slow. Said I, "In this business, Mac, if you're not fast, you're not good." Copywriting is harder than it looks. Over time, I interviewed a lot of people.

"Don is a detective at heart," Wilkie's obliging lady friend told me over lunch in Kansas City. They had come to Kansas City for no greater purpose than to meet with me and to attend a Rusty Humphies show, which they had done the night before. In addition to being a syndicated radio host, Humphries is a talented performer and satirist. Oregon-based, he just happened to be doing a gig in Kansas City. Thanks to Rich Davis, a former producer for Humphries and one of my most stalwart supporters, I had become a semiregular guest on Rusty's show. As with Mr. Southwest, this is where Wilkie first heard me—a couple of rogue asteroids hooking up in the far reaches of the "lunatic orbit."

As a way of making sense out of a given mystery, I have found 14th century philosopher William of Occam to be a useful guide. We know his approach to problem solving by the label "Occam's razor," an axiom often stated in shorthand as, "The simplest explanation is usually the best." The original Latin—"Pluralitas non est ponenda sine necessitate"—adds some nuance. This translates roughly, "One ought not posit multiple variables unnecessarily."

In implicating Ayers in the writing of *Dreams*, I do not need to force a single variable. Ayers had the talent, the motive, and the proximity. He and Obama shared a worldview. He read the same books as Obama and many more. He knew black culture as well as any outsider to the culture could, better certainly than Obama. He had worked as a community organizer. He has written authoritatively about the postmodern style that runs through *Dreams*. He knows his nautical metaphors from his days at sea. He had even visited Hawaii the year before *Dreams* was written. Other than the fact that his name is not on the book, no variable disqualifies Ayers or forces the observer to doubt his involvement.

To credit *Dreams* to Obama alone, one has to posit any number of nearly miraculous variables: he somehow found the time; he somewhere mastered nautical jargon and postmodern jabberwocky; he in some sudden, inexplicable way developed the technique and the talent to transform himself from stumbling amateur to literary superstar without any stops in between. To credit *Audacity* to Obama alone, one has to posit at least two additional variables: one is his adoption of a modified and less competent style, and the second is his ability to write such a book given the punishing schedule of a freshman senator.

Wilkie and I were applying Occam to a distinct but related mystery—Obama's origins. To this point, I had steered clear of the "birther" business. The fever swamps surrounding Obama's citizenship were swallowing reputations whole, and so I stuck to literary analysis. Still, Team Obama's squirrelly response to just about any inquiry regarding records—birth, grades, test scores, theses, parents' marriage, passport, mother's passport applications, adoption by Soetoro, status in Indonesia—raised the eyebrows of anyone who was looking.

David Mendell came to this understanding as early as 2004. While covering the Illinois Senate race for the *Chicago Tribune*, he approached the Obama camp about interviewing friends and family in Hawaii. To his surprise, he sensed an initial hesitance. Given that his was the state's largest newspaper, and it had endorsed Obama even in his ill-fated campaign for Congress, Mendell writes, "Turning down the *Tribune*'s request for family interviews would not seem a wise decision at this point in the Senate campaign." Mendell's next sentence demands attention: "However, Obama's aides must have been wary about what I would turn up."

Obama agreed to assist Mendell on the condition that an attendant, a deputy press aide named Nora Moreno Cargie, accompany him to track his reporting and "monitor the content of my interviews." The interview that seems to have made everyone most anxious was the one with Obama's maternal grandmother, Madelyn Dunham. Mendell spoke to "Toot" in the living room of her spare tenth-floor Honolulu apartment, the one in which Obama was raised. Eighty-two at the time of the interview, Dunham struck Mendell as "cautious and protective." She called the interview off after half an hour, grabbed Mendell's arm, and told him, "Be kind to my grandson."

When Toby Harnden of the British *Telegraph* visited Hawaii early in the 2008 campaign, he too ran into a wall of resistance. One of Obama's closest friends declined his request for an interview, telling Harnden, "He and others had been instructed to stop talking to the press."

Wilkie too had misgivings about the Gardol Shield around the Obama legend. In his first email to me a few months earlier, he told me he had a "different theory" as to why this was so, but he cautioned me, "My theory is really off the wall." That caution struck me as encouraging. Too many people whose theories really are off-the-wall don't know it. Wilkie pitched his idea as a literary project. "I remembered you talking about Obama's poetry," he continued. "I have read

'Pop' now maybe 20 or 30 times, and I think it is about Obama telling us that 'Pop' really is, his pop." That was all the pretext I needed to jump into the swamp.

From the beginning I had been aware of Obama's poetry. As a nineteen-year-old sophomore, Obama had two poems— "Underground" and "Pop"—published under his name in the spring 1981 edition of Occidental College's literary magazine, *Feast*. If Obama wrote any other poems, they have not emerged. Occidental student writer Kevin Batton first exhumed the poems in an article titled "Ode to Obama" in the March 2007 edition of the *Occidental Weekly*. In the first sentence of the article, the prescient Batton observes, "The remarkable details of Barack Obama's heritage and biography are coming to be some of the most important aspects of his campaign." As Batton understood, much depended on those details. If they proved less remarkable than advertised, the Obama brand would have suffered, perhaps fatally. Given the brand's illusory nature, this was one "Pop" that Team Obama had hoped would remain absentee.

Like Obama's early prose, "Underground" suggests no particular promise. Other than being goofy and easy to make fun of, however, it presented no immediate problems, either. Republishing this poem may have been the cruelest swipe an otherwise friendly media took at Obama during the campaign.

UNDERGROUND

Under water grottos, caverns
Filled with apes
That eat figs.
Stepping on the figs
That the apes
Eat, they crunch.
The apes howl, bare
Their fangs, dance,

Tumble in the
Rushing water,
Musty, wet pelts
Glistening in the blue.

"What 'Underground' certainly shows," writes Batton hopefully, "is Obama's eye for detail and ear for rhythm, which anticipate his later writing style." Another friendly critic has described the poem as a "vivid if obscurely symbolic description of a tribe of submarine primates." Although "Underground" is arguably the best poem ever written about submarine primates, most of Obama's literary acolytes have largely—and charitably—chosen not to notice it. The surprisingly mature and sophisticated poem "Pop" has drawn considerably more attention.

POP

Sitting in his seat, a seat broad and broken
In, sprinkled with ashes,
Pop switches channels, takes another
Shot of Seagrams, neat, and asks
What to do with me, a green young man
Who fails to consider the
Flim and flam of the world, since
Things have been easy for me;
I stare hard at his face, a stare
That deflects off his brow;
I'm sure he's unaware of his
Dark, watery eyes, that
Glance in different directions,
And his slow, unwelcome twitches,
Fail to pass.
I listen, nod,

Listen, open, till I cling to his pale,

Beige T-shirt, yelling,

Yelling in his ears, that hang

With heavy lobes, but he's still telling

His joke, so I ask why

He's so unhappy, to which he replies . . .

But I don't care anymore, cause

He took too damn long, and from

Under my seat, I pull out the

Mirror I've been saving; I'm laughing,

Laughing loud, the blood rushing from his face

To mine, as he grows small,

A spot in my brain, something

That may be squeezed out, like a

Watermelon seed between

Two fingers.

Pop takes another shot, neat,

Points out the same amber

Stain on his shorts that I've got on mine, and

Makes me smell his smell, coming

From me; he switches channels, recites an old poem

He wrote before his mother died,

Stands, shouts, and asks

For a hug, as I shink [sic] my

Arms barely reaching around

His thick, oily neck, and his broad back; 'cause

I see my face, framed within

Pop's black-framed glasses

And know he's laughing too.

Batton describes this poem as "an autobiographical evocation of a moment" between a young Obama and "his maternal grandfather, with whom Barack lived for many years of his youth." That grandfather would be Stanley Armour Dunham. Born in Wichita in 1918, Dunham had a rough go of it as a kid. His mother committed suicide when he was eight and his father abandoned the family soon afterward. Sent to live with his grandparents in nearby El Dorado, Dunham rebelled, punched out his principal, skipped town, rode the rails, then returned home and settled down to marry high school senior Madelyn Payne in 1940. From the outset, Madelyn was the proper member of the family, the rooted one, and, ultimately, its primary breadwinner.

In the month following Pearl Harbor, Dunham enlisted in the army. Before heading overseas, he shared a moment or two with Madelyn. Their daughter, the cruelly named Stanley Ann Dunham (henceforth "Ann"), was born as a result in November 1942. (This was the same year, as it happens, that mother figure Bernardine Dohrn was born in Wisconsin.) For no reason anyone quite knows, the little family moved to the Seattle area in 1955 and remained there until their abrupt departure for Hawaii in the summer of 1960, immediately after Ann had completed her senior year of high school.

As the *Seattle Times* reported in 2008, Ann was something of a teen beatnik. At her high school, she felt most at home in "anarchy alley," a wing of Mercer Island High where the school's most progressive teachers held forth. She attended a Unitarian church affectionately known as "the little Red church on the hill" and hung out in Seattle's coffee shops talking jazz, foreign films, and liberal politics. By all accounts, Ann did not want to leave for Hawaii.

Obama romanticizes the move in *Dreams*. As he tells it, the manager of the furniture company where "Gramps" worked as a salesman informed him about a new store opening in Hawaii. Inspired by the "limitless" business prospects there, the restless Dunham proceeded to "rush home that same day and talk my grandmother into selling their house and packing up yet again, to embark on the final leg of their journey, west, toward the setting sun."

Dunham never did achieve much in Hawaii. At some point he switched from selling furniture to selling insurance and relied increasingly on Madelyn to keep the family afloat. Young Barry moved into their modest, two-bedroom apartment when he was ten and remained there—save for a few years nearby with his mother and sister—until leaving for college.

In his original article, Batton considers Dunham "a natural choice for the subject of a poem." Batton cites the line from *Dreams* in which Obama writes that his grandfather "had come to consider himself as something of a free thinker—a bohemian, even. He wrote poetry on occasion, listened to jazz." Virtually all reviewers of consequence seem to have accepted Batton's analysis. Rebecca Mead, for instance, writing in the *New Yorker*, unhesitatingly describes the poem as a "loving if slightly jaded portrait of Obama's maternal grandfather." Remnick makes the same point. " 'Pop,' " he says as though a given, "clearly reflects Obama's relationship with his grandfather Stanley Dunham." I could find no mainstream publication that even suggests otherwise.

This interpretation, if a bit lazy, is not unreasonable. "I can still picture Gramps leaning back in his old stuffed chair after dinner," writes Obama in *Dreams*, "sipping whiskey and cleaning his teeth with the cellophane from his cigarette pack." The orthodox read of "Pop," however, leaves a basic question unanswered. It caught Wilkie's eye, and it should have caught everyone's: if the poem really is about Stanley Dunham, why didn't Obama simply call it "Gramps"? If I were to write about the man I knew as "Gramps," I might not necessarily call the poem "Gramps," but I surely would not call it "Pop." That latter title, after all, has obvious implications.

Those implications find support in some of the poem's more provocative lines, particularly the references to Obama looking and smelling like the old man. Although I confess to having little patience with poems that require more work than a sudoku grid, especially ones that don't rhyme, the boy in the poem does seem to be confronting the older man with his paternity, especially given that he calls him "Pop." Wilkie's original question to me was this: is it possible that Stanley Dunham was actually Obama's father?

Wilkie was not implying incest, but rather that the loose-living Dunham hooked up with a black woman somewhere, and that Dunham accepted responsibility for the offspring. A few bits of evidence argue for this. One is the poem in question. The second is the fact that Stanley happily took the boy in and treated him like a son. A third, although I would count it as pure gaffe, is Obama's claim "My father served in World War II." The fourth is the fact that Obama strongly resembles the young Stanley Dunham. The likeness is powerful and undeniable. "You know," Stanley's brother Ralph has said of Obama, "he looks exactly like Stanley. He looks exactly like my brother, only he's dark."

Occam reminds his followers that when challenging accepted wisdom, they pose an alternative with fewer unnecessary variables and, ideally, no loose ends. The case for Gramps as father, however, collapses when assessing Ann's behavior. If there is a logic to Barack Sr. serving as proxy father, there is none for Ann's accepting the full burden of parenthood especially, as shall be seen, in the first year of young Barry's life.

The case is further weakened by the line in the poem "he switches channels, recites an old poem / He wrote before his mother died." Although Obama credits Gramps with a little poetic dabbling, he was more of a dirty limerick kind of guy than a real poet. More to the point, Dunham's mother died when he was eight years old. Obama knows this. He says so in *Dreams*. Dunham would not have read a poem he wrote "before his mother died." Besides, it is not unusual for a male to look more like his grandfather than his father.

In sum, Gramps did not sire Obama. Nor did Obama write this poem about Gramps. That so many critics have assumed he did testifies to the shallowness of their enterprise. To his credit, Wilkie accepted this verdict and kept on working his way through the enigma that is Barack Obama.

BARACK SR.

In assessing the origins of "Pop," I finally came to see what others had seen before me: namely that there were holes in the standard campaign story wide enough to drive a truck through—unless, of course, you were Barack Sr., who had a fatal weakness for driving not through things but into them.

The day after Obama was elected president, the *Guardian* summarized his "incredible" story. This was what the campaign disseminated and what is still widely believed.

He was a son of the Luo tribe who, when not in school, had herded his father's goats; she was the daughter of white Protestant prairie folk from the American heartland. And yet they fell in love. They married and in 1961 they had a child, who would also be called Barack Hussein Obama. The marriage did not last. Obama Sr took up a scholarship in Harvard—alone—and eventually went back to Africa.

Essential to the story are the notions of love and marriage. "My parents shared not only an improbable love," said Obama famously in his 2004 convention keynote, "they shared an abiding faith in the possibilities of this nation." If the "love" is suspect, so then is the "faith" in America. So too is the equally improbable ascent of Barack Obama.

In *Dreams*, Ann Dunham tells the now college-age Obama the story of her love for his father and their eventual split; her chin trembles as she speaks. Yes, Barack Sr. had previously bonded with a woman in Kenya, but they had separated and since this had been a mere "village wedding" there was no legal document showing divorce. He had wanted to take Ann and Barry back to Kenya after finishing his studies, but grandfather Hussein was sending threatening letters saying he did not want "Obama blood sullied by a white woman," and Toot had become hysterical worrying that Mau-Maus would chop off Ann's head.

Despite the familial resistance, the marriage "might have worked out." When, however, Harvard offered Barack Sr. a fellowship to finish his Ph.D., he anguished his way to acceptance. "How can I refuse the best education?" he lamented. "It wasn't your father's fault that he left, you know," Ann tells Obama. "I divorced him."

In September 2009, President Obama was poised to address the nation's schoolchildren writ large, an innovation that struck many on the right as a wee bit Big Brotherly. Team Obama responded to the protest by feinting back to the center, if not the right, in the actual speech. Afterward, the media scolded the right for its misplaced anxiety and persisted in seeing Obama as a centrist and not as a crafty fake-out artist.

In the talk, Obama asked America's students to take personal responsibility. That was all well enough. Missed in the media hubbub, however, was his take on why this could be difficult for some students. "I get it," he told the kiddies. "I know what that's like. My father left my family when I was two years old, and I was raised by a single mother." In *Dreams*, Obama made the same claim. "He had left

Hawaii back in 1963," he wrote of Barack Sr., "when I was only two years old." When he wrote this in *Dreams*, he probably knew better. By 2009, he certainly knew better, but so invested was he in the story, and so useful had it been in his rise, that he continued to dissemble, even before millions of schoolchildren.

In his research, Don Wilkie unearthed a letter written by Barack Sr. to his Kenyan mentor, Tom Mboya, on the 29th of May, 1962. In the letter, he told Mboya that he was leaving "this June" for Harvard. This would have been two months shy of young Barry's *first* birthday. It gets worse. "You know my wife is in Nairobi there," he continues, "and I would really appreciate any help you may give her." This was no "village wedding." He had met Kezia in Nairobi and married her in that capital city. The couple had two children by 1962. Not surprisingly, Barack Sr. does not mention Ann or Barry in the letter.

Barack Sr.'s departure for Harvard and a grand tour of mainland universities en route was actually reported by the *Honolulu Advertiser* on June 22, 1962. *Washington Post* ace reporter David Maraniss observes, "The story did not mention that he had a wife and an infant son." Obama himself noticed this oversight years later when he discovered the article "folded away among my birth certificate and old vaccination forms." He writes in *Dreams*, "No mention is made of my mother or me, and I'm left to wonder whether the omission was intentional on my father's part, in anticipation of his long departure."

This one passage raises a few other questions. If Obama had access to his own birth certificate, why did he not simply produce it when it became a subject of controversy? If Obama had read the article in question, would he not have seen the date and realized that his putative father had left Hawaii before his first birthday? And finally, if the grandparents saved the article about this seemingly deadbeat dad, might they have had a reason to be more favorably disposed to Barack Sr. than circumstances would suggest?

Frank Marshall Davis makes a throwaway observation in his memoir, *Livin' the Blues*, that might have some bearing on Barack Sr.'s motivation to abscond. Davis observes that in Hawaii's relaxed racial environment African exchange students "wreaked havoc among co-eds at the university." Then he specifically cites a "student from Kenya" who quit the islands "leaving two pregnant blondes." Writing about ten years after Barack Sr.'s departure, Davis may or may not be alluding to Obama, but he has no reason to exaggerate the temptations.

The address on the letter to Mboya is 1482 Alencastre Street in Honolulu. This is a new address in Obama lore. The August 1961 birth announcement had placed the happy young couple, "Mr. and Mrs. Barack Obama," at 6085 Kalaniana'ole Highway, where they presumably shared their improbable love before Harvard drew Barack Sr. away. In fact, it is doubtful that Ann and Barack Sr. ever lived together.

An innocent post-election article in the *Honolulu Advertiser* about Obama's boyhood homes notes that at the time of Obama's birth, Barack Sr. "also had a residence at 625 11th Avenue in Kaimuki." Like all of his other known residences, this one was within walking distance of the campus. The Kalaniana'ole address is eight miles away. It was the home at the time of Stanley and Madelyn.

Baby Obama did not stay there long in any case. As my *WND* colleague Jerome Corsi reported in August 2009, a month before Obama's speech to the schoolkids, "Stanley Ann Dunham Obama" enrolled for two night classes at the University of Washington at Seattle that began on August 19, 1961—Anthropology 100, "Introduction to the Study of Man," and Political Science 201, "Modern Government." This was just fifteen days after the listed date of Obama's birth. She would attend class at the university through the winter and spring semesters.

Corsi was confirming the earlier research of conservative activist Michael Patrick Leahy, who self-published a book, *What Does Barack Obama Believe?*, in the summer of 2008. From the remove of, say, the *Washington Post* offices or those of the *New Yorker*, it would have been easy to dismiss Leahy, but he was doing the legwork the media were not doing. He interviewed Ann Dunham's high school friends and fixed her in Washington long before anyone else had. If credentials matter, Leahy has a B.A. from Harvard and an MBA from Stanford. He writes well and researches carefully. Corsi, for that matter, has a Harvard Ph.D. as well.

The apolitical Washington state historical blog HistoryLink now confirms Ann's presence in August 1961, identifies her Capitol Hill apartment in Seattle, names the courses she took, and documents an extended stay by Ann and little Obama into the summer of 1962. The 1961–62 Polk Directory confirms an "Obama Anna Mrs studt" at this Thirteenth Avenue address.

Somehow, this information escaped the four book-length biographies I consulted (including one by the *New York Times*), several long-form magazine and newspaper bios including Maraniss's comprehensive August 2008 article, the official campaign biography, and Obama himself in *Dreams*. Not one of these accounts places Ann and/or Obama anywhere other than Hawaii during Obama's first two years. This is not an incidental detail. Their exile to Washington means no less than that the famed multicultural marriage, the rock on which Obama built his political career, was so much Silly Putty, as malleable as the occasion demanded.

Remnick was the first of the orthodox scribes to break the silence with the spring 2010 publication of *The Bridge*. He mentions the Washington exile casually as if to suggest that it was common knowledge. He buffers the news further by claiming that Ann took "extension courses" in the fall and implies that she did not arrive until the winter. As Corsi reported, however, "The university confirmed Dunham's classes starting in the fall of 1961 were night classes." For added cover, Remnick quotes at length Ann's high school friend Susan Blake Botkin to the effect that "it was sad to me when her marriage disintegrated."

"After a year," writes Remnick imprecisely of Ann's comings and goings, "she decided to return to Honolulu, move in with her parents, and go to the University of Hawaii." Given that Barack Sr. had left

Hawaii in June 1962, this timeline suggests that he may never have seen little Barry as a baby. Remnick claims otherwise. As he tells it, in the fall of 1962 Ann and Barry went to visit Barack Sr. at Harvard, "but the trip was a failure, and she returned to Hawaii."

Again Remnick attempts to shore up this crumbling mythology, but the facts pound up against it. In his *Washington Post* piece, Maraniss calls the Harvard trip "an unresolved part of the story." The only evidence for Ann's trip to Harvard is the testimony of Botkin. "She was on her way from her mother's house to Boston to be with her husband," Botkin reportedly tells Maraniss. "[She said] he had transferred to grad school and she was going to join him."

Earlier interviews with Botkin, one of which has been posted on the Internet, yield a much clearer picture. In these, Ann had come to visit "briefly" with Barry at Botkin's family home. She placed the time as "a late August afternoon . . . when Barry was just a few weeks old." In the interview, she did not give the impression of being deceptive. As she told the *Seattle Times* in April 2008, Ann was excited about her husband's plans to return not to Harvard but to Kenya.

Botkin said the same to Leahy, who interviewed her early in the summer of 2008. Here too Botkin adds a clarifying detail: "She left [Hawaii] just as soon as she had clearance from her doctor to travel with her new baby." Maraniss failed to make the same connection and puts the visit a year later. As Botkin acknowledged in several interviews, she never saw her friend again. This visit at Botkin's mother's house had to be in 1961, a year before Barack Sr. left for Harvard.

A week or two after the Botkin visit, Ann stopped by to see another high school friend, Maxine Box. Box relates essentially the same story Botkin had. "Ann was only a year out of high school and was already married with a child," she tells Leahy. The baby was brand-new. "She was on her way to join her husband," she adds, "but I don't know where." Box never saw Ann again, either.

Despite the fact that he was writing a lengthy biographical piece on the next president three months before the election, and at the

Washington Post no less, Maraniss made a hash of it. "But as Botkin and others later remembered it," he writes, "something happened in Cambridge, and Stanley Ann returned to Seattle. They saw her a few more times, and they thought she even tried to enroll in classes at the University of Washington, before she packed up and returned to Hawaii."

Here virtually every fact is wrong. Her friends saw Ann in 1961 a year before Barack Sr. went to Harvard. They saw her only once, and she *did* enroll at the University of Washington. Maraniss seems to have interpreted their comments to fit his preconceptions, and Remnick built upon the mistakes of Maraniss and others.

Maraniss, however, is a solid reporter. In his defense, it is possible that Botkin and Box misled him. There is ample evidence that the Obama camp was attempting, with some success, to shape the testimony of Obama's friends, if not silence them outright. Don Wilkie, for one, is convinced that Obama operatives got to Botkin and Box when they realized the problems with "the story" and had them reread *Dreams* to refresh their memories. He has a good case. In *Dreams*, Ann explains the breakup to her son:

> "Then you were born and we agreed that the three of us would return to Kenya after he finished his studies. But your grandfather Hussein was still writing to your father, threatening to have his student visa revoked. By this time Toot had become hysterical—she had read about the Mau-Mau rebellion in Kenya a few years earlier, which the Western press really played up—and she was sure that I would have my head chopped off and you would be taken away."

In her interview with Remnick nearly fifty years after she last saw Ann, Botkin manages to cite the exact excuses for the breakup that Ann had offered in *Dreams*:

> "Barack Sr.'s father wrote and said, Don't bring your white wife and that half-breed child, they will not be welcome. There were Mau-Mau

uprisings, they were beheading white women and doing unspeakable things. Ann's parents were very worried when they heard that."

"It seems like there are two groups of people in Obama's past," Mr. Southwest observes wryly. "Those who decline to comment or aren't allowed to talk and those who talk freely and glowingly and usually with amazing detail even after many years."

The two friends in question fall into the latter category. Although their stories challenge the accepted chronology, they do not seriously threaten the master narrative. Yes, of course, Ann loved Barack Sr. She told us so in letters. No, she was just visiting Washington on her way to see her husband. Yes, the baby was a newborn, precisely "three weeks old" according to Botkin. Yes, it was a shame when the marriage fell apart. Wilkie may be on to something. The official story held through the election. When bloggers sensed that something was wrong, they may have gone after the wrong something, an African birth. From the Obama perspective, a Maui birth or a Seattle birth would have been almost as problematic. Either would have punctured the "improbable love" balloon.

Ann was staying with a friend of the family when she visited Botkin and Box. Where she lived those next few months is uncertain. The fact that she is listed in the 1961–62 Polk Directory for Seattle makes one wonder whether she had arrived in Washington earlier in 1961, possibly before Obama was born. She was not enrolled at the University of Hawaii that spring 1961 semester, and at that time in Hawaii one could register a live birth "at home" through a notarized mail order form. That registration would automatically trigger the birth announcement in the two relevant papers.

If Botkin and Box were being straightforward in their interviews, they may not have known whether Ann was spinning face-saving stories or whether she had herself been deluded by the stories Barack Sr. had spun. In his conversation with Botkin, Leahy had gotten the sense that Barack Sr. had not been present for the birth, and he certainly did not prevent Ann from fleeing with the baby immediately afterward. Her departure for Washington would have required preparation and parental support. The evidence suggests that if there had ever been a marriage, it had collapsed by the time of Obama's birth.

In reconstructing this story, I am reminded again why I so distrust the media, especially on the question of Obama. Leahy had broken a major story months before the election, a story that put a lie to the carefully crafted Obama mythology, and the media refused to notice. This stunning oversight raises a fundamental question: why are we to trust the narrative that the mainstream collective has contrived about the year leading up to Obama's birth?

In researching that critical year, one quickly sees that much of this narrative depends on two less-than-reliable sources: Obama himself and a chatty Hawaii Democratic congressman and now Hawaii governor, Neil Abercrombie. Of the Dunhams, only Madelyn was alive in 2004, and she did not survive the 2008 campaign.

Abercrombie knew Barack Sr. back in the day at the University of Hawaii. "[Barack Sr.] was an intellectual in every sense of the word," Abercrombie gushed to the *Washington Post* in 2007. "He was the sun, and the other planets revolved around him." Sound like a pattern developing here? A member of the House's progressive caucus, Abercrombie has been talking excitedly about the relationship for years, playing John the Baptist to Obama's Jesus.

"Little Barry, that's what we called him," Abercrombie told the *Chicago Tribune*, while "recalling his days with Obama Sr. and his future wife, Ann Dunham, at the University of Hawaii." If Obama was born on August 4, 1961, however, there could not have been many such days with the loving couple and little Barry. Ann was in Seattle two weeks later. Even before she returned in late summer or fall 1962, Barack Sr. had left for Harvard for good.

Citing Abercrombie as a source, a 2007 Hawaii TV news report claimed that Ann "became estranged from her husband, Barack Obama Sr., after his departure for Harvard." I don't know about

Hawaii, but in Missouri if you flee from your husband with baby in tow two weeks after his birth, that qualifies as "estrangement."

According to divorce papers filed in 1964, Barack Sr. and Ann married in Wailuku, Maui, on February 2, 1961. But one has to wonder whether it was a marriage in anything but name or whether there was a marriage at all. Obama himself writes in *Dreams*, "In fact, how and when the marriage occurred remains a bit murky, a bill of particulars that I've never quite had the courage to explore." The fact that one page of the divorce records is missing does not help clarify matters.

No one attended the wedding, not Abercrombie, not Ann's parents. In fact, no one in Barack Sr.'s clique seemed to know there was a relationship, let alone a wedding. Neil's brother, Hal, never saw Ann and Barack Sr. together. Another clique member, Pake Zane, who had distinct memories of Barack Sr., could not recall Ann at all. When Neil Abercrombie and Zane visited their friend in Nairobi in 1968, Barack Sr. shocked them by never once inquiring about his putative wife and six-year-old son.

The seventeen-year-old Ann had met the twenty-four-year-old Barack Sr. in Russian class at the University of Hawaii. Why they were studying Russian is a question for another day. In 1960, people like Lee Harvey Oswald studied Russian. Barack Sr. was his ideological kin. A month before he left Hawaii, he had spoken along with former Communist Party USA head Jack Hall at a "Mother's Peace Rally."

In *Dreams*, Ann provides only the sketchiest detail of their first date—he came an hour late and with friends—and nothing more. Botkin claims to have received a letter or two from Ann in which she spoke about Barack Sr., but beyond this, there is no evidence of a relationship, and the only evidence for the marriage is the divorce papers, which are real and have been posted online.

One reason people marry in a county other than their own—Maui

County, for instance—is to keep the announcement of the marriage license out of the local paper. By claiming a Maui wedding, and perhaps even attaining a Maui license, the Dunhams could have assured the baby an identity without drawing attention to the relationship.

Leahy, for one, does not believe the couple ever got married. If Obama had, in fact, been born out of wedlock, that would not have affected his eligibility for higher office, but it would have surely deglamorized him. "Barry Dunham" does not exactly tease the imagination. "It's the exotic name," argues Leahy, "that succinctly captures the unusual life narrative Obama has been publicly promoting for over thirteen years."

Whatever his contribution, Barack Sr. lent young Barry a name, an identity, and a romantic story line. Obama's mother and grandparents sustained this narrative throughout Obama's childhood. Until made permanently "not available" by the Obama campaign, "Toot," Madelyn Dunham, confirmed the story but without enthusiasm. Wrote Mendell of his interview with Madelyn, "Madelyn did appear to hold back some in our interview." Perhaps more than we know.

As related in *Dreams* and reported in any number of sources, Obama's African relatives have accepted Obama as one of their own. And yet there is even less clarity on the Kenyan side. As the story is told, Barack Sr. had children with at least four different women, two of them American, and he occasionally circled back to the first of the four, Kezia. Ruth, an American, was forced to raise Kezia's two oldest children, just as the woman Obama knows as "Granny," the family storyteller, was forced to raise Barack Sr. as her own. In another time and place, the Obamas would have had their own reality TV show.

Questions linger about the paternity of most of these offspring. In *Dreams*, Obama's contrarian aunt Sarah would tell her nephew that "the children who claim to be Obama's are not Obama's." Young Barry must have had doubts about his own perch in the family tree. On the occasion of his father's death, lawyers contacted anyone who might have claim to the estate. "Unlike my mum," Obama tells his sister Auma in *Dreams*, "Ruth has all the documents needed to prove who Mark's father was." Ruth obviously could produce a marriage license and a birth certificate for her son, Mark. Ann Dunham apparently could not. As I was beginning to see, the search for those documents was a legitimate one.

UNKNOWN BLACK MALE

O ne of the signs my camera crew recorded in the 2009 March for Life read simply and pointedly, "Obama, your mother chose life." Yes, she did. In pre-*Roe* 1961, only the depraved, the desperate, and/or the wealthy did otherwise. Ann chose not only to bear the baby, but also to keep him, a doubly brave move in 1961 in light of his interracial parentage.

In roughly the same year that Ann Dunham found herself with child, the Wisconsin niece of one of my neighbors showed up on my New Jersey block for a sojourn of several months. I was just old enough to figure out what was going on, and the girl was still young enough to feel more comfortable talking to me than to her aunt. Strange nieces showed up in a lot of neighborhoods back then. We sent a few of our own packing as well. Before the moral emancipation of the late 1960s, sufficient shame accompanied out-of-wedlock births to make relocation a likely option.

Given these understandings, serious people have questioned

whether the adventurous Ann might not have coupled with a young "negro" she had met at one of the hip Seattle coffeehouses that she frequented. Ann never dated "the crew-cut white boys," affirmed friend Susan Botkin. If a black guy had impregnated Ann, this would explain the family's abrupt departure to Hawaii, the one state in the union where a mixed-race baby could grow up almost unnoticed. It certainly explains the move to Hawaii better than the illusory rationale Obama offers in *Dreams*.

This scenario makes sense of any number of details, including Stanley Dunham's sudden eagerness to move without promotion to Hawaii; Madelyn's willingness to quit her job as an escrow officer in nearby Bellevue, Washington; Ann's angry resistance to the move; her poor performance in her limited first-semester courses at the University of Hawaii; her failure to enroll for the second semester; and, most of all, her otherwise inexplicable return to Washington in August 1961—if not earlier.

True, to make this scenario work, we have to add one major variable, but it is a plausible one. Imagine Ann coming home from class one day in Hawaii in fall 1960 in one of her all-concealing muumuus— she had written Botkin that muumuus were worn on campus—and telling her father that there was this charming, larger-than-life Kenyan in her class. The scheming Stanley asks her to invite him over for dinner.

Stanley befriends Barack Sr. and enlists him in his plot. He explains that a boy named Barack, the legitimate son of a Kenyan, could move through American life more seamlessly than a boy named, say, Johnny, the illegitimate son of an American black. It may not have been fair, but it was true. He tells Barack Sr. that he can make it worth his while. Ann understands. Madelyn is dubious about all of this—she is paying the bills—but she plays along.

As to Barack Sr., he has to contribute nothing to the proceedings but his name. No marriage announcement will appear in the Honolulu papers. Ann will leave in time for the fall semester at the University of Washington—perhaps months before—and she will not return until he leaves for graduate school. The address she provides for the birth announcement is eight miles from the university, so she will not embarrass him by hanging around campus.

In January 1961, Ann leaves for an extended stay at a home for unwed mothers in, say, Maui. Barack Sr. flies in briefly to apply for a marriage license and perhaps even to formalize the charade with a discreet ceremony. The baby is born in a Maui clinic in February. Soon afterward, Ann returns to Honolulu.

In August, ten months after she first meets Barack Sr., she or her mother fills out a mail order registry of birth, as was legal, claiming that the baby was born at home on August 4. This information automatically finds its way into a weekly release of birth announcements to the two local newspapers. The famed "certificate of live birth" that the Obama camp posted online in 2008 lists no hospital and cites Barack Sr.'s "race" as "African," all the better to reinforce the baby's distinctive identity.

This charade, if it happened as described, would help explain why Barack Sr. blithely blew off his new family when he headed for Harvard less than a year after the announced birth date. Apparently he rejected an opportunity to take both wife and child to New York and began dating as soon as he arrived at Harvard. Barack Sr.'s cooperation would also put Stanley Dunham's affection for him in perspective.

A group photo taken at the time of his departure for Harvard in 1962 shows not only Stanley's stunning resemblance to the future president, but also his inexplicable fondness for a black man who allegedly knocked up his seventeen-year-old daughter and is now abandoning her and his grandson. Of the eighteen adults in the photo, it is Stanley who stands next to the multi-leied Barack Sr. Both are smiling broadly. Neither Madelyn nor Ann is in the picture.

This photo is not an anomaly. In *Dreams*, Gramps speaks so respectfully of his prodigal son-in-law that the knowing reader has to question the credibility of the narrative. "Your dad could handle just about any situation, and that made everybody like him," says Gramps at the end of a jovial storytelling session about the absentee dad. Even the young Obama gets the sense that the tales being told to him about his father are "apocryphal." Whether or not Barack Sr. fathered the child, what seems undeniable is that the Dunhams made an elaborate effort to enshrine him in the family lore.

Some who believe Obama was born in Kenya have argued that the Kenyan exile was part of the deal and they cite any number of Kenyans who claim Obama was born there. From Occam's perspective, however, this wrinkle adds still one more major variable to an already burdened theory.

For all of its explanatory power, the unknown-black-male scenario runs aground—or at least seems to—on Susan Botkin's testimony. She remembers the baby being about three weeks old. She also recalls, as mentioned, that Ann arrived in Washington as soon as the doctor gave her clearance to travel. These comments argue for an August birth.

In my conversations with Don Wilkie, however, he wondered whether these details were too perfect, too precise. How likely is it, he asked, that someone would describe a baby as "three weeks old" more than forty-five years after the fact? Just a little suspicious, he wondered whether the Obama camp had gotten to Botkin and asked her to conform to its timeline. A more likely explanation is that by the time anyone asked Botkin about Ann, Obama was a celebrity. Botkin knew when he was reportedly born, knew roughly when Ann had visited, and did the math.

Leahy, however, had talked to both Botkin and Box early on and sensed no guile from either. Both reported that Ann seemed happy and proud. This happiness is more easily explained if Ann had returned to find her lost love than if she were fleeing a failed marriage. In either case, neither Botkin nor Box saw Ann again. They did not know she had enrolled at the University of Washington. Having worked hard to create an identity for her baby, Ann may not have wanted them to see the reality.

A third high school friend, Barbara Cannon Rusk, caught up with

Ann and little Barry in the summer of 1962. They were still in Washington a year after her arrival. "I recall her being melancholy at the time," Rusk told Leahy. "I had a sense that something wasn't right in her marriage. It was all very mysterious." Soon afterward, in all scenarios, a defeated Ann Dunham returned to Honolulu with one-year-old Barry.

Although hypothetical, the unknown-black-male explanation solves so many plot problems and leaves so few holes I can't quite bring myself to dismiss it. The same cannot be said for the "Malcolm X as father" theory. This theory got a fair amount of cyber ink, most of it playful on the right, and patronizing in the irony-free zones of the left. "So if you thought the paranoid theories about Obama couldn't get any crazier, clearly you were wrong." So wrote Alex Koppelman in *Salon* in a too-typical, too-solemn slam of a clearly mischievous piece on Malcolm X, this one in Pam Geller's blog *Atlas Shrugs*.

In truth, if Malcolm X had gone anywhere near Seattle in 1960, he would not have dallied with Ann Dunham. Malcolm may have been the least likely candidate of any race to sire Obama. From the time he entered prison until the time he married Betty Sanders twelve years later, he did not touch a woman "because of Mr. Muhammad's influence upon me." He presumed the same principled restraint from his fellow Black Muslims, especially from honcho Elijah Muhammad. When he learned otherwise and protested vigorously, Muhammad put a fatwa on his head that his goons eventually carried out.

For those who insist on a celebrity father for Obama, Seattle served up a much better candidate than Malcolm X. In 1960, a fellow named "Johnny" was making his reputation in Seattle's club scene as a left-handed guitarist with a local band known as the Rocking Kings. Two days older than Ann, this tall, thin young black man was not at all abashed about dating white women. Indeed, he was allegedly thrown out of high school for holding a white girl's hand. After Ann left for Hawaii, Johnny joined the army. He caused enough trouble to get himself quickly booted. Ann was living in Seattle at the time, but instead of returning home, Johnny decided to try his luck in Nashville. In the spirit of mischief, I have to ask whether this was the reason Ann seemed so down in the summer of 1962.

Of course, as you may have guessed, Johnny decided to use the stage name "Jimi" and changed the spelling of his last name from "Hendricks" to "Hendrix." In a further Paul-is-dead kind of twist, Obama cites as his personal marker for 1967 the fact that "Jimi Hendrix performed at Monterey." At a Labor Day festival in Milwaukee in 2010, Obama said of his critics, "They talk about me like a dog." Bloggers were quick to note that this line was lifted verbatim from Hendrix's song "Stone Free." In *Dreams*, he also names a friend in Chicago "Johnny." And, of course, Obama, like Hendrix, is left-handed. I can envision the mirthless *Huffington* headline now, "Whack job from Web's farthest lunatic orbit says Hendrix Obama's father!" The weird thing is that the imagined tale of Ann and Jimi is only slightly less credible than the tale as told of Ann and Barack Sr. Weird too is that Obama can remember the year of Monterey but not the year he met Michelle, the year his half brother died, the year he first visited Africa, or the year his parents married.

FRANK

I would guess that not one Obama voter out of one hundred could identify the late Frank Marshall Davis, and I doubt if one media person out of a thousand has read his memoir, *Livin' the Blues*. This is unfortunate on any number of levels. For one, his book captures the ebb and flow of 20th century black American life as well as any ever written. For another, no individual influenced the young Obama more than Davis did. This combination should have made him a staple of the multicultural canon and a pinup in every reporter's cubicle, but it did neither.

Like Boo Radley, Davis remains in the shadows for one reason: the media fear what the light would do to him. For all of Davis's gifts, and they are many, his lifelong flirtation with darkness makes him a little too creepy for his own display case in the Barack Obama presidential library. That darkness flavors the poem "Pop," the title character of which, as shall be seen, is clearly Davis himself. Less clear are two issues of equal import: Who wrote the poem? And how literally are we to take its title?

As mentioned, the critics who have reviewed "Pop" have failed to identify the subject of the poem and ducked the implication of its title. They prefer "Pop" to be a musing, a benign one at that, about "Gramps," Stanley Dunham. At least a few have seen in these cryptic verses an early flowering of the decency that progressives see as their birthright. Writes poet Ian McMillan in the *Guardian*, "There's a humanity in the poem, a sense of family values and shared cultural concerns that give us a hint of the Democrat to come." McMillan's review reminds me why I distrust poetry almost as much as I do the people who critique it.

Frank Marshall Davis was not dependably a Democrat. In fact, he campaigned for Republican presidential candidates Alf Landon and Wendell Willkie—no relation to Don—before veering hard to the left. By 1948, he had moved well beyond Democrat Harry Truman, whose devious Marshall Plan, Davis argues, was "aimed directly at the Soviets." In the latter half of his fifteen years in Chicago, that left turn would lead him to the barricades on any number of hot political fronts. When not protesting, he served as executive editor of the Associated Negro Press. At night he wrote poetry and haunted the city's jazz clubs. His progressive politics and his exceptional poetry had made him many friends in Chicago's white community as well as in the black.

And then, in 1948, two years after his marriage to Helen Canfield, a white socialite eighteen years his junior, Davis left his job and growing reputation behind and headed for Hawaii. In *Livin' the Blues*, he credits an article in a women's magazine for the inspiration to leave. Helen read it wistfully, shared her thoughts with Davis, and he promptly "suggested we investigate."

Writing in the era of Watergate, after the death of J. Edgar Hoover, Davis felt safe in acknowledging that his friend Paul Robeson "enthusiastically supported the idea" and that union honcho Harry

Bridges greased the skids for him in Hawaii. To understand Davis's elusive politics, one does well to understand theirs, especially Robeson's, whose political evolution mirrors Davis's own.

About Bridges, head of the International Longshoremen's and Warehousemen's Union (ILWU), there can be no doubt. A Soviet hard-liner, he hewed to the party line through the Molotov-Ribbentrop pact when it was hard and through the war when it was easy. After the war, when Stalin declared America the *glavni vrag*, the "main enemy," Bridges hung in with Team Stalin.

So did Robeson. The media-educational complex, however, has so successfully airbrushed his reputation that today public schools named "Paul Robeson" dot the landscape. If educators don't know or don't care about Robeson's background, historians are beginning to. Among them is the Greek-born British author Tim Tzouliadis. His 2008 bestseller, *The Forsaken*, should be read by every school board member anywhere who thinks "Robeson" might make a good name for a middle school.

When Robeson first visited the Soviet Union in 1934, he found a community of more than two thousand Americans, black and white, already in place. Although many of these were political activists, most were ordinary laborers and craftsmen lured during the Depression by the promise of steady work. At the time, they were the toast of the Soviet Union.

By 1937, when Robeson returned to Russia for a lengthy concert tour, Stalin had unleashed his famously paranoid "Terror" against all suspected intriguers. He was no longer killing kulaks in the middle of nowhere but Americans in the heart of Russia. Robeson pretended not to notice. His son Pauli, then ten, could see what his father refused to: the parents of his school chums were being arrested and assassinated. In his memoirs, Pauli lamented how his father had turned his back even on his closest black friends now marooned in the Soviet Union. By 1949, almost all of the Americans had been incarcerated or liquidated in the Terror along with several million Russians and other foreign nationals. That did not stop Robeson from returning to the Soviet Union that year to entertain.

By the time Stalin died in 1953, no adult with an active brain wave could have failed to understand the depths of his depravity, none but the winner of the 1952 Stalin Peace Prize, Paul Robeson. "Yes, through his deep humanity, by his wise understanding, he leaves a rich and monumental heritage," Robeson eulogized his beloved Uncle Joe. "He leaves tens of millions all over the earth bowed in heart-aching grief." Stalin had left tens of millions under the earth as well.

Robeson's involvement colors Davis's Hawaii venture, which could not have been as whimsical as Davis makes it sound. In leaving Chicago, Davis abandoned his life's great passion—jazz. He dedicates page after page of his memoir to jazz: the records he collects, the concerts he attends, the dances he frequents, the classes he teaches, the radio show he hosts, the performers he meets. In Hawaii, all of this goes by the wayside save for the records. In his memoir post-1948, he talks about jazz not at all.

Davis jokes that he "launched his invasion of Hawaii" by leaving Chicago on December 7, 1948, the seventh anniversary of Pearl Harbor. He arrived with a massive ILWU strike imminent. Within months of his arrival, the union virtually shut Hawaii down. "The 178-day strike gnawed at the island's lifelines," observed the *Honolulu Star-Bulletin* on the occasion of the strike's fiftieth anniversary, "forcing small businesses into bankruptcy, causing food shortages and in the end, making the ILWU one of the Territory's major powers." Davis cheered on the strikers through a weekly column in the progressive, ILWU-funded newspaper, the *Honolulu Record*, a post he had gotten through Bridges.

One has to wonder whether the Party made Davis an offer he could not refuse. For all of Hawaii's charms, the then forty-two-year-old walked away from a life of rising prominence as poet and editor to work as a self-employed paper wholesaler and part-time columnist. "I do not recommend any black settling in Hawaii," Davis would write years later, "unless he has special skills, a sizeable bank account, or an assured monthly income from outside sources." Unless propaganda was his special skill or the Party was subsidizing him, Davis would have had none of the above.

In Chicago and in Hawaii, the FBI kept a nineteen-year watch on Davis and amassed a file that runs six hundred pages as posted online. At least one cooperating informant met with Davis "on Communist Party matters" for a period of several years and collected Davis's Party dues. These were the Korean War years in the early 1950s. By this time, the dewy-eyed idealists had long since fled the CPUSA, a wholly owned Soviet subsidiary.

When Stanley Dunham first met Davis is uncertain. There is ample evidence that Dunham's politics listed leftward, but unlike Davis, he had little to offer any cause, let alone the KGB. Investigator Cliff Kincaid submitted a request to the FBI to see if the Bureau had kept a file on Dunham. "Records which may be responsive to your Freedom of Information Act (FOIA) were destroyed on May 01, 1997," responded the FBI cryptically in March 2010. Reading into the text of the letter, it seems likely that Dunham's name was listed in the FBI's "main index record," but that proves little.

The case for Davis as "Pop" does not depend on the nature of the liaison between Davis and Stanley Dunham or on its date of initiation. There is a variety of evidence including a 1987 interview with Davis recorded by the University of Hawaii for a documentary on his life. Watching it, one can visualize "Pop": the drinking, the smoking, the glasses, the twitches, the roaming eyes, the thick neck and broad back. "I could see Frank sitting in his overstuffed chair," Obama remembers in *Dreams*, "a book of poetry in his lap, his reading glasses slipping down his nose."

As to the sharing of sage advice, that description fits Davis better than it does Dunham. "I was intrigued by old Frank," Obama writes in *Dreams*, "with his books and whiskey breath and the hint of hardearned knowledge behind the hooded eyes." More conclusively still,

"Pop" does something that Davis would naturally do but that Dunham would not: he "recites an old poem / He wrote before his mother died."

The first time the reader meets Davis in *Dreams*, he is referred to as "a poet named Frank." Obama remembers, "[Davis] would read us his poetry whenever we stopped by his house, sharing whiskey with Gramps out of an emptied jelly jar." On one occasion in *Dreams*, the teenage Obama stops by alone and Davis pours him his own shot. To close the case, Dunham's mother died when he was eight. Davis's mother died when he was twenty and had already established himself at Kansas State as a poet of promise.

Toby Harnden of the *Telegraph* credibly traces the first meeting of boy and man to the fall of 1970, when young Barry was nine. Obama admittedly spent the summer of 1970 in Hawaii, but he was supposed to have been in Indonesia in the fall. Then again, he was also believed to have lived full-time in Indonesia the year before until photos of him as a third grader at Noelani Elementary in Honolulu surfaced after the election. Mystery surrounds the man.

Maya Soetoro-Ng, Obama's half sister, would describe Davis as her brother's "point of connection, a bridge . . . to the larger African-American experience." *Dreams'* treatment of Davis testifies to his importance in the boy's life. On nine separate occasions in *Dreams*, Obama refers to "Frank." Other than public figures like Jeremiah Wright and members of the Obama family, no one else is called by his or her real name.

Not many Chicagoans would understand who "Frank" was, but some of those who did still mattered. One was Vernon Jarrett. As a young journalist, he and Davis had worked together in a communist front, the Citizens' Committee to Aid Packinghouse Workers. By the time Obama arrived in Chicago, Jarrett, at that point a syndicated columnist, was a proven kingmaker. "He stoked the political embers in Chicago that led to the 1983 election of the city's first African American mayor, Harold Washington," wrote the *Washington Post* of Jarrett in its 2004 obituary. His daughter-in-law, Valerie Jarrett, would become Obama's closest adviser.

Obama wanted black Chicago to know his connectedness, but he was savvy enough to omit Davis's last name, as well as any reference to his politics. Had Obama written this book with the presidency in mind, he would likely have eliminated *all* references to Davis—and Wright too, for that matter.

For whatever reason, Obama introduced "Frank" to the world, and he deserves his day in court. Of the two charges he stands accused of, let me start with the most salient, paternity. What follows is unproven but not ungrounded. The evidence that ties Ann Dunham to Davis in 1960 is a series of nude photos of a young woman who looks strikingly like Ann. Figuring their authenticity easier to disprove than prove, I turned to that venerable fact checker, Snopes.com. Some on the right have accused Snopes of shilling for Democratic causes. A comparable service, TruthOrFiction.com, investigated this claim and cleared Snopes, finding "no discernible pattern of bias or deception, nor any evidence of advocacy for or against."

I do not believe this for a minute. In its assessment of the Ayers-Obama relationship, for instance, Snopes—which is really no more than California couple David and Barbara Mikkelson—concludes that the two "aren't (and never were) close." As proof, the Mikkelsons cite statements by Ayers, the Obama camp, and the mainstream media. That's it. A weak defense is one thing. A fraudulent defense is another. It suggests a hidden truth, and such is the case with Ann Dunham.

The Mikkelsons give the Dunham-as-nude-model rumor a big, fat "False." Although conceding that the photos are genuine and not retouched, they dismiss them as "pictures of late 1950's pinup model Marcy Moore, who just happened to bear a vague facial resemblance to a young Ann Dunham." This is bunkum. On facial features alone, the Mikkelsons should have ruled out the much prettier Moore, but it is not the face that betrays intent. Moore's all-pro body has useful mass in places the perky amateur body of the Dunham look-alike does not. Moore even gets her own featured spot in a wonderfully trashy reference service called "Boobpedia, the Encyclopedia of big boobs." The Mikkelsons had to see the difference. Their site provides a photo of Moore.

The woman in the nude photos looks not vaguely like the young Ann Dunham. She looks stunningly like her, right down to the long Dunham chin, the petite mouth, and the arched eyebrows. The timing is also perfect. Seen on the table in one photo is the Stan Kenton LP *Cuban Fire*, a jazz album, this version of which was released in 1960, the year Ann arrived in Hawaii.

Unlike Marcy Moore's professionally lit pinup shots, the photos in question are as amateurish as the model. The decorations clearly suggest Christmas, and yet the woman has a tan line. In her letters back to Seattle, Ann had enthused about wearing shorts to class, and the tan begins where the shorts would have ended. The young woman's hair is sufficiently short that her earlobes show just as Ann's do in her high school graduation photo. Tarted up as she is, the woman in the photos looks older than Ann as a high school senior, but her body looks appropriately young.

To close a case, all evidence finally has to point in the same direction. If this is Ann, the photo could have been taken only in December 1960, before she let her hair grow. If this is Ann, she could not have been more than about a month or so pregnant at the time. If this is Ann, the timing undoes the "unknown black male" on the mainland theory. If this is Ann, the intimacy of the photos makes the photographer a suspect in the Obama paternity mystery.

It should not surprise to learn that Frank Marshall Davis was an avid photographer. When he was thirty and living in Chicago, a neighbor who worked for an optical firm started supplying Davis with purloined photography magazines, cameras, and darkroom equipment. "I was hooked," recalls Davis in *Livin' the Blues*. "As I gained confidence behind the lens," he adds, "I turned to nudes." He photographed single women, married women, black women, white women.

"I was amazed," he writes, "at the number of gals eager to strip and stand unclothed before the all-seeing eye of the camera."

Davis's passion for nude photography complemented his sideline as a pornographer. In 1968, he chronicled his sexual adventures in a book titled *Sex Rebel: Black* under the pseudonym "Bob Greene." There is no doubt he wrote the book. In his memoir, when approached in a San Francisco bookstore by a savvy reader who inferred his authorship from the text, Davis owned up. Writes he coyly, "I could not then truthfully deny that this book, which came out in 1968 as a Greenleaf Classic, was mine." The editor of *Livin' the Blues*, John Edgar Tidwell, confirms the same.

In *Sex Rebel*, the Davis persona, the narrator, insists that the book's adventures are all "taken from actual experiences." His sexual preferences in the relatively discreet *Livin' the Blues* largely correlate with those in *Sex Rebel*, as do many of his life experiences, but *Sex Rebel* is a novel, not an autobiography—a good thing, as the book documents his seduction of a thirteen-year-old girl. The girl's name, by the way, is Anne.

In a more telling encounter, the Davis persona hooks up with a college student named "Gloria." He places the meeting in Chicago in the 1940s, but dates, places, and names are routinely changed to protect identities. Gloria is described as a short, shapely, sad-eyed, dark-haired girl who "felt herself responsible, because of her white skin, for the evils of color hate and wanted to atone to Negro males individually." To appease her guilt, Gloria presents her rump to the narrator and demands to be spanked. I cite this last detail because Davis admits to being something of a "derriere" man and two of the three alleged Dunham photos are fully derriere-centric, and the third is nearly so.

When it comes time for actual sex, Gloria insists that the Davis persona not wear a condom. "What if you become pregnant?" he asks. "That's what I'd hoped for," she says. "I'd like nothing more than a baby by a colored man." When Gloria expresses indifference to her parents' likely rejection, the man asks how she would live. "Oh I'd find a way," she answers. In both the memoir and *Sex Rebel*, by the way, the author boasts that the only women he has ever impregnated were white. In the memoir, he claims three such scores.

In *Dreams*, Obama shows his mother from a different angle—thankfully—but with a passion not unlike Gloria's. In this particular vignette during Obama's Columbia years, Ann is visiting New York when she insists on dragging her son to a revival of *Black Orpheus*. Writer/director Marcel Camus based this film on the myth of Orpheus and Eurydice and sets it in the favelas of Rio de Janeiro during Carnival.

Ann claims to have seen the film as a sixteen-year-old during the summer she allegedly served as an au pair in Chicago. This is one of the rare instances in the book where the dates actually work. *Black Orpheus* was originally released in 1959. Watching her watch the movie, Obama gets a glimpse into the "unreflective heart of her youth." What he sees is "a reflection of the simple fantasies that had been forbidden to a white middle-class girl from Kansas, the promise of another life: warm, sensual, exotic, different."

One can only guess whether Dunham introduced his daughter to Davis in 1960 as he did his grandson some years later. (In *Sex Rebel*, the Davis persona dwells on a loving three-way encounter with a Seattle couple, Dot and Lloyd.) Ann, a progressive seventeen-year-old with a yen for the dark and exotic, would have been red meat for Davis. He might well have responded to the opportunity as Chicago congressman Mel Reynolds did when offered similarly ripe, career-killing fare: "Did I win the Lotto?"

The most credible evidence for Davis as Obama's father is embedded in the title of the poem about him, "Pop." Passages in the poem would seem to reinforce the case. Like so much contemporary poetry, however, "Pop" is sufficiently obscure in meaning that one does not so much review the poem as decrypt it. All such efforts, of course, are subjective, including the one that follows.

The young man in the poem appears restive, frustrated with the evasiveness of the older man, who "switches channels," twitches, glances from side to side, rambles. Finally, the boy wearies of the old joke the man has been telling, holds a mirror up to the man's face, and demands answers. The old man breaks, "Makes me smell his smell, coming / From me" and then "Stands, shouts, and asks / For a hug." A very good case could be made that Obama has asked Davis, "Pop," to acknowledge his paternity, and he has finally done so. At least a few of my correspondents have argued for this interpretation.

If the title of the poem "Pop" was meant to be literal, if Davis seduced Ann and impregnated her, he would have had every reason to find a proxy father who was black. He was married at the time to a white socialite and had young children. Once again, for all the same reasons, Barack Sr. would have made the perfect "beard." Davis acknowledged knowing Kenyans at the university and might well have met Barack Sr. at a communist front event, not unlike the ILWU-sponsored "Mother's Peace Rally" at which the senior Obama spoke in 1962.

In this scenario, there would have been no need to alter the timeline. An August birth would be entirely appropriate, and Ann would be understandably eager to leave the mess behind. What causes me to question this scenario is my own belief that Davis not only is "Pop," but that he also wrote "Pop." My suspicion here is more hunch than science. Still, it is an educated hunch.

Nowhere else in his unaided oeuvre, such as it is, does Obama show the language control he does in "Pop." Two years later, in the pages of Columbia's weekly newsmagazine, *Sundial*, he would be writing semiliterate clunkers like "The belief that moribund institutions, rather than individuals are at the root of the problem, keep SAM's energies alive."

Ian McMillan writes of the nineteen-year-old Obama, "He's obviously read the Beat poets and writers like Gary Snyder and Charles

Bukowski." Obviously? Obama, an indifferent student and doper at the time, has given us no evidence of an interest in anything besides "neocolonialism, Franz Fanon, Eurocentrism, and patriarchy."

More telling, of course, is Obama's poem "Underground," which appeared alongside "Pop" in the spring 1981 edition of Occidental College's literary magazine, *Feast*. This silly adolescent ode to "apes that eat figs" in underwater grottoes has none of the style or sophistication of "Pop." In fact, "Underground" sounds as if it were written by another, lesser poet, namely Obama himself. Others have noted the difference. Poet and novelist Warwick Collins, for instance, believes "Pop" to be "by far the more powerful and complex" of the two poems, and his is the consensus opinion.

Mr. Southwest, who has done yeoman's work on the Ayers-Obama connection, has long believed Davis to be the subject of "Pop." His preliminary textual analysis leads him to believe that Davis is the author of "Pop" as well. As he will be the first to admit, however, working with only one poem as base makes comparison with other Davis work tricky, especially since Davis experimented with a range of free verse styles.

In my own reading, I see "Pop" as a self-reflection by Davis. Distressed to be losing the young Obama to the lure of the mainland, he writes a poem about himself as seen through Obama's eyes. In the way of support for this theory, consider a poem published by Davis in 1975—six years earlier—called "To a Young Man."

I had hoped to show in this space the poem itself, but that was not to be. When I contacted the poem's publisher, the University of Illinois Press, a representative cheerfully suggested that reprinting the poem would not be a problem.

A month after my initial request, having heard nothing back, I inquired about the state of my request. For the first time, I was asked my reason for wanting to reprint the poem. Biting my tongue, I responded as follows:

In *Deconstructing Obama*, I analyze the influences on Barack Obama's oeuvre. In the case of the Davis poem, I attempt to show how Davis influenced the poetry of the young Obama, specifically Obama's poem "Pop," which is clearly about Davis and not his grandfather as reporters have lazily asserted.

"I have forwarded your request to the estate of Frank Marshall Davis for approval," responded the university's Kathleen Kornell. "If they consent to the reprint I will let you know and mail a letter of permission and invoice for the permission fee."

This was the first I had heard of the need for Davis family approval. "With all due respect we initiated this request four and a half weeks ago," I wrote to Kornell. "I was promised a response within two to four weeks. Now, it seems like we are just beginning the process." I asked for a prompt up or down as this delay was beginning to threaten the book's scheduled release.

The response came promptly. "I have heard from the Frank Marshall Davis estate," wrote Kornell a few days later, "and unfortunately, they have denied your request to reprint the poem, 'To a Young Man.'" She offered no reason why.

The motivations of at least one member of the family, Frank's son Mark, seem self-evident. As a blogger on Obama's Organizing for America website, Mark Davis worked to protect Obama from the "smear" originating in "Right-Wing Fantasy Land" that Davis had passed his Stalinist values on to Obama.

In any number of disingenuous posts during the 2008 campaign, Mark Davis argued that although his father may have been affiliated with the Communist Party, there was no evidence that he was a Stalinist—a neat trick in the Stalin era—or that he instructed Obama in the same.

Unfortunately, Davis is silent on the issue at hand, namely, whether his father influenced Obama's poetry, perhaps to the point of writing

"Pop" for him. The parallels between that poem and "To A Young Man" are powerful.

In each of the two poems in question, the old man, the Davis character, is discussed in the third person. In the 1981 poem, the narrator calls him "Pop"; in the 1975 poem, he is called "the old man." In each poem, when this older character speaks to the young man, he does so without benefit of quotation marks.

In "To a Young Man," the Davis character says on one occasion, "Since then I have drunk / Half a hundred liquid years / Distilled / Through restless coils of wisdom." Note in "Pop" the similar flow of language: "Pop switches channels, takes another / Shot of Seagrams, neat, and asks / What to do with me, a green young man."

Both poems are written in free verse and make ready use of what is called enjambment, that is, the abrupt continuation of a sentence from one line into the next. There are parallels in word choice as well as in style. "Neat" means without water or ice. "Neat" and "Distilled" both suggest a kind of alcoholic purity. The author emphasizes each of these words by isolating it from the flow of the text.

In "Pop," the older man "Stands, shouts, and asks / For a hug, as I shink." Most reviewers simply dismiss *shink* as a typo, the right word being *shrink*. Still, as poet McMillan notes in the *Guardian*, *shink* literally means "to be hit in the face with a penis." I am not making this up.

In each case, too, the older man shares his wisdom with a "young man" who may not be eager to hear it. The young man of "Pop" dismisses that wisdom as a mere "spot" in his brain, "something / that may be squeezed out, like a / Watermelon seed between / Two fingers." Comparably, the old man in the Davis poem "walked until / On the slate horizon / He erased himself." Whether "squeezed out" or "erased" from the young man's consciousness, the older character understands just how tenuous is his hold on the lad's soul.

For all his awareness, however, the older man finds a certain drunken satisfaction in the exchange. Toward the end of "To a Young Man," the old man "turned / His hammered face / To the pounding stars / Smiled / Like the ring of a gong." "Pop" also concludes on an upbeat note: "I see my face, framed within / Pop's black-framed glasses / And know he's laughing too."

There is no way to know whether the "young man" of the 1975 poem is Obama. The reader is told that the younger fellow is twenty years old and that the old man is fifty years older. Davis was precisely seventy in 1975, but Obama was no more than fourteen. This may be just a note of discretion on Davis's part. Lacking too in the 1975 poem are the intimacy and anxiety that characterize "Pop," but in 1975 Davis was just getting to know Obama, and he was not worried about losing him.

Each poem hints at a love that is something other than paternal. A therapist who blogs under the name "Neo Neocon" offers the most insightful reading of the poem that I was able to identify. She too is convinced that "Pop" is Davis and she finds the following sequence disturbing in the extreme:

> *Pop takes another shot, neat,*
> *Points out the same amber*
> *Stain on his shorts that I've got on mine, and*
> *Makes me smell his smell, coming*
> *From me . . .*

The most innocent explanation for the "amber stain" on the shorts of both mentor and initiate or "his smell, coming / From me" is that Davis got the teenage Obama drunk, and they both spilled whiskey on themselves. That reading does not explain, however, why the spill is specifically on their shorts and not on their shirts or how Davis's breath now comes from Obama. The therapist senses a darker exchange. She cannot be certain about "outright sexual abuse," but, she notes, "there is no question that the poem is describing a boundary violation on several levels: this child feels invaded—perhaps even taken over—by this man, and is fighting against that sensation."

This would be easier to dismiss were it not for the narrator's concession in *Sex Rebel* that "under certain circumstances I am bisexual" as well as "a voyeur and an exhibitionist." In the introduction to *Sex Rebel*, an alleged Ph.D. named Dale Gordon goes further. He describes the pseudonymous author, Bob Greene, as having "strong homosexual tendencies in his personality." He specifies, "When Bob Greene takes another man's penis in his mouth, he does so to provide pleasure for the man." There is enough talk in *Sex Rebel* about the taste and texture of semen to merit the suspicion that the "breath" and "amber stain" references in "Pop" refer to the exchange of something other than whiskey. There may have been a whole lot of "shinking" going on chez Davis after all.

In *Livin' the Blues*, Davis is considerably more discreet. Although he talks at length about his romantic life, he spares the reader the nitty-gritty. He makes an exception to speak of a particular enthusiasm, what he calls on one occasion his "lifelong oral orientation" and on another his "hitherto repressed oral desires," but he places these in a heterosexual context. He restricts talk of homosexuality to the theoretical. "I am unalterably opposed," he thunders indignantly, "to any attempt at regimentation of the sex drive into the rigid outlets customarily prescribed by our religious traditions." At least a decade before anyone else did, Davis argued for a united front between gays and blacks: "Blacks and Homos, Arise!" If it matters, he was also the first guy on his block to get his ear pierced.

I had been skeptical of the tabloid allegations of bisexuality that have dogged Obama until realizing that Obama imported the only romance that appears in *Dreams*. Bolstering those allegations is the fact that his most notorious accuser, Larry Sinclair, limits Obama's role to that of the passive partner in oral sex, a role that could have been ingrained chez "Frank" given Davis's obsession with pleasing people orally.

The fierce and frequent public debate about gay-related issues makes Obama's sexual history relevant. If what Sinclair says is true—and he has written a book about the same, titled, a wee bit sensationally, *Barack Obama & Larry Sinclair: Cocaine, Sex, Lies & Murder?*—there may be others out there even more exploitive and extortive than Sinclair.

The media's discretion would be understandable had they not spent so much energy trying to discern the "real" mother of Trig Palin or to find the apocryphal dealers who sold cocaine to George Bush or marijuana to Dan Quayle. As became embarrassingly clear in their aggressive noncoverage of John Edwards and his love child, the media alter outcomes even of primary races by ignoring the escapades of favored Democrats.

Remnick, of course, turns a blind eye to Davis's dark side. In one of those hot flashes that give liberalism a bad name, he describes Dunham's introduction of his grandson to Davis as "one of the more thoughtful and consequential things Stanley did in his role as surrogate grandfather," almost as thoughtful perhaps as when Mom introduced her thirteen-year-old to Roman Polanski. Forget about the communist part. Davis was an admitted "sex rebel" with, at the very least, a fictional taste for the underage and the male.

As compensation for exploiting the young Obama, Davis may well have slipped this "green young man" a poem for publication. Such an everyday scam would not have seemed unethical to an old man used to the "flim and flam" ("Pop") of a world where "one plus one" does not necessarily make "two or three or four" ("To a Young Man"). Trained to believe that nothing adds up and the deck is stacked against him, Obama has seemed from the beginning entirely comfortable with a counterfeit literary career.

AX

Before signing on with Obama for the 2004 U.S. Senate race, David Axelrod met with the man favored to win the Democratic primary, multimillionaire Blair Hull. Known for his aggressive oppositional research, beginning with his own candidate, Axelrod quickly learned of Hull's Achilles' heel, a protection order that Hull's second wife had applied for during a nasty divorce proceeding. Axelrod did not think Hull could survive its disclosure and opted instead to work with underdog Obama.

About a month before primary election day, the *Chicago Tribune*, Axelrod's former employer, broke the news of the protective order. With the *Tribune* pushing for disclosure, Hull's ship sunk even more swiftly than Howard Dean's had after his "I Have a Scream" speech earlier that year in Iowa. Although Axelrod has denied involvement in leaking the story, the *Tribune* reporter who broke it would later concede that Team Obama had "worked aggressively behind the scenes" to get the story out.

In April 2007, the *New York Times Magazine* ran a lengthy feature on Axelrod with the aptly postmodern title "Obama's Narrator." Wrote reporter Ben Wallace-Wells, "Axelrod has worked through Obama's life story again and again, scouring it for usable political material." By April 2007, Axelrod had surely scoured it for the unusable as well. Knowing the holes in the Obama story, he restricted David Mendell's movements in Hawaii, discouraged any number of Obama friends from talking to the press, and refused to give even the *New York Times* leads about Obama's days in New York.

When Axelrod combed through the official records—the grades, the SAT and LSAT scores, the college theses, the passport, Obama's parents' marriage license, the college applications, the birth certificate—he likely saw more red flags than in his own parents' May Day parades and so decided to bury them all. The media would not have let a Blair Hull skate by like this, let alone a Sarah Palin, but Axelrod knew the media well enough to know their weakness for bright, clean, articulate, dialect-free black Democrats.

What did Axelrod know? If I can speculate, he knew that Obama's very paternity resembled the punch line of a racist taunt he had heard as a kid on the mean streets of lower Manhattan: "At least I got a father, not fourteen black suspects." On the information available, he could not know for sure who the father was.

The best suspect remained Barack Sr. Yet every time he looked at that picture of a smiling Stanley Dunham waving aloha to his supposed scoundrel of a son-in-law he had to wonder even about that. For sure, the narrative Obama painted in *Dreams*—not even Ax suspected Ayers's role—and rolled out for the 2004 keynote was false in almost every detail. Barack Sr.'s coupling with Ann Dunham was no Kumbaya moment. If it symbolized anything, it symbolized third-world eagerness to exploit mindless liberal idealism, and that was not the kind of story line that would get a president elected. Better to leave Obama believing in the Dorothy-and-the-goatherd fable. The campaign would need his sincerity. But how sincere was Obama? In the 1995 introduction to *Dreams*, he writes, "I learned long ago to distrust my childhood and the stories that shaped it."

Try as he might, Axelrod could not scratch Frank Marshall Davis from the paternity sweepstakes. Davis was more than the sum of his parts—communist, pornographer, possible pedophile—but those parts were enough to sink a candidacy, that is, if the media chose to pursue the connection. Axelrod was confident they would not. Davis's race and obscurity would keep them well at bay. It was the live ones, Ayers and Wright, who had him double dosing on Compoz, but at least they could not be the father. Could they?

The only person who knew the story behind the story lay on her deathbed as the 2008 campaign wound down. She was a sometime Republican, the ant in a family of grasshoppers, and just a little bit bitter about the same. Could Ax count on her to protect her grandson? Ten days before the 2008 election, Obama abandoned the campaign trail to make sure. He flew to Hawaii to visit Toot one last time. The *Washington Post* innocently hinted at a secondary motive for the visit: "The trip served to remind not only of Obama's biracial heritage but also the unusual and even exotic upbringing that shaped his life." Yes, one more reminder of the improbable love that would teach the world to sing.

The media, however, could not bring themselves to question any of this, not the story, and certainly not the authorship of the story. In recognizing Obama's unique genius, they validated their own. They have so much emotional equity staked in this recognition that they would rather believe Obama a failed president than a fraudulent human being or a fake writer. In May 2010, in the midst of the Gulf oil mess, the Pulitzer Prize–winning *New York Times* columnist Maureen Dowd plumbed new depths of self-deception:

> In "Dreams From My Father," Obama showed passion, lyricism, empathy and an exquisite understanding of character and psychological context—all the qualities that he has stubbornly resisted showing as

president. It was a book that promised a president who could see into the hearts of other people. But there's so much you don't learn about candidates in campaigns, even when they seem completely exposed.

To those of us west of Times Square, "completely exposed" obviously means something different than it does to the willfully blind Ms. Dowd.

HUBRIS

I n 1872, amateur archeologist Charles C. Abbot found some ancient Indian tools on his farm in western New Jersey. After consulting a Harvard geologist, he surmised that the remains dated
back about ten thousand years. At the time, the official orthodoxy, en-
forced by a haughty Smithsonian Institute, was that American Indians
had moved into North America much more recently. Accordingly, the
Smithsonian sent its skeptic in chief, William Henry Holmes, to review the site and put this upstart amateur in his place. Abbott got his
revenge by publishing a poem in *Science*. It reads in part:

> *The stones are inspected*
> *And Holmes cries, "rejected,*
> *They're nothing but Indian chips."*
> *He glanced at the ground,*
> *Truth, fancied he found,*
> *And homeward to Washington skips. . . .*

During the presidential campaign of 2008, there were more than a few of us who could identify with Mr. Abbott. One was author and activist Michael Patrick Leahy. In the summer of 2010, Leahy called me and asked whether I would be in western New York state in early August. His parents live in Jamestown, and I spend much of my summer nearby on Lake Erie. As it turned out, we had only one day on which we could meet, and that day was August 4.

We met at Andriaccio's, a congenial Italian restaurant on Chautauqua Lake, the setting for my one and only novel, *2006: The Chautauqua Rising*. Published in 2000 and set, as the reader might surmise, in 2006, this mildly futuristic action thriller tells the tale of a grassroots insurrection that in many ways anticipated the Tea Party insurgency of 2009. As it happens, Leahy—a good-spirited, unpretentious guy for a Harvard grad—had just signed a contract to do a book on the ideological roots of the Tea Party movement. As an aside, those thinking of writing a book should be sure to give it a title that people can pronounce. I learned this the hard way. The lake is pronounced "sha-TAWK-wa."

When a member of our party observed that the day, August 4, happened to be Barack Obama's birthday, Leahy and I both chimed in, "alleged birthday." It might very well be his birthday, we explained, but one simply could not be sure. In fact, there is very much about Obama's life that must still be preceded by the word *alleged*. When, for instance, I put the question of Obama's paternity to Leahy, Don Wilde, and Mr. Southwest, I got three different answers. And these are serious guys who know more about Obama's past than does anyone at the *New York Times*.

And therein lies the problem. For the first time in the modern era, the major media—the *New York Times*, the *Washington Post*, the TV networks, CNN, PBS, NPR, *Time, Newsweek*—chose not to know the background of a leading presidential candidate. The biographical information they served the public about Obama was consistently shallow, often synchronized, and more than occasionally wrong. Worse, the establishment media, left and right, chastened investigators like Leahy and myself for daring to look for evidence that challenged the orthodoxy. They would simply glance at our work, dismiss it out of hand, and, yes, homeward to Washington skip.

During the fall and summer of 2008, Leahy and I had each addressed one of the two questions that this book poses: In my case, did Barack Obama write *Dreams from My Father*? In Leahy's, was the story Obama told in *Dreams* true? As we both discovered well before the November election—discoveries that could have altered the outcome if widely known—the answer to each of our questions was an unequivocal "no."

If I might tie the threads together, here is what the media chose to ignore. In 1994, at Michelle's urging, a desperate Barack Obama turned his mess of a manuscript over to Bill Ayers and asked for help. Obama knew that his mentors at Harvard had cut some corners, and if they could get away with it, why not he?

Obama had not yet run for office, but he was itching to. As far as Ayers knew, Obama had set his sights no higher than mayor of Chicago, and that was fine by Ayers. With an indebted African American protégé as mayor, Ayers could undertake the kind of educational reform he had been conjuring since quitting the underground. So together he and Obama conspired to tell the kind of story that would make Obama electable. Ayers's political insights tempered Obama's steely ambition to produce a shrewdly crafted book, one whose architecture, if sometimes a plumb or two off bubble, is not terribly hard to decode.

The media never tried. They point, for instance, to *Dreams*' inclusion of Obama's lotus-eating years as a sign of his honesty and the book's artlessness. It was neither. Ayers and Obama here were cauterizing a wound. By exposing Obama's drug use, they denied his future opponents the news value of doing the same. Besides, Bill Clinton had suffered more in the 1992 campaign from his denials—"I did not inhale"—than from his indulgences. If the collaborators were being honest, they would have exposed Obama's sex life, but that they chose to conceal and/or concoct.

By the time of the 2008 campaign, Obama had reason to suspect that his parents had never married, that the three members of this little family had never lived together, and that Barack Sr. had skipped out on the family before his first birthday. He clung to the belief, though he may have had his doubts, that he was Obama's son. He had to. The larger point of *Dreams* was to establish Obama's African legacy. Given the importance of that legacy, Obama buried his doubts and allowed his origins story to stand. Scrutiny came only from independent investigators. They may have chased leads down a rabbit hole or two, but to their credit, they sensed something amiss and kept on digging.

In the official retelling of the origins story, Obama spent his first six years in Hawaii and then moved to Indonesia. Had Obama included the Washington state sojourn in the narrative, he would have spoiled the plotline. Indonesia enhanced the plot. By recounting his years there—five according to *Audacity*, four according to *Dreams*, and about three in reality—he reinforced his exotic appeal and his international savvy.

The collaborators took pains to play down Obama's Muslim identification and education. Islam had no political capital in Illinois. Christianity did. Central to the story told in *Dreams* was Obama's showy embrace of the same. Given his long-term ambitions, Obama miscalculated by tying himself to the Reverend Wright. Ayers did not. In Chicago politics, the affiliation with Wright only helped.

The Chicago connection was critical. Although Obama spent five years altogether at Columbia and Harvard, he does not write so much as a single sentence about campus life at either Ivy institution. By contrast, he dedicates more than a third of *Dreams* to his three years as a community organizer in Chicago, easily the book's most tedious section. The narrative foreshadows his arrival there with prophetic signs like his putative childhood trip to Chicago and his mentoring by legendary Chicagoan Frank Marshall Davis.

There was no point, however, in getting too explicit about Obama's relationship to Davis. If Ayers was a small-*c* communist, Davis was a capital-*C* one. In 1994, even in Chicago, communism did not play well. Ayers knew enough to soft-sell "Frank" and write himself out of the book. The benignly progressive, aggressively black Obama the reader meets in *Dreams* had been produced and packaged expressly for political shelf appeal. The intended consumers were lakefront liberals and South Side African Americans, and both consumer groups bought as projected.

Had Obama restricted his ambitions to Chicago or even Illinois, *Dreams* would have gone unchallenged. Nothing in it would have troubled the media or the state's comfortable Democratic majority. For its part, the blogosphere would have had no more reason to dig into Obama's past than into that of any other self-aggrandizing senator.

Obama, however, wanted more. He doubled down on his hubris in choosing a collaborator who also wanted more. Had Ayers done what book doctors usually do—mined the thoughts and mimicked the voice of the named author—no one would have been suspicious. Instead he imposed his own voice, his own thoughts, even his own lost love on an already unreliable narrative. The resulting construction propped up the myth of Obama's genius but so obviously as to invite deconstruction. In his vanity, Ayers had made little attempt to conceal the struts.

As the myth of Obama collapses, and it will, our established media will sort through the rubble and wonder who or what brought it down. At the end of the day, they will be no more gracious in giving credit than the Smithsonian was to the many amateurs who finally forced it to rethink its position on Indian origins. Today, if illusions die easily, establishments still die hard.

NOTES

INTRODUCTION

PAGE

1 USA Today *had accurately:* Craig Wilson, "A Glowing 'Portrait' of the Obamas' Rock-Solid Marriage," *USA Today*, September 21, 2009.

3 *"There is no underestimating":* David Remnick, The Bridge: The Life and Rise of Barack Obama (New York: Knopf, 2010), p. 420.

4 *"our constructed reality":* Bill Ayers, *Fugitive Days: Memoirs of an Anti-War Activist* (Boston: Beacon, 2001), p. 44.

4 *"But another part of me":* Barack Obama, *Dreams from My Father: A Story of Race and Inheritance* (New York: Crown, 2004), p. 63.

10,000 HOURS

PAGE

13 *"ten-thousand-hour rule":* Malcolm Gladwell, *Outliers: The Story of Success* (New York: Little, Brown, 2008), p. 40.

13 *In his recent memoir:* Christopher Hitchens, *Hitch-22: A Memoir* (New York: Twelve, 2010).

13 *Obama's Hawaii mentor:* Frank Marshall Davis, *Livin' the Blues: Memoirs of a Black Journalist and Poet* (Madison: University of Wisconsin Press, 1992).

14 *"the best-written memoir":* Joe Klein, "The Fresh Face," *Time*, October 19, 2006.

14 *"the best writer":* Jonathan Raban, "All the Presidents' Literature," *Wall Street Journal*, January 10, 2009.

14 *"Whatever else people"*: Oona King, "Oona King on Barack Obama's *Dreams from My Father,*" *Times* (London), September 15, 2007.

14 *"I was astonished"*: "Writers welcome a literary U.S. president-elect," Associated Press, November 6, 2008.

THE STORY

18 *"signature appeal"*: Remnick, p. 360.

18 *"carefully constructed narrative"*: Toby Harnden, "Barack Obama's true colours: The making of the man who would be US president," *Telegraph*, August 21, 2008.

19 *Almost exactly ten years:* For an extended discussion of the Clinton myth, see Jack Cashill, *Ron Brown's Body: How One Man's Death Saved the Clinton Presidency and Hillary's Future* (Nashville: WND Books, 2004), pp. 94–104.

19 *"our first black president"*: Toni Morrison, "Talk of the Town," *New Yorker*, October 5, 1998.

20 *"Nobody ever loved"*: Virginia Kelley, *Leading with My Heart* (New York: Simon and Schuster, 1994), p. 28.

20 *They turned the living room:* David Maraniss, *First in His Class: The Biography of Bill Clinton* (New York: Touchstone, 1996), p. 37.

BURYING PERCY

23 *"to let a serious crisis"*: Rahm Emanuel, White House chief of staff, after his nomination by president-elect Barack Obama in November 2008, said, "You never want to let a serious crisis go to waste."

24 *As George Orwell acknowledged:* George Orwell, "Politics and the English Language," *Horizon*, April 1946.

24 *"We invented words"*: Bill Ayers, Bernardine Dohrn, and Jeff Jones, eds., *Sing a Battle Song: The Revolutionary Poetry, Statements, and Communiques of the Weather Underground, 1970–1974* (New York: Seven Stories, 2006), p. 151.

24 *When asked about Obama:* "Inside City Hall," NY1, March 25, 2008.

26 *Shortly after the story:* Ben Smith, "Obama camp denies Sutton story," *Politico*, September 4, 2008.

26 *A self-appointed:* Ben Smith, "Sutton family retracts Obama story," *Politico*, September 6, 2008.

27 *Unconvincingly, he claimed:* Kenneth R. Timmerman, "Obama's Harvard Years: Questions Swirl," *Newsmax*, September 23, 2008.

27 *In March 2009:* Michael Calderone, "JournoList: Inside the echo chamber," *Politico*, March 17, 2009.

Amiable Dunces

PAGE

30 *"all the contradictions"*: Thomas Frank, *What's the Matter with Kansas?* (New York: Henry Holt, 2004), p. 161.

31 *"I wanted [Jimmy] Carter in"*: "Chevy Chase: I wanted Carter to win," CNN.com, November 3, 2008.

31 *"After the last eight years"*: Alex Spillius, "Sir Paul McCartney 'should apologise to American people for Bush insult,'" *Telegraph*, June 4, 2010.

32 *"probably the smartest guy"*: Imus in the Morning, Citadel Media, November 10, 2008.

33 *"What am I going to tell"*: "Teleprompter Falls and Biden Jokes: 'What am I going to tell the president when I tell him his teleprompter is broken?,'" ABCNews.com, May 27, 2009.

Beautiful Old House

PAGE

34 *"probably the best-known intellectual"*: Tony Judt, "The Rootless Cosmopolitan," *Nation*, July 19, 2004.

34 *"against settlements, against Israeli apartheid"*: Peter Wallsten, "Allies of Palestinians See a Friend in Obama," *Los Angeles Times*, April 10, 2008.

35 *In late October 2007:* Janny Scott, "Obama's Account of New York Years Often Differs From What Others Say," *New York Times*, October 30, 2007.

35 *Nearly three years later:* Remnick, p. 113.

35 *Said, you see:* For a more in-depth look at Said's lifelong fraud, see Jack Cashill, *Hoodwinked: How Intellectual Hucksters Have Hijacked American Culture* (Nashville: Thomas Nelson, 2005), pp. 129–34.

35 *"Orientalism is written"*: Edward Said, *Orientalism* (New York: Vintage, 1994), p. 337.

35 *"Mr. Said was born in Jerusalem"*: Janny Scott, "A Palestinian Confronts Time," *New York Times*, September 19, 1998.

36 *"Virtually everything I learned"*: Justus Reid Weiner, " 'My Beautiful Old

House' and Other Fabrications by Edward Said," *Commentary*, September 1999.

37 *In a glowing obituary:* Richard Bernstein, "Edward Said: Leading Advocate of Palestinians Dies at 67," *New York Times*, September 25, 2003.

FUGITIVE DAYS

38 *"I inform Martha":* "Democratic National Convention," petercoyote .com, August 25, 1996.

39 *Dinitia Smith begins:* Dinitia Smith, "No Regrets for a Love of Explosives; In a Memoir of Sorts, a War Protester Talks of Life With the Weathermen," *New York Times*, September 11, 2001.

39 *"Is this, then, the truth":* This quote comes from the Smith article. It is not in *Fugitive Days*.

40 *In February:* Ben Smith, "Ax on Ayers," *Politico*, February 26, 2008.

41 *"storm of criticism":* "Stephanopoulos defends his questions to Obama," *Los Angeles Times*, April 17, 2008.

41 *"such tired tripe":* Tom Shales, "In Pa. Debate, The Clear Loser Is ABC," *Washington Post*, April 17, 2008.

41 *"obscure sixties radical":* Michael Grunwald, "The Democrats Play Trivial Pursuit," *Time*, April 17, 2008.

41 *"The real story":* Scott Whitlock, "Stephanopoulos Quizzes Obama on Relationship to Member of Terrorist Group; Olbermann Enraged," Newsbusters.org, April 16, 2008.

41 *"top ten":* Michael Calderone, "Top ten media blunders of 2008," *Politico*, December 22, 2008.

42 *"Dig it":* Vincent Bugliosi and Curt Gentry, *Helter Skelter* (New York: Norton, 2001), p. 297.

42 *"Diana was fair":* Ayers, *Fugitive Days*, p. 97.

42 *"The woman on the other end":* Ibid., p. 3.

43 *"The old gods failed":* Ibid., p. 115.

43 *John Brown:* Ibid., p. 264.

43 *"imagines their actions":* Ibid., p. 287.

44 *"It was this knowledge":* Sam Green and Bill Siegel, *Weather Underground*, 2002.

44 *"intentions were evil":* Ayers, *Fugitive Days*, p. 105.

44 *"capitalism promotes racism":* Robert Farrow, "Who is William Ayers and Why You Should Care," October 16, 2008, baltimorereporter .com/?p=5811.

44 *"still the biggest threat"*: Ayers et al., eds., *Sing a Battle Song*, p. 37.

45 *"obsessed with the march"*: Obama, *Dreams*, p. 43.

45 *When her then husband*: Ibid., p. 47.

45 *"a lonely witness"*: Ibid., p. 50.

45 *"ugly conquest"*: Ibid., p. 23.

46 *"I chose my friends"*: Ibid., p. 100.

46 *"Joseph Stalin was a great man"*: W. E. B. Du Bois, "On Stalin," *National Guardian*, March 16, 1953.

46 *"It's useful to remind"*: Barack Obama, *The Audacity of Hope* (New York: Random House, 2008), p. 359.

47 *"struggle—between worlds"*: Obama, *Dreams*, p. x.

47 *"I have seen, the desperation"*: Ibid., p. x.

47 *"Soweto or Detroit"*: Ibid., p. 314.

THE WORD-SLINGER

PAGE

48 *"I picture the street"*: Ayers, *Fugitive Days*, p. 191.

48 *"Night now fell"*: Obama, *Dreams*, p. 187.

49 *"I had the thing"*: Ayers, *Fugitive Days*, p. 53.

49 *"We were ill-equipped"*: Ayers et al. eds., *Sing a Battle Song*, p. 25.

50 *Remnick dismisses*: Remnick, p. 547.

50 *As Kurtz reported*: Stanley Kurtz, "Founding Brothers," *National Review Online*, September 24, 2008.

50 *"further evidence"*: Kurtz, "Chicago Annenberg Challenge Shutdown," *National Review Online*, August 18, 2008.

51 *"Ayers had nothing to do"*: Kurtz, "Obama and Ayers Pushed Radicalism on Schools," *Wall Street Journal*, September 23, 2008.

51 *"Ayers helped bring"*: Remnick, p. 280.

51 *"I met [Obama]"*: Walter Shapiro, "Bill Ayers talks back," *Salon.com*, November 17, 2008.

51 *"He wanted to be mayor"*: David Mendell, *Obama: From Promise to Power* (New York: Harper, 2007), p. 92.

POETIC TRUTHS

PAGE

53 *Boxing great Muhammad Ali*: For an in-depth look at the Ali myth see Jack Cashill, *Sucker Punch: The Hard Left Hook That Dazed Ali and Killed King's Dream* (Nashville: Thomas Nelson, 2006).

53 *According to Early:* Gerald Lyn Early, *The Muhammad Ali Reader* (New York: Rob Weisbach Books, 1998), p. 30.

54 *"Suddenly I knew":* Muhammad Ali, *The Greatest: My Own Story* (New York: Ballantine, 1975), p. 38.

54 *"Honkies sure bought":* Mark Kram, *Ghosts of Manila: The Fateful Blood Feud Between Muhammad Ali and Joe Frazier* (New York: HarperCollins, 2002), p. 78.

54 *"a collection of* Life *magazines":* Obama, *Dreams,* p. 29.

55 *Remnick concedes:* Remnick, pp. 235–39.

56 *"I wanna cut his nuts off":* "Jackson says Obama comments not about envy," CNN.com, July 10, 2008.

56 *Obama's deterministic approach:* Shelby Steele, *The Bound Man: Why We Are Excited About Obama and Why He Can't Win* (New York: Free Press, 2008), p. 71.

56 *"to think and act":* Ibid., p. 54.

57 *"full of inarticulate resentments":* These and the following excerpts are all found in *Dreams from My Father.* To locate similar brief excerpts going forward, the reader is encouraged to consult the digitized version on Google Books.

57 *"I also thought I was black":* Ayers, *Fugitive Days,* p. 92.

57 *"distinguished theologian":* Bill Ayers and Bernardine Dohrn, *Race Course: Against White Supremacy* (Chicago: Third World, 2009), p. 281.

57 *Ayers tells of how:* Unless specified otherwise, these and the following brief excerpts are all found in *Fugitive Days.* To locate similar brief excerpts going forward, the reader is encouraged to consult the digitized version on Google Books.

58 *"I felt the warrior":* Ayers, *Fugitive Days,* p. 158.

58 *"deep-seated cultural malady":* Tim Wise, *Between Barack and a Hard Place: Racism and White Denial in the Age of Obama* (San Francisco: City Lights Books, 2009), p. 8.

58 *The student writes:* Ibid., p. 13.

59 *"Maybe I'm the last":* Ron Chepesiuk, *Sixties Radicals, Then and Now: Candid Conversations with Those Who Shaped the Era* (Jefferson, N.C.: McFarland, 1995), p. 102.

CRYSTAL CHAOS

60 *Barack Obama gave a speech:* "Barack Obama's Iraq Speech," wikisource .org/wiki/Barack_Obama's_Iraq_Speech.

60 *As Katz tells it:* Mendell, pp. 172–74.

62 *"What's worse":* Stuart Silverstein, "The Nazi Death Camp that Barack Obama's Great-Uncle Helped Liberate," *Los Angeles Times,* May 27, 2008.

62 *"The story in our family":* "Obama admits reference to Auschwitz was wrong," Reuters, May 27, 2008.

62 *"My father served":* Gateway Pundit, "Huh? . . . Obama Says His Father Served in World War II???," *First Things,* August 17, 2010.

62 *Six years later:* Lynn Sweet, "Transcript of Obama, McCain at Saddleback Civil Forum with Pastor Rich Warren," *Chicago Sun-Times,* August 18, 2008.

63 *"most courageous" speech:* Mendell, p. 175.

63 *"wrote the speech long hand":* Ibid., p. 174.

64 *"An official at Local 50":* Larry Rohter and Liz Robbins, "Joe in the Spotlight," Caucus Blog, *New York Times,* October 16, 2008.

65 *"That's the speech":* Mendell, p. 276.

66 *"The streets became sparkling":* Ayers, *Fugitive Days,* p. 179.

CONSPIRACY COMMERCE

PAGE

67 *According to the document:* John Harris and Peter Baker, "White House Memo Asserts a Scandal Theory," *Washington Post,* January 10, 1997.

67 *In late 2009: Meet the Press,* NBC, September 27, 2009.

68 *A few weeks earlier: Meet the Press,* NBC, September 6, 2009.

68 *As I learned:* David Thibodeau and Leon Whiteson, *A Place Called Waco* (New York: PublicAffairs, 1999). At the end of this well-reviewed book, survivor Thibodeau lists the names and ethnicity of all the victims. He makes no issue of it. He may have presumed that everyone knew.

68 *Authorities dumped the bodies:* Denice Stephenson, ed., *Dear People: Remembering Jonestown: Selections from the People's Temple Collection at the California Historical Society* (Berkeley, Calif.: Heyday, 2005), p. 160.

70 *"diabolical potency":* Remnick, p. 253.

70 *As Osnos relates:* Peter Osnos, "Barack Obama and the Book Business," *Century Foundation,* October 30, 2006.

71 *When he switched topics:* Remnick, p. 220.

71 *Intimate friend Valerie Jarrett:* Remnick, p. 227.

71 *"impostor phenomenon":* Benedict Carey, "Feel Like a Fraud? At Times, Maybe You Should," *New York Times,* February 5, 2008.

72 *In speaking of Obama:* "Biden's description of Obama draws scrutiny," CNN.com, January 31, 2007.

72 *"no Negro dialect"*: John Heilemann and Mark Halperin, *Game Change: Obama and the Clintons, McCain and Palin, and the Race of a Lifetime* (New York: Harper, 2010), p. 37.

72 *"Blacks like Obama"*: Steele, p. 14.

72 *"Obama had missed deadlines"*: Remnick, p. 228.

72 *According to Christopher Andersen*: Christopher Andersen, *Barack and Michelle: Portrait of an American Marriage* (New York: William Morrow, 2009), p. 162.

73 *"He and Michelle accepted"*: Remnick, p. 268.

73 *"I would work off an outline"*: Daphne Dunham, "20 Second Interview: A Few Words with Barack Obama," Amazon.com.

73 *"muddled" essays*: Remnick, p. 117.

73 *Remnick quotes Henry Ferris*: Remnick, p. 228.

74 *"hopelessly blocked"*: Andersen, p. 162.

74 *And a major payday*: Garance Francke-Ruta, "Obama Earned Nearly $2.5 Million in Book Royalties in 2008," *Washington Post*, March 19, 2009.

Ballast

PAGE

77 *"The confrontation in the Fishbowl"*: Ayers, *Fugitive Days*, p. 56.

77 *"I heard all our voices"*: Obama, *Dreams*, p. 394.

77 *"A steady attack"*: Ibid., p. 198.

78 *"I'd thought that when"*: Ayers, *Fugitive Days*, p. 47.

78 *"a vision of falling overboard"*: Ibid., p. 197.

78 *"I realized that no one"*: Ibid.

78 *"Memory sails out"*: Ibid., p. 76.

78 *one of four times* murky: Unless specified otherwise, this and the following short excerpts are found in either *Dreams from My Father* or *Fugitive Days*. To locate these brief nautical excerpts going forward, the reader is encouraged to consult the digitized version on Google Books.

80 *"a shining sea of blues"*: Bill Ayers, *A Kind and Just Parent: The Children of Juvenile Court* (Boston: Beacon, 1997), p. 82.

SECRET SHARER

PAGE

82 *"While we packed"*: Obama, *Dreams*, p. 31.

83 *"a treacherous appeal"*: Joseph Conrad, *Heart of Darkness* (1902), Plain Label Books available through Google Books, p. 87.

83 *"The man filled"*: Ibid., p. 153.

84 *"It was an affirmation"*: Ibid.

84 *"He inhabited"*: Ayers, *Fugitive Days*, p. 150.

84 *"He continued"*: Ibid.

84 *"We swarmed"*: Ibid., p. 179.

84 *"trees are shattered"*: Ibid., p. 160.

84 *"the mixed blood"*: Obama, *Dreams*, p. xv.

84 *"Her face powdered"*: Ibid., p. 56.

84 *"his eyes were closed"*: Ibid., p. xi.

85 *"The point was"*: Conrad, p. 28.

85 *"He appealed to me"*: Joseph Conrad, "The Secret Sharer (1910)," Plain Label Books available through Google Books, p. 22.

85 *"An accidental discovery"*: Ibid., p. 63.

86 *"random acts of terror"*: Don Terry, "The Calm After the Storm," *Chicago Tribune Magazine*, September 16, 2001.

86 *"penetrate the blank stares"*: Obama, *Dreams*, p. x.

86 *"penetrate" what the American terrorists*: Ayers, *Fugitive Days*, p. 294.

86 *"terrorism . . . practiced in the countryside"*: Terry.

THE POSTMODERN PRESIDENT

PAGE

87 *In this essay:* Barack Obama, "Why Organize?" *Illinois Issues*, University of Illinois at Springfield, 1988, http://illinoisissues.uis.edu/archives/2008/09/whyorg.html.

88 *"that rare politician who can actually write"*: Michiko Kakutani, "Obama's Foursquare Politics, With a Dab of Dijon," *New York Times*, October 17, 2006.

88 *"mixture of verifiable fact"*: Remnick, p. 231.

89 *It was a huge relief:* Maureen Dowd, "Oprah's Bunk Club," *New York Times*, January 8, 2006.

89 *"I was talking to a friend of mine"*: Belinda Luscombe, "Is Maureen Dowd Guilty of Plagiarism?," *Time*, May 18, 2009.

90 *What makes* Dreams: Remnick, p. 231.

90 *"is this then the truth"*: Dinitia Smith, "No Regrets for a Love Of Explosives; In a Memoir of Sorts, a War Protester Talks of Life With the Weathermen," *New York Times*, September 11, 2001.

90 *In early October 2008*: Bill Ayers, "Narrative Push/Narrative Pull," Bill Ayers blog, January 19, 2008.

90 *"And so what was"*: Obama, *Dreams*, p. xi.

90 *"Our trials and triumphs"*: Ibid., p. 294.

91 *"I understood that"*: Ibid., p. xvi.

91 *"I had felt"*: Ibid., p. 105.

91 *"Truth is usually"*: Ibid., p. 434.

91 *"As far as race in America"*: Bill Ayers, *Teaching Toward Freedom: Moral Commitment and Ethical Action in the Classroom* (Boston: Beacon, 2004), p. 146.

91 *"But I suspect"*: Ibid., p. 434.

92 *"But all in all"*: Ibid., p. xiv.

92 *"I was engaged"*: Ibid., p. 76.

92 *"At best"*: Ibid., p. 85.

92 *"Forgetting can be confused"*: Ayers, *Fugitive Days*, p. 233.

92 *"I know how strongly"*: Obama, *Dreams*, p. 21.

92 *"When history"*: Ayers, *Fugitive Days*, p. 297.

93 *"It corresponds"*: Obama, *Dreams*, p. 21.

93 *"I've come to see"*: Ayers, *Fugitive Days*, p. 294.

93 *"rotten and unjustifiable"*: Ibid., p. 207.

93 *"perhaps three-quarters"*: Ibid., p. 300.

93 *"I saw a dead body once"*: Ibid., p. 279.

94 *"during the summer"*: Obama, *Dreams*, pp. 144–45.

95 *"four American boys"*: Ayers, *Fugitive Days*, p. 56.

95 *"I remembered the whistle"*: Obama, *Dreams*, p. 145.

WEIRD SCIENCE

PAGE

98 *"No one who cannot rejoice"*: Ron Rosenbaum, "Literary Sleuth Absolves Bard of a Bad Poem," *New York Observer*, June 23, 2002.

ACKNOWLEDGMENTS

PAGE

101 *In April of that year*: Peter Wallsten, "Allies of Palestinians see a friend in Obama," *Los Angeles Times*, April 10, 2008.

102 *"A major news organization"*: Ben Smith, "McCain camp demands L.A. Times release video," *Politico*, October 28, 2008.

102 *"First, chronologically"*: Rashid Khalidi, *Resurrecting Empire: Western Footprints and America's Perilous Path in the Middle East* (Boston: Beacon, 2005), p. 212.

103 *"the Elsa Maxwell of Hyde Park"*: Remnick, p. 280.

103 *"I believe that after failing"*: Jack Cashill, "Evidence Mounts: Ayers Co-Wrote Obama's Dreams," *American Thinker*, October 17, 2008.

103 *"These oral histories"*: Andersen, p. 164.

104 *"a searing and timely account"*: Barack Obama, untitled review of *A Kind and Just Parent*, *Chicago Tribune*, December 21, 1997.

104 *Among them are*: Ayers, *A Kind and Just Parent*, p. 82.

REFORMERS

PAGE

105 *The answer:* William Ayers and Michael Klonsky, "Navigating a restless sea: The continuing struggle to achieve a decent education for African American youngsters in Chicago," *Journal of Negro Education* (Winter 1994).

106 *"remained in a state of perpetual crisis"*: Obama, *Dreams*, p. 256.

106 *"bloated bureaucracy"*: Ibid., p. 256.

106 *"Self-interest"*: Ibid.

106 *"defend the status quo"*: Ibid., p. 257.

106 *"an indifferent state legislature"*: Ibid., p. 256.

106 *"school reform"*: Ibid.

107 *In* Dreams, *all deeper:* Ibid., p. 97.

107 *" 'The first thing' "*: Ibid., p. 258.

107 *"In an authoritarian system"*: Ayers, *Teaching Toward Freedom*, p. 8.

107 *"The message to Black people"*: Ayers, *Fugitive Days*, p. 271.

107 *"From day one"*: Obama, *Dreams*, p. 258.

109 *"teachers, principals"*: Ibid., p. 256.

109 *"not so true"*: Ibid.

RUSH

PAGE

111 *"Shy of a confession"*: Jack Cashill, "Who Wrote Dreams From My Father," *American Thinker*, October 9, 2008.

112 *"Cashill's assertions"*: Remnick, p. 254.

113 *"This may not have"*: Ibid.

113 *"libel about Obama's memoir"*: Ibid., p. 254.

113 *If asked:* James Shapiro, *Contested Will: Who Wrote Shakespeare?* (New York: Simon & Schuster, 2010), p. 70.

113 *So unsettled:* Ibid., p. 72.

113 *An 1852 entry:* Ibid., p. 69.

114 *The literary fraud:* For a more in-depth look at Haley's fraud, see Jack Cashill, *Hoodwinked: How Intellectual Hucksters Have Hijacked American Culture* (Nashville: Thomas Nelson, 2005), pp. 113–18.

114 *"Would this trip to Kenya"*: Obama, *Dreams*, p. 302.

115 *his father had also been involved:* Ted Sorensen, *Counselor: A Life at the Edge of History* (New York: HarperCollins, 2008), pp. 144–51.

116 *"did a first draft of most chapters"*: Ibid., p. 146.

116 *"This was a charge"*: Remnick, p. 253.

CHANNELING BILLY

PAGE

120 *In his 1993 book,* To Teach: Bill Ayers, *To Teach: The Journey of a Teacher* (New York: Teachers College Press, 2001), p. 94.

121 *As Obama tells it:* Obama, *Dreams*, p. 143.

121 *The passage in question:* Ayers, *A Kind and Just Parent*, p. 86.

121 *When the other students:* Obama, *Dreams*, p. 62.

121 *"Barry never rejected Joella"*: Remnick, p. 73.

122 *"Education is for self-activating"*: Ayers, *To Teach*, p. 132.

122 *"Understand something, boy"*: Obama, *Dreams*, p. 97.

123 *The years he spent:* Davis, *Livin' the Blues*, p. 78.

123 *In fact, he dedicated:* Ibid., p. 79.

123 *In his memoir:* Ibid., p. 328.

123 *"two Marxists"*: Obama, *Dreams*, p. 140.

124 *"When the war ended"*: Chepesiuk, p. 104.

124 *He knew him personally:* Ayers, *To Teach*, p. 106; Ayers and Dohrn, *Race Course*, p. 20.

124 *"a consulting house"*: Obama, *Dreams*, p. 135.

124 *"serious exaggeration"*: Denko, "Barack Obama Embellishes His Resume," AnalyzeThis.net, July 9, 2005.

124 *"a spy behind enemy lines"*: Obama, *Dreams*, p. 135.

124 *the phrase "behind enemy lines"*: Ayers, *Fugitive Days*, p. 164.

125 *"Amerikan imperialism"*: Ayers, Dohrn, and Jones, eds., *Sing a Battle Song*, p. 149.

125 *"a patrol in the Mekong Delta"*: Ayers, *Fugitive Days*, p. 104.

125 *When mourning:* "Bob Feldman interviews Bernadine Dohrn," Morningside-Heights.net, 1998.

Space Limitations

126 *In one comic example:* Remnick, p. 546.

127 *"wider currency"*: Ibid., p. 254.

127 *"Internet hobo"*: "Did You Know This," *Wonkette: The DC Gossip*, June 29, 2009.

129 *"engaged in irresponsible"*: James Taranto, "Bogged Down," *American Spectator*, February 2009.

129 *"I think trying to claim"*: Jonah Goldberg, "Unconvinced," The Corner, *National Review Online*, June 28, 2009.

131 *In the weeks leading up:* Bruce Heiden, "Obama in Plain Sight: Intro to 'Dreams' Implies He Didn't Write It," *Postliberal*, October 17, 2009.

Swiftboating

137 *Of the twenty-three officers:* John O'Neill, "Factual support for the advertisement 'Any Questions?,' " letter posted on FoxNews.com, August 2, 2004.

140 *"Internet zanies"*: Ken Blackwell, "Dreams—or Nightmares—From Obama's Father," *Big Hollywood*, July 8, 2009.

Vichy

146 *"A partial manuscript"*: Andersen, p. 164.

147 *"the Supreme Court never"*: Barack Obama, "The Courts and Civil 147," *Odyssey*, WBEZ-FM, January 18, 2001.

149 *"I've read Obama's books"*: Christopher Buckley, "Sorry, Dad, I'm Voting for Obama," *Daily Beast*, October 10, 2008.

149 *"I remember distinctly an image"*: David Brooks, "Run, Barack, Run," *New York Times*, October 19, 2006.

LONDON FOG

151 *On Sunday, under Sarah Baxter's:* Sarah Baxter, "Republicans try to use Oxford don to smear Barack Obama," *Times* (London), November 2, 2008.

152 *In that same day's paper:* Peter Millican, "How they tried to tarnish Barack Obama: Peter Millican reveals how he was drawn into a plot to link the Democrat to a former radical," *Times* (London), November 2, 2008.

154 *As I observed, Millican:* Jack Cashill, "Oxford don trips badly on 'Dreams' analysis," *WorldNetDaily*, November 4, 2008.

MILLI VANILLI

160 *"the Special Olympics or something":* "President Obama Jokes About Being a Bad Bowler: 'It's Like the Special Olympics,' " ABCNews.com, March 19, 2009.

160 *or when TOTUS:* "Obama Thanks Himself, Irish PM Repeats Speech in Teleprompter Meltdown," FOXNews.com, March 18, 2009.

160 *"No recent inaugural":* Jonathan Raban, "The golden trumpet," *Guardian*, January 24, 2009.

160 *"It was so rhetorically flat":* Charles Krauthammer, "Obama's Inaugural Surprise," RealClearPolitics.com, January 23, 2009.

160 *It is simply mysterious:* Michael Gerson, "The Speech? Dare I Say: Yuck. And Yet: Wow," *Washington Post*, January 21, 2009.

161 *"Not one of his greatest":* Dawson Bell, "Bill Ayers denies '70s plot to blow up Detroit police sites," *Free Press*, January 25, 2009.

161 *Just a week earlier:* Barack Obama, "Breaking The War Mentality," *Sundial*, March 1983, posted in full at ironicsurrealism.com.

168 *In 1990, Obama contributed:* "Tort Law—Prenatal Injuries—Supreme Court of Illinois refuses to recognize cause of action brought by fetus against its mother for unintentional infliction of prenatal injuries," *Harvard Law Review*, 1990.

168 *Sentences that begin:* Barack Obama, "Humane Alternatives to State Budget Cuts," *Hyde Park Herald*, February 20, 2002.

168 *The one column:* Barack Obama, "Family Duties Took Precedence," *Hyde Park Herald*, January 12, 2000.

169 *even more subversive:* Krista Gesaman, "Who's Missing at the 'Roe v. Wade' Anniversary Demonstrations? Young Women," *Newsweek*, January 22, 2010.

GENIUS SCHOOL

PAGE

171 *"won" a full scholarship:* Mendell, p. 56.

171 *"unspectacular":* Remnick, p. 116.

171 *"I don't think":* Ibid., p. 178.

172 *"Harvard, Yale, Stanford":* Obama, *Dreams,* p. 275.

172 *"Obama would soon":* Mendell, p. 85.

172 *"Told by counselors":* Andersen, p. 88.

172 *"Michelle frequently deplores":* Liza Mundy, *Michelle* (New York: Simon & Schuster Paperbacks, 2008), p. 64.

172 *"dense and turgid":* Mundy, p. 82.

172 *The less charitable:* Christopher Hitchens, "Are We Getting Two for One?," *Slate,* May 5, 2008.

172 *"The study inquires":* Michelle Robinson, "Princeton-Educated Blacks and the Black Community," 1985, available at politico.com/pdf/080222_MOPrincetonThesis_1-251.pdf.

173 *"It doesn't take a Bart Simpson":* "Bart the Genius," *The Simpsons,* January 14, 1990.

173 *"I must say":* Remnick, p. 215.

173 *"American universities impose":* Steele, p. 14.

174 *He boasts:* Remnick, p. 199.

174 *This competition:* Fox Butterfield, "First Black Elected to Head Harvard's Law Review," *New York Times,* February 6, 1990.

174 *"By the time":* Remnick, p. 187.

175 *"A search of the HeinOnline database":* Matthew Franck, "Obama the Titan or the Cipher," *National Review Online,* February 12, 2008.

175 *Of course, that would not stop:* Remnick, p. 267.

175 *"If Obama was a white man":* "Clinton-backer Ferraro: Obama Where He Is Because He's Black," ABCNews.com, March 11, 2008.

175 *"I am livid at this thing":* Katharine Seelye and Julie Bosman, "Ferraro's Obama Remarks Become Talk of Campaign," *New York Times,* March 12, 2008.

176 *"demagogic fool":* Remnick, p. 406.

176 *"I'm black":* *60 Minutes,* CBS News, September 27, 2007.

177 *"the liberal pieties":* Clarence Thomas, *My Grandfather's Son: A Memoir* (New York: HarperCollins, 2007), p. 252.

177 *"Obama's faith":* Jonathan Alter, *The Promise: President Obama, Year One* (New York: Simon & Schuster, 2010), p. 64.

COPYCATS

PAGE

178 *After the 2008 election:* Lawrence Tribe, "Morning-After Pride," Forbes .com, November 5, 2008.

178 *"I'm so excited about this candidacy":* Mark Zaborney, "Obama Impressed Harvard Law Professor," *Toledo Blade*, March 2, 2008.

179 *"a phenomenon of some significance":* Joseph Bottum, "The Big Mahatma," *Weekly Standard*, October 4, 2004.

179 *Velvel promptly responded:* Lawrence Velvel, "Re: Larry Tribe, Larry Summers, And Elena Kagan: Because Of The Larry Tribe Affair, It Is Time For Larry Summers To Go," *Velvel on National Affairs*, April 22, 2005.

179 *The tipster reported:* Bottum, "The Big Mahatma."

180 *That same April:* Velvel, "Re: Larry Tribe."

181 *They may have been taking:* Bo Crader, "A Historian and Her Sources," *Weekly Standard*, January 28, 2002.

181 *"mistakes can happen":* Doris Kearns Goodwin: "How I Caused That Story," *Time*, January 27, 2002.

182 *When the student editors:* "The Consequence of Plagiarism," *Harvard Crimson*, March 11, 2002.

182 *He scolded them:* Tribe's complete response can be found at http://johnin northcarolina.blogspot.com/2006_02_19_archive.html.

182 *"a wonderful book":* "Obama Proposes 'Team of Rivals' Cabinet," ABC News.com, May 22, 2008.

GREEN PEPPERS

PAGE

184 *"Cosby never got the girl":* Obama, *Dreams*, p. 52.

185 *Obama's Chicago mentor:* Remnick, p. 139.

185 *Another Chicago friend, John Owens:* Ibid., p. 181.

185 *an "old girlfriend":* Ibid.

185 *"He had a serious girlfriend":* Mendell, p. 94.

185 *"I couldn't outcompete him":* Andersen, p. 60.

185 *"There are several black ladies":* Obama, *Dreams*, p. 211.

185 *"She was white":* Ibid., p. 210.

186 *"on this particular evening":* Ibid., p. 269.

187 *"She had been to the manor born":* Ayers, *Fugitive Days*, p. 97.

187 *"brought Bill Ayers":* "Memories of Diana," *Time*, March 30, 1970.

187 *Ayers expressed similar anxieties:* Ayers, *Fugitive Days*, p. 95.

188 *"We spoke in a language"*: Ibid., p. 230.

188 *"a perfect marriage"*: Ibid., p. 97.

188 *"for his callous treatment"*: Jane Alpert, "Mother Right: A New Feminist Theory," *Documents from the Women's Liberation Movement: An On-line Archival Collection*, http://scriptorium.lib.duke.edu/wim/mother/.

189 *In his 1997 book:* Ayers, *A Kind and Just Parent*, p. 2.

189 *"No one," he writes:* Andersen, p. 60.

189 *Long before Obama:* Obama, *Dreams*, p. 103.

189 *"Her voice"*: Ibid., p. 104.

190 *"Do you mind"*: Ibid.

190 *"uncles and aunts"*: Obama, *Audacity*, p. 389.

190 *A black campaign worker:* Remnick, p. 502.

190 *"I don't think Obama"*: Ibid., p. 505.

190 *"I am married to a black American"*: Barack Obama, "A More Perfect Union," March 18, 2008, full text available at: http://www.huffington post.com/2008/03/18/obama-race-speech-read-th_n_92077.html.

191 *"In her eminent practicality"*: Obama, *Dreams*, p. 439.

191 *"I met Michelle"*: Obama, *Audacity*, p. 386.

WINE-DARK SEA

PAGE

192 *"assumes the role"*: Jack Cashill, "The Improvised Odyssey of Barack Obama," *American Thinker*, December 28, 2008.

193 *"a quest in which"*: Michiko Kakutani, "From Books, New President Found Voice," *New York Times*, January 18, 2009.

193 *"Memory sails out"*: Ayers, *Fugitive Days*, p. 76.

194 *"mariner's chart,"* Ibid.

194 *"the geography of his life"*: Ibid., p. 50.

194 *"an intellectual journey"*: Obama, *Dreams*, p. xiv.

194 *"to see a new map"*: Ibid., p. 85.

194 *"That first encounter"*: Ibid., p. 277.

194 *"map of my life"*: Ayers and Dohrn, *Race Course*, p. 8.

194 *"at some uncharted border"*: Obama, *Dreams*, p. 86.

195 *"charting his way"*: Ibid., p. xvi.

195 *"What I needed"*: Ibid., p. 115.

195 *"Junkie. Pothead"*: Ibid., p. 93.

195 *"They did fight"*: Ibid., p. 117.

196 *"I remember often eating"*: Phil Boerner, "Barack Obama '83, My Columbia College Roommate," *Columbia College Today*, January/February 2009.

196 *"Like a tourist"*: Obama, *Dreams*, p. 122.

197 *"uncertain of my ability"*: Ibid., p. 120.

197 *As the scene unfolds*: Ibid., pp. 3–5.

198 *Apparently, Ayers so liked*: Ayers, *Fugitive Days*, pp. 2–3.

198 *"You god-driven man"*: Homer, *The Odyssey*, translated by Ian Johnston, http://www.mlahanas.de/Greeks/Texts/Odyssey/Odyssey10.html.

198 *"guide that might show me"*: Obama, *Dreams*, p. 121.

199 *The CNN lead*: Kate Bolduan, "Chief of firm involved in breach is Obama adviser," CNN.com, March 22, 2008.

200 *"not an especially convincing sequence"*: Remnick, p. 245.

200 *"a roadside tavern"*: Obama, *Dreams*, p. 302.

201 *"The Old Man's here"*: Ibid., p. 323.

202 *The words he speaks*: Ibid., p. 442.

202 *"He lied excessively"*: Patrick O'Brian, *The Far Side of the World* (New York: Norton, 1992), p. 141.

Hog Butcher

205 *"Not an uncommon slip-up"*: Steven Levingston, "Obama's Ghostwriter?," Washingtonpost.com, July 2, 2009.

205 *"What do you know about Chicago"*: Obama, *Dreams*, p. 142. Unless specified otherwise, all short excerpts are found in either *Dreams from My Father* or *Fugitive Days*. To locate these, the reader is encouraged to consult the digitized versions on Google Books. The one exception is Ayers's "Sharpesville," found on page 18 of *Race Course*.

205 *"broad-shouldered brute"*: Davis, *Blues*, p. 128.

Audacity

208 *"Barry was a Muslim"*: Remnick, p. 61.

209 *his mother's 1968 passport renewal*: Jerome Corsi, "New documents point to Indonesian citizenship," *WorldNetDaily*, August 4, 2010.

209 *"made faces"*: Obama, *Dreams*, p. 154.

209 *"Barack, huh"*: Ibid., p. 149.

209 *"The government wanted"*: Ibid., p. 265.

209 *"Although my father"*: Obama, *Audacity*, p. 242.

210 *"my Muslim Faith"*: Christina Bellantoni, "Obama's verbal slip fuels his critics," *Washington Times*, September 7, 2008.

210 *"White folks' greed"*: Obama, *Dreams*, p. 293.

210 *"Obama, without fail"*: Mendell, p. 77.

210 *"as much more of a political document"*: Kakutani, "Obama's Foursquare Politics."

211 *"He procrastinated"*: Remnick, p. 444.

211 *"committee markups, votes"*: Obama, *Audacity*, p. 383.

211 *"Like a traditional pol"*: Remnick, p. 445.

212 *"There was another inkblot"*: Mendell, p. 308.

212 *"His best writing time"*: Jay Newton-Small, "How Obama Writes His Speeches," *Time*, August 28, 2008.

213 *"He was punching the clock"*: Remnick, p. 444.

213 *"read the manuscript"*: Obama, *Audacity*, p. 430.

214 *"In crafting a speech"*: Mendell, p. 315.

214 *"those who work"*: Barack Obama, "Teaching Our Kids in a 21st Century Economy," speech delivered at the Center for American Progress, October 25, 2005.

214 *"And in fact"*: Obama, *Audacity*, p. 191.

215 *"Indeed, the single biggest 'gap' "*: Barack Obama, Call to Renewal conference, June 28, 2006.

215 *"The single biggest gap"*: Obama, *Audacity*, p. 238.

215 *"a joint Obama/Favreau production"*: Raban, January 24, 2009.

216 *Although not one word*: For these comparisons, I used as sources only two Ayers books: *Fugitive Days* and *Teaching Toward Freedom*. For "tolerant" I also searched *To Teach* and *Kind and Just Parent*.

218 *"But travel a few blocks"*: Obama, *Audacity*, p. 297.

218 *"during my very first days"*: Obama, *Dreams*, p. 252.

218 *"Here a knot"*: Ayers, *A Kind and Just Parent*, p. 82.

218 *"Knots of men"*: Ayers and Dohrn, *Race Course*, p. 10.

219 *"A steady attack"*: Obama, *Dreams*, p. 198.

219 *"one is tempted"*: Obama, *Audacity*, p. 247.

219 *"Hey, I understand"*: Sean Hannity, "Cable Exclusive With 'Courage and Consequence' Author Karl Rove," FOXNews.com, March 10, 2010.

THE PLAN

PAGE

221 *"unabashed liberal"*: Mendell, p. 308.

221 *"the most liberal"*: "2007 Vote Ratings," *National Journal*, March 7, 2008.

221 *"a healer, not a divider"*: Mendell, p. 313.

221 *The maneuver left:* Remnick, p. 207.

221 *"white man in blackface":* Ibid., p. 328.

221 *"politically calculating chameleon":* Ibid., p. 516.

221 *"generally adoring press coverage":* Ibid., p. 449.

221 *"The Color Purple":* Newsweek, December 27/January 3, 2005.

222 *"The chapters boil down":* Michael Tomasky, "The Phenomenon," *New York Review of Books,* November 30, 2006.

222 *In his otherwise flattering:* Klein, "The Fresh Face."

222 *"a shrewd candidate's book":* Remnick, p. 456.

222 *"Reagan spoke":* Obama, *Audacity,* p. 38.

222 *His appeal:* Ibid., p. 39.

223 *The call reminded him:* Ibid., p. 264.

224 *"an internal conceit":* Mendell, p. 354.

224 *"a tool of the white liberals":* Remnick, p. 328.

224 *"He was so bored":* Ibid., p. 444.

224 *"The job was too small":* Ibid.

224 *"He's just too talented":* Ibid., p. 274.

224 *Jonathan Alter openly marvels:* Alter, pp. 64–65.

224 *College friend John Drew:* Ronald Kessler, "Obama Espoused Radical Views in College," *Newsmax,* February 8, 2010.

225 *"I think he's an arrogant":* Remnick, p. 404.

225 *The Alice Palmer drama:* Ibid., pp. 279–82.

226 *"one of the great speeches":* " 'Hardball' with Chris Matthews' for March 18," MSNBC.com, March 18, 2008.

226 *"the most remarkable utterance":* Frank Rich, "The Republican Resurrection," *New York Times,* March 23, 2008.

226 *"If Senator Obama did not say":* "Obama strongly denounces former pastor," MSNBC.com, April 29, 2008.

227 *"divisive and destructive":* Ibid.

227 *"the cheap rhetorical tricks":* Charles Krauthammer, "The 'Race' Speech Revisited," *Washington Post,* May 2, 2008.

227 *"And what I think":* "Obama strongly denounces former pastor," MSNBC.com, April 29, 2008.

228 *"We've seen this happen before":* "Alan Colmes Highlights Bill Ayers Exclusive," FOXNews.com, February 24, 2009.

228 *"The Pentagon was ground zero":* Ayers, *Fugitive Days,* p. 265.

229 *An informed observer:* Hanspeter Born, "Der Präsident und sein Bombenleger," weltwoche.ch, October 14, 2009.

230 *To prove the encounter:* Anne Leary, "Bill Ayers No Dream," *Backyard-Conservative,* October 6, 2009.

231 *"Here's what I'm going to say"*: Jonah Goldberg, "Ayers's 'Confession,' " *National Review Online*, October 7, 2009.

231 *"Ayers is messing with conservatives"*: David Weigel, "Yes, Bill Ayers Is Messing With People," *Washington Independent*, October 7, 2009.

NOBEL LAUREATE

PAGE

232 *"Clearly, the award"*: "Bill Ayers speaks to Naresh Vissa about Obama's Nobel prize and Afghanistan," *Student Voice*, December 3, 2009.

233 *That honor falls to one Rigoberta Menchú:* For a more in-depth look at Menchú's fraud, see Cashill, *Hoodwinked*, pp. 141–49.

233 *Menchú describes:* Rigoberta Menchú, *I, Rigoberta Menchú: An Indian Woman in Guatemala* (Brooklyn, N.Y.: Verso, 1984).

233 *"I just wanted to do something"*: Ibid., p. 179.

234 *In 1989, Stoll found himself:* David Stoll, *Rigoberta Menchú and the Story of All Poor Guatemalans* (Boulder, Colo.: Westview, 1999), p. 69.

234 *"We have an unfortunate tendency"*: Ibid., p. 247.

234 *"mythologies of purity"*: Ibid.

234 *"protected revolutionary sympathizers"*: Ibid., p. 246.

235 *"Rigoberta's story of oppression"*: Ibid., p. 245.

235 *"They say it doesn't matter"*: Robin Wilson, "Anthropologist Challenges Veracity of Multicultural Icon," *Chronicle of Higher Education*, January 15, 1999.

235 *"All autobiographies embellish"*: "Quote of the Day," *New York Times*, December 15, 1998.

235 *Said Bill Maher: Real Time with Bill Maher,* HBO, October 9, 2009.

235 *"Obama is becoming Jimmy Carter"*: Eric Erickson, "Barack Obama Wins Nobel Peace Prize: He's Becoming Jimmy Carter Faster Than Jimmy Carter Did," Redstate.com, October 9, 2009.

236 *"His speech in Strasbourg went further"*: Toby Harnden, "Barack Obama: 'Arrogant US has been dismissive' to allies," *Telegraph*, April 3, 2009.

GOING ROGUE

PAGE

237 *"her indispensable help"*: Sarah Palin, *Going Rogue: An American Life* (New York: HarperCollins, 2009), p. 410.

237 *"I love meat"*: Ibid., p. 18.

237 *"Sarah Palin—now don't laugh"*: Chris Matthews, *Hardball*, MSNBC, May 12, 2009.

238 *David Brooks would call Palin: This Week*, ABC, November 15, 2009.

238 *"know-nothing"*: Dick Cavett, *News Live*, MSNBC, November 20, 2009.

238 *"a dangerous person"*: Martha Stewart, *Showbiz Tonight*, HLN, November 22, 2009.

239 *"marginal report cards"*: Obama, *Dreams*, p. 74.

239 *"life truly began"*: Palin, p. 51.

240 *"Can you get the back end"*: Ibid., p. 188.

GRAMPS

244 *"Turning down the* Tribune's *request"*: Mendell, pp. 20–21.

244 *"He and others"*: Toby Harnden, "Barack Obama's true colours: The making of the man who would be US president," *Telegraph*, August 21, 2008.

245 *Occidental student writer*: Kevin Batton, "Ode to Obama," *Occidental Weekly*, March 2007.

246 *"vivid if obscurely symbolic"*: Rebecca Mead, "Obama, Poet," *New Yorker*, July 2, 2007.

248 *As the* Seattle Times *reported*: Jonathan Martin, "Obama's Mother Known Here as 'Uncommon,' " *Seattle Times*, April 8, 2008.

248 *"rush home that same day"*: Obama, *Dreams*, p. 16.

249 *"loving if slightly jaded"*: Mead, "Obama, Poet."

249 *Remnick makes the same point*: Remnick, p. 106.

250 *"You know"*: Nancy Benac, "Obama's grandfather Stanley Dunham," Associated Press, May 30, 2009.

BARACK SR.

251 *"He was a son of the Luo tribe"*: Jonathan Freedland, "The Obama story," *Guardian*, November 6, 2008.

252 *Yes, Barack Sr. had*: Obama, *Dreams*, p. 126.

252 *"I get it"*: "Prepared Remarks of President Barack Obama: Back to School Event," Arlington, Virginia, September 8, 2009, whitehouse.gov.

252 *"He had left Hawaii"*: Obama, *Dreams*, p. 5.

253 *"The story did not mention"*: David Maraniss, "Though Obama Had to Leave to Find Himself, It Is Hawaii That Made His Rise Possible," *Washington Post*, August 22, 2008.

253 *"folded away among my birth certificate"*: Obama, *Dreams*, p. 26.

254 *"wreaked havoc among co-eds"*: Davis, *Livin' the Blues*, p. 318.

254 *An innocent post-election article*: Will Hoover, "Obama's Hawaii boyhood homes drawing gawkers," *Honolulu Advertiser*, November 9, 2008.

254 *"Stanley Ann Dunham Obama"*: Jerome Corsi, "Obama 'mama': 15 days from birth to Seattle class," *WorldNetDaily*, August 4, 2009.

255 *"extension courses"*: Remnick, p. 56.

255 *"it was sad to me"*: Ibid.

256 *posted on the Internet*: Jerome Corsi, "Official Obama nativity story continues to unravel," *WorldNetDaily*, September 1, 2009.

256 *"She left [Hawaii] just as soon"*: Michael Patrick Leahy, "What Does Obama Believe," unpublished manuscript, p. 48.

256 *"Ann was only a year"*: Ibid., p. 49.

257 *"Then you were born"*: Obama, *Dreams*, p. 126.

257 *"Barack Sr.'s father"*: Remnick, p. 56.

259 *"an intellectual in every sense"*: "Father's Abandonment Molded Obama," *Washington Post*, December 14, 2007.

259 *"Little Barry"*: Mary Ann Akers, "Aloha, Little Barry Obama for President," *Washington Post*, October 18, 2007.

260 *According to divorce papers*: available at http://www.scribd.com/doc/18130 \289/Obama-1964-Divorce-Papers-13-Pages-Missing-Pg-11.

260 *"In fact, how and when"*: Obama, *Dreams*, p. 22.

260 *"Mother's Peace Rally"*: "Barack Obama Sr." (with photo), Keywiki.org.

261 *"It's the exotic name"*: Leahy, private correspondence.

261 *"Madelyn did appear"*: Mendell, p. 23.

261 *"the children who claim"*: Obama, *Dreams*, p. 439.

262 *"Unlike my mum"*: Ibid., p. 345.

Unknown Black Male

PAGE

264 *"the crew-cut white boys"*: Janny Scott, "Obama's Mother—An Unconventional Life," *New York Times*, March 14, 2008.

265 *A group photo*: Jerome Corsi, "Photo challenges Obama nativity story," *WorldNetDaily*, January 5, 2010.

267 *"I recall her being melancholy"*: Leahy, "The Myth of Barack Obama's Early Life," Scribd.com, October 31, 2008.

267 *"So if you thought the paranoid theories"*: Alex Koppelman, "October Surprise: Who's Obama's Real Father," *Salon*, October 31, 2008.

268 *"Jimi Hendrix performed at Monterey"*: Obama, *Dreams*, p. 11.

268 *"They talk about me like a dog"*: Charles Johnson, "President Obama quotes Jimi Hendrix," *LittleGreenFootballs*, September 6, 2010.

FRANK

270 *"There's a humanity in the poem"*: Ian McMillan, "The Lyrical Democrat," *Guardian*, March 29, 2007.

270 *"aimed directly at the Soviets"*: Davis, p. 297.

270 *"suggested we investigate"*: Ibid., p. 311.

270 *"enthusiastically supported"*: Ibid.

271 *When Robeson first visited*: Tim Tzouliadis, *The Forsaken: An American Tragedy in Stalin's Russia* (New York: Penguin, 2008), pp. 267–69.

272 *"launched his invasion"*: Davis, p. 311.

272 *"The 178-day strike gnawed"*: Richard Borreca, "Political, Economic Clout Carried ILWU to Power," *Honolulu Star-Bulletin*, October 18, 1999.

272 *"I do not recommend"*: Davis, p. 321.

273 *"on Communist Party matters"*: Davis's FBI files are posted at usasurvival .org.

273 *Investigator Cliff Kincaid*: Jerome Corsi, "FBI destroyed file on Obama's grandfather," *WorldNetDaily*, April 12, 2010.

273 *There is a variety of evidence*: Interview available at http://www.youtube .com/watch?v=C422SbiYHoU.

273 *"a book of poetry in his lap"*: Obama, *Dreams*, p. 89.

273 *"I was intrigued by old Frank"*: Ibid., p. 77.

274 *"a poet named Frank"*: Ibid., p. 78.

274 *Toby Harnden of the* Telegraph: Toby Harnden, "Frank Marshall Davis, alleged Communist, was early influence on Barack Obama," *Telegraph*, August 22, 2008.

274 *"point of connection"*: Ibid.

274 *"He stoked the political embers"*: *Washington Post*, May 25, 2004.

275 *Figuring their authenticity*: "Photographs show Barack Obama's mother posing in the nude?," Snopes.com.

275 *"no discernible pattern of bias"*: truthorfiction.com.

276 *"I was hooked"*: Davis, *Livin' the Blues*, p. 230.

277 *"I could not then truthfully deny"*: Ibid., p. 346.

277 *In* Sex Rebel, *the Davis persona*: Frank Marshall Davis alias "Bob Greene," *Sex Rebel: Black (Memoirs of a Gash Gourmet)* (San Diego: Greenleaf Classics, 1968), p. 14.

277 *his seduction of a thirteen-year-old girl*: Ibid., p. 71.

277 *In a more telling encounter:* Ibid., p. 116.

278 *In both the memoir:* Davis, *Sex Rebel,* p. 119; *Livin' the Blues,* p. 333.

278 *In this particular vignette:* Obama, *Dreams,* p. 123.

279 *"He's obviously read the Beat poets":* McMillan, "The Lyrical Democrat."

280 *"by far the more powerful and complex":* Warwick Collins, "Barack Obama's early poems," publicpoems.com, February 8, 2008.

280 *In the way of support:* Frank Marshall Davis, "To A Young Man," 1975, from *Black Moods—Uncollected and Unpublished Poems* (Champagne: University of Illinois Press, 2007), p. 186.

283 *"outright sexual abuse":* "Obama and the disturbing influence of Frank Marshall Davis," NeoNeocon.com, April 3, 2009.

283 *"under certain circumstances":* Davis, *Sex Rebel,* p. 13.

283 *"When Bob Greene":* Ibid., p. 8.

284 *"I am unalterably opposed":* Davis, *Livin' the Blues,* p. 206.

284 *If what Sinclair says:* Larry Sinclair, *Barack Obama & Larry Sinclair: Cocaine, Sex, Lies & Murder?* (Chicago: Sinclair Publishing, 2009).

285 *"one of the more thoughtful":* Remnick, p. 94.

Ax

PAGE

286 *Known for his aggressive:* Mendell, p. 171.

286 *"worked aggressively behind the scenes":* Mendell, "Obama Lets Opponent Do Talking," *Chicago Tribune,* June 24, 2004.

287 *"Axelrod has worked through":* Ben Wallace-Wells, "Obama's Narrator," *New York Times Magazine,* April 1, 2007.

288 *"The trip served to remind":* Robert Barnes, "Obama Visits Grandma Who Was His 'Rock,' " *Washington Post,* October 25, 2008.

288 *new depths of self-deception:* Maureen Dowd, "A Storyteller Loses the Story Line," *New York Times,* June 1, 2010.

Hubris

PAGE

290 *In 1872, amateur archeologist:* Charles Mann, *1491: New Revelations of the Americas Before Columbus* (New York: Knopf, 2005), pp. 168–71.

ACKNOWLEDGMENTS

T his story could never have been told without the active help of many citizen journalists, technical advisers, media supporters, and miscellaneous friends of the truth. Forgive me in advance if I overlook anyone.

In the citizen journalist department, let me list my helpmates more or less in the order in which they came into my orbit: Peter Verzola of California, Mark Justin of Hawaii, Ryan Geiser of Nebraska, Jay Spencer of Massachusetts, "Ishmael" of North Carolina, Bruce Dunstan of Australia, Bruce Heiden of Ohio, Shawn Glasco of Colorado, Don Wilkie of Michigan, and Michael Patrick Leahy of Tennessee.

Those providing technical advice and/or literary forensic studies include Patrick Juola of Pennsylvania, Ed Gold of Florida, Andrew Longman of California, Chris Yavelow of North Carolina, and Debra Blackstone of California—my worthy webmaster.

Consistent media support came from a few solid sources, most notably *WorldNetDaily* publisher Joseph Farah, *American Thinker* publisher Thomas Lifson, talk-radio host Rusty Humphries, Sinclair Broadcasting VP Mark Hyman, and Swiss journalist Hanspeter Born. Thanks too to those local radio and Internet hosts who stayed with me throughout.

Among the more stalwart friends of the truth have been radio producer Rich Davis of Kansas, former congressman Chris Cannon of Utah, and especially Bob Fox of California.

Thanks to those of my friends and family who believed in what I was doing, none of whom put up with more than my wife, Joan. My esteemed agent, Alex Hoyt, hung tight as well, and Anthony Ziccardi of Simon & Schuster showed more than a little courage in approving the project.

Finally, a word of appreciation for the good folks at Threshold Editions and Simon & Schuster for their competence and congeniality, editor Kevin Smith most notably.

INDEX